AFFECT, COGNITION, AND CHANGE

Affect, Cognition, and Change:
Re-Modelling Depressive Thought

John D. Teasdale

and

Philip J. Barnard

*Medical Research Council
Applied Psychology Unit
Cambridge, England*

 LAWRENCE ERLBAUM ASSOCIATES, PUBLISHERS
Hove (UK)   Hillsdale (USA)

Reprinted in paperback 1995

Lawrence Erlbaum Associates Ltd., Publishers
27 Palmeira Mansions
Church Road
Hove
East Sussex, BN3 2FA
U.K.

British Library Cataloguing in Publication Data

Teasdale, John D.
   Affect, Cognition, and Change: Re-modelling Depressive Thought.—
   (Essays in Cognitive Psychology Series, ISSN 0959 4779)
   I. Title   II. Barnard, Philip J.
   III. Series
   153.4

   ISBN 0-86377-372-9

Printed and bound in the UK by Redwood Books, Trowbridge

To Jackie and Geraldine

Contents

Acknowledgements

This book reflects the influence of many people. We gratefully acknowledge the contributions of our teachers, students, colleagues, patients, and friends, and the many writers who have played a part, knowingly or unknowingly, in shaping the ideas we describe.

More practically, we are indebted to Caroline Muncey for the hundreds of thousands of keystrokes she has cheerfully word-processed into the final manuscript, and into many previous versions. Sharon Gamble and Moira Stephenson have also contributed their skills, on occasion. We are very grateful to them, and to Alan Copeman for his careful photographic work, and to Jon May and Lisa Tweedie for their invaluable assistance in the preparation of figures.

We also wish to thank Ben Teasdale for his vital assistance in the final stages of manuscript preparation, and Joe Teasdale for doing the gardening.

Brendan Bradley, Chris Brewin, David M. Clark, Tim Dalgleish, D. John Done, Leslie Henderson, Charlotte Lloyd, Andrew Mathews, and Michael Power made most helpful comments on a draft of this book. We thank them all.

Finally, it is a pleasure to thank Alan Baddeley, Director of the Applied Psychology Unit, for the initial invitation to write this book, and for creating an environment in which the collaboration on which it depended could develop.

PART I

The Problem; Some Evidence;
Previous Answers

CHAPTER ONE

Negative Thinking and Depression

A young woman is walking her dog. It is a beautiful September morning. It is her birthday. She is very aware of her thoughts: "What a flop my life has been all these years—another rotten year gone and lots more to go—how full of failures and miseries my life has been."

She is depressed. Is this the reason she thinks in this gloomy pessimistic way, or has her life really been so bad? Does thinking this way contribute to keeping her depressed? If we were to change the way she thinks would this change the way she feels? If we were to change the way she feels would this change the way she thinks? Can we, by changing the way she thinks and feels, help reduce the chances that she will continue to be depressed, both now and in the future?

These questions provided the stimulus to the enquiry of which this book is a part. The answers are likely to be of more than theoretical interest. Cognitive models of depression (Beck, 1976) suggest that negative pessimistic thinking is an important factor maintaining depression. Cognitive therapy, a form of psychological treatment based on these ideas, is designed to teach patients to change the way they think and feel. This psychological therapy has already been shown to be at least as effective as tricyclic antidepressant medication in the treatment of outpatients with major depressive disorder. There is also encouraging evidence that cognitive therapy is more effective than pharmacotherapy in preventing future relapse, once initial treatment has been discontinued (Hollon, Shelton, & Loosen, 1991; Williams, 1992). Cognitive therapy is currently quite complex and time-consuming. Better understanding of the psychological processes involved in the maintenance and modification of depression is likely to be an important factor in the further development of improved methods of psychological treatment. More generally, it is likely that the attempt to understand the processes involved in maintaining and changing depression will cast light on the wider range of mild unpleasant mood states that afflict us all from time to time.

An Overview:
The Applied Science Approach to Understanding
Depressive Thinking

Our general strategy is to adopt an applied science approach. This provides a method by which practical problems can be solved while, at the same time, basic psychological understanding is advanced. This strategy takes a concrete "real-world" problem as an initial point of departure, and as a continuing reference point against which the relevance of subsequent experimentation and theorisation can be gauged. It then exploits existing investigative paradigms, or creates new paradigms, to capture in the laboratory essential aspects of the applied problem. Taking advantage of the precision of measurement and the power of experimental methodology offered by these laboratory paradigms, theoretical accounts of experimentally demonstrated phenomena are developed. These theories can then be applied and refined by reference both to the initial "real-world" problem, and to continuing laboratory investigations designed to test key features of the theories. By a continuing iterative interaction between experiment, theory, and attempts to solve the applied problem, more detailed empirical information is accumulated and theoretical accounts are improved. The eventual outcome is that our ability to deal with the practical target problem is improved, and we also have a clearer understanding of related aspects of psychological function, rooted in controlled empirical investigations.

In this book we focus on the problem of the negative thinking shown by depressed patients, its possible role in the production and maintenance of depression, and how, by changing this thinking, or processes associated with it, we can improve psychological treatments for depression. We begin by considering the cognitive model of depression, developed by clinicians from their astute observation of depressed patients. Although not couched in precise scientific terms, these ideas have been invaluable in developing effective psychological treatments for depression. However, these ideas, in their original form, have encountered considerable difficulties as more detailed evidence has accumulated. Further, the effectiveness of treatments based on these ideas, although encouraging, still leaves room for improvement. Thus, there is reason to look to the applied science strategy to see whether it can provide better understanding of depressive thinking, and guidelines for the development of further improvements in treatment. We describe the application of this strategy, drawing both on our own work and that of others.

We describe the development of the applied science approach to depressive thinking in approximate chronological order. The first stage involved empirical investigation of aspects of information-processing in depressed patients, and in normal subjects in whom depressed mood had been induced experimentally. The findings of these studies provided the challenge to develop explanatory theoretical accounts. Gordon Bower's associative network theory of mood and memory offered an initially attractive and useful way of understanding the results of these and many related studies. We describe and evaluate this approach. Application of Bower's theory to the problem of depression overcomes many of the difficulties encountered by the original, clinically derived, accounts and provides valuable new insights into the clinical problem.

A virtue of experimentally derived theories is that their precision enables their weaknesses to be identified. As more and more experimental evidence of the effects of moods on cognitive processes has accumulated, it has become increasingly clear that Bower's associative network theory is inadequate. Interestingly, some of the difficulties of this theory, recognised by cognitive psychologists, parallel difficulties with the clinically derived cognitive model recognised by cognitive therapists.

Problems at both the experimental and clinical levels are resolved in an alternative conceptual framework, Interacting Cognitive Subsystems (ICS). As this is a relatively novel approach it is presented in some detail. Unlike both the clinical cognitive model and Bower's associative network theory, which recognise only one specific level of meaning, ICS recognises both a specific and a more holistic, generic, level of meaning. ICS suggests that affect is directly related only to the more generic level of meaning. ICS enables us to capture, within an explicit information-processing framework, the distinction between "knowing with the head" and "knowing with the heart".

The application of ICS to understanding mood-related biases in memory and judgement is described. The proposal that such biases arise from the effects of affect-related schematic models allows ICS to provide an integrative account of existing empirical evidence in these areas. In the course of accounting for the variability of experimental results in laboratory studies of mood and memory, the ICS analysis offers new insights into the nature of moods themselves.

The analysis of mood-related biases in memory and judgement provides the basis for an account of negative depressive thinking and its role in the maintenance of depression. The suggestion that information-processing can become "interlocked" in vicious cycles, processing only a limited range of depressive themes, is central to this account. The account is wholly consistent with the empirical evidence available in this area. The motivational bases of "interlocked" patterns of cognitive processing are explored in relation to self-regulatory theories of depression. The analysis that emerges suggests that such processing reflects attempts to resolve discrepancies in situations where centrally important goals can neither be attained nor relinquished.

The ICS account of negative thinking and depression is compared with that offered by Beck's clinical cognitive model. In contrast to the initial formulations of the clinical model, ICS emphasises the importance of higher-level meanings, associated with the processing of affect-related schematic models. These models integrate sensory contributions, particularly those derived from bodily experience, with patterns of lower-level meanings. The processing of schematic models is marked by the subjective experience of "felt senses" with implicit meaning content.

Interacting Cognitive Subsystems provides a comprehensive framework within which we can understand the effectiveness not only of existing, standard, forms of cognitive therapy for depression but also of more recent developments in cognitive therapy, and of a range of other psychological treatments. ICS provides an explicit account within which the strengths of earlier statements of the clinical cognitive model, and of conventional forms of cognitive therapy, can be retained while at the same time acknowledging the contribution of more recent developments. In this way, ICS can provide a theoretical foundation for achieving further progress in improving psychological treatments. In particular, ICS provides an information-processing framework within which accounts of experientially oriented treatments can be developed.

The book concludes with a discussion of ways of improving our understanding of complex phenomena such as the inter-relationship between cognitive and affective processes. A virtue of the Interacting Cognitive Subsystems approach presented is that it is, potentially, a conceptual framework that we can use to understand not only experimental and clinical phenomena, but also ourselves.

Negative Thinking and Depression: Beck's Original View

Systematic studies demonstrate that patterns of negative thinking are a very common characteristic of depressed people in general, not just of our young lady walking her dog. On the basis of clinical observation, Beck (1967; 1976) identified a pattern of reportable depressive thoughts, which he termed the negative cognitive triad. This consists of a negative view of the *self* (perceived as deficient, inadequate, or unworthy), of the *world* (interactions with the environment are perceived as representing defeat or deprivation), and of the *future* (current difficulties or suffering will continue indefinitely). Studies employing quantitative measures have generally confirmed the existence of these patterns of thinking in depressed samples (e.g. Haaga, Dyck, & Ernst, 1991).

Beck (1967; 1976; 1983) and his colleagues (Beck, Rush, Shaw, & Emery, 1979; Beck, Epstein, & Harrison, 1983; Kovacs & Beck, 1978) have outlined a theoretical account of the origins and role of negative thinking in the aetiology of depression. These ideas have had enormous influence in shaping treatment and research in depression. Before presenting and evaluating this account it should be pointed out that it is, avowedly, a clinical rather than a scientific theory. By this, its proponents mean that the main purpose of the theory is to guide the clinician in understanding and treating patients, rather than to provide a detailed exposition articulated in precise theoretical terms. It has, nonetheless, generated a considerable body of research and controversy (e.g. Coyne & Gotlib, 1983).

A major difficulty in evaluating Beck's cognitive model stems from the fact that it is a clinical theory. Consequently, presentations of the model have tended to be relatively imprecise, to have varied from one statement to another, and to have shifted in their emphasis over time. We present and evaluate what is generally regarded as the "original" version of the cognitive model, citing original sources wherever possible. In doing so, it is important to acknowledge that there have been subsequent developments in the corpus of ideas subsumed within the clinical cognitive model. Some of these developments have, indeed, been in response to criticisms similar to those which we shall describe. Nonetheless, the "original" version of the model is still widely used, and, historically, was the form of the model prevailing at the time that our "narrative of applied science" begins.

"The cognitive model views the other signs and symptoms of the depressive syndrome as consequences of the activation of the negative cognitive patterns. For example, if the patient incorrectly *thinks* he is being rejected, he will react with the same negative affect (for example, sadness, anger) that occurs with *actual* rejection. If he erroneously believes he is a social outcast, he will feel lonely" (Beck et al., 1979, p. 11). This view suggests that negative cognitions produce depressed affect. Beck et al. (1979, pp. 12–13) define cognitions "as any ideation with verbal or pictorial content". Similarly (Beck et al., 1983, p.2): "Cognitions are stream-of-consciousness or automatic thoughts that tend to be in an individual's awareness ... Examples of negative cognitions are 'I'm a failure', 'No one will ever love me', and 'I've made a mess of my life'." The use of the term "cognitions" in this way to refer solely to consciously experienced thoughts and images clearly diverges from the much wider use of the term in cognitive psychology, where it is assumed that the majority of cognitive processing is not experienced as consciously accessible thoughts or images. This difference in the use of terms has been the basis of a number of misunderstandings (e.g. see discussions by Lang, 1988; Leventhal & Scherer, 1987).

Where do the negative cognitions that produce depression come from?

In Beck's cognitive model, distorted *cognitions* are produced when a stressful event (e.g. divorce, loss of a job) activates an individual's unrealistic *schemata* ... Schemata are ... stable, general underlying beliefs and assumptions about the nature of the world and how one relates to it. These assumptions are based on past experience and serve to direct the individual's attention to, and interpretation of, current experiences. Examples of schemata are 'If I am not loved by others, I am not a worthwhile person' and 'I must achieve great things or I will be a failure in life'. ... The person's underlying assumptions constitute a vulnerability to events. (Beck et al., 1983, p. 2.)

It is suggested that, in vulnerable individuals, negative cognitions arise from the application of dysfunctional assumptions to "matching" events, much as in the derivation of conclusions from premises in an argument (Kovacs & Beck, 1978, p. 528). So, for example, given the premise "If I am not loved by others, I am not a worthwhile person", evidence of indifference by someone leads to the conclusion, expressed in a negative cognition, "I'm a failure". This negative cognition in turn, it is proposed, leads to depressed affect. Figure 1.1 summarises the key features of the cognitive model of depression.

Problems with Beck's Cognitive Model

As it has been investigated more closely, Beck's cognitive model has encountered a number of difficulties. Some of these are summarised here.

1. Purely "cognitive" accounts of depression, and depressive thinking, are embarrassed by evidence suggesting that negative thinking may be a *consequence* of depression rather than an *antecedent* to depressed feelings. For example, most measures of negative thinking recover towards normal levels with remission of the episode of depression even when, as in treatment with antidepressant drugs, no attempt is made to deal with environmental events, negative cognitions, or dysfunctional beliefs or assumptions (Simons, Garfield, & Murphy, 1984). Similarly, when

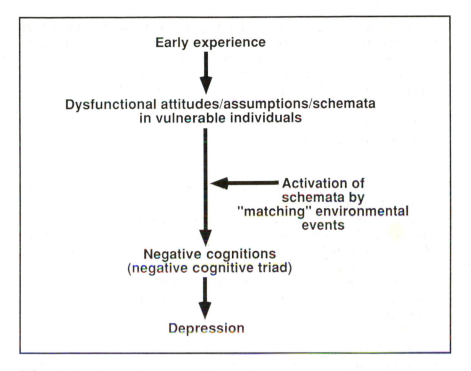

FIG. 1.1. Beck's cognitive model of depression.

psychological treatments directed at changing behaviours or interpersonal processes, rather than cognition, are successful in reducing depression, they reduce negative thinking to an extent comparable to that achieved by equally effective treatments targeted on cognition (e.g. Imber et al., 1990; Rehm, Kaslow, & Rabin, 1987). It is difficult to reconcile such evidence with the view that negative thinking is solely an antecedent to depression. Rather, these findings suggest that negative thinking is, either as well or instead, a consequence of depression.

2. Beck's model suggests that vulnerability to depression depends on possessing, as a relatively enduring characteristic, dysfunctional assumptions, attitudes, and beliefs. This view has been interpreted to predict that groups of depressed patients, after they have recovered from their episode of depression, should still show higher scores than normal controls on measures of dysfunctional attitudes. Most of the studies that have examined this issue have found, counter to the prediction from Beck's model, that although scores on measures of dysfunctional attitudes are elevated in episode they return to normal levels with recovery (see, e.g., Teasdale, 1988).

3. Beck's cognitive model has been interpreted to suggest that environmental events may only be important to the extent that they "trigger" dysfunctional cognitive structures; thereafter, the development of depression is primarily a function of these structures "activated" by matching events. This essentially "intrapsychic" view has been criticised for its neglect of the demonstrated importance of social and environmental factors in the aetiology of depression (Barnett & Gotlib, 1988; Brown & Harris, 1978; Coyne & Gotlib, 1983).

4. Beck's cognitive model recognises only one level of meaning, and for that reason has considerable difficulties with the distinction between "intellectual" and "emotional" belief, or, more generally, between "cold" and "hot" cognition. So, when a depressed patient says something like "I know I'm not worthless but I don't believe it emotionally", the Beck approach suggests that this simply reflects *quantitative* variations in a single level of meaning: "The therapist can tell the patient that a person cannot believe anything 'emotionally' ... when the patient says he believes or does not believe something emotionally, he is talking about *degree of belief*" (Beck et al., 1979, p. 302, original italics). Many clinicians have found this analysis unconvincing, regarding "emotional" belief as qualitatively distinct from "intellectual" belief, and functionally more important.

The original form of Beck's cognitive model, although it has been of enormous heuristic value in generating both an effective psychological treatment for depression (Beck et al., 1979; Williams, 1992) and a considerable body of research, clearly has its problems.

An important source of difficulty is the possibility that negative thinking is a *consequence* of depression rather than *antecedent* to it. It is therefore appropriate that the starting point for our "narrative of applied science" should be a series of empirical studies examining possible biasing effects of depression on aspects of memory assumed to be related to negative thinking.

CHAPTER TWO

Effects of Depressed Mood on the Accessibility of Autobiographical Memories

Autobiographical Memory in Depressed Patients

Unlike Beck, most psychiatrists have regarded the negative thinking reported by depressed patients as an effect of the depressed state, depression in some way biasing cognitive processing in a negative direction.

In a seminal study, Lloyd and Lishman (1975) translated this rather vague notion into a more precise hypothesis that could be investigated experimentally: In depression, the relative ease of recall of unpleasant experiences is increased; in contrast, the relative ease of recall of pleasant experiences is decreased. Ease of recall was measured by the time taken to retrieve memories, faster retrieval indicating easier recall. Depressed patients were presented with neutral cue words, such as "window", and asked to recall to each word a personal experience that was in some way associated with the word. For half the words, the patients were asked to retrieve a pleasant experience; for the remainder they were asked to recall an unpleasant experience. The ratio of the time taken to recall unpleasant memories to the time taken to recall pleasant memories (U/P) was calculated for each patient, and used as a measure of the relative ease of recall of the two types of memory. The relationship of U/P to patients' scores on a measure of severity of depression, the Beck Depression Inventory, is shown in Fig. 2.1.

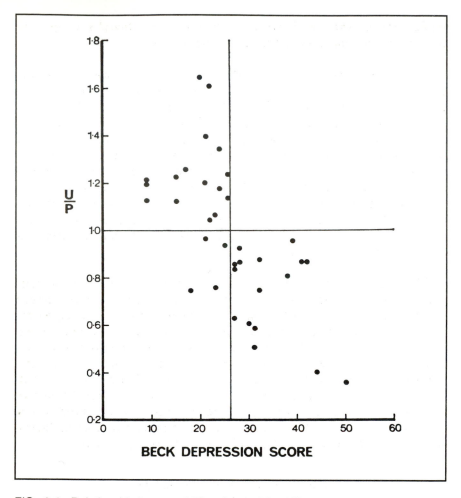

FIG. 2.1. Relationship between U/P ratios and Beck Depression Inventory scores. U/P > 1 means that unhappy memories are retrieved more slowly than happy memories, U/P < 1 means the converse (vertical line indicates mean depression score for the group). Reproduced from from Lloyd & Lishman (1975) with permission.

U/P progressively diminished with increasing depression, the correlation being substantial and significant (-0.64). Mildly depressed subjects, like most normal subjects, showed U/P ratios greater than unity, whereas most of the more severely depressed patients showed ratios less than one, unpleasant experiences being recalled more quickly than pleasant experiences.

Lloyd and Lishman's results were certainly consistent with the idea that depression in some way affected the relative ease of recall of pleasant and unpleasant experiences. However, they were correlational findings and thus open to a number of alternative interpretations:

1.   the life experience of patients who get more severely depressed, compared to those who get less severely depressed, contains more unpleasant experiences and fewer pleasant experiences, and it is this which produces the correlations between depression and recall times;

2.   people who possess, as an enduring trait-like characteristic, a tendency to recall unpleasant experiences more quickly and pleasant experiences more slowly will, when they get depressed, get more severely depressed, and this produces the observed pattern of correlations;

3.   depression affects not so much the accessibility of pleasant and unpleasant experiences as the tendency to categorise the experiences that are recalled as pleasant or unpleasant, and it is this factor that accounts for the observed correlations.

With respect to the second possibility, Lloyd and Lishman included in their study a measure intended to assess relatively enduring personality characteristics, the Eysenck Personality Inventory (Eysenck & Eysenck, 1964). Neuroticism scores from this measure showed a significant negative correlation with U/P (-0.56). Neuroticism and depression were themselves highly intercorrelated. However, partial correlations showed that the relationship for each of these with U/P remained significant when the effect of the other was held constant. Lloyd and Lishman concluded that the disturbance of hedonic selectivity of memory they had observed was a reflection both of the effects of the depressive process and an enduring characteristic of those individuals who are prone to depression.

Induced Mood and Accessibility of Autobiographical Memories

If Lloyd and Lishman's findings were at least partly attributable to effects of the depressed state on the relative accessibility of pleasant and unpleasant experiences, then experimentally manipulating depressed mood should affect the relative times to retrieve pleasant and unpleasant experiences. Teasdale and Fogarty (1979) tested this prediction in a study in which they manipulated the mood of students using a procedure similar to that developed by Velten (1968). After preliminary instructions that they should try to feel the mood suggested by each statement, subjects studied 30 cards bearing self-referent mood-inducing statements. For the depressed mood induction, statements progressed from mild to more depressing content: "Things aren't quite like I would like them to be"; "Looking back on my life I wonder if I have accomplished anything really worthwhile"; "I feel downhearted and miserable". For the happy mood induction, statements were increasingly positive: "All in all I am pretty pleased with the way things are going"; "Life is so full and interesting it's great to be alive!"; "I feel so good I almost feel like laughing". The Velten procedure has now been used in many experiments. It appears to produce happy and unhappy mood states that differ reliably on a range of measures, for example, writing speed and speech rate, in addition to self-reports of subjective state (Clark, 1983a).

In the Teasdale and Fogarty study, each subject retrieved memories to cue words in both happy and depressed moods. As predicted, U/P ratios were significantly smaller in the depressed mood than in the happy mood. The effects of depressed mood appeared to be restricted to increasing the time to retrieve pleasant memories, the time to retrieve unpleasant memories being very similar in the two conditions (Fig. 2.2). This might suggest an asymmetry in the effects of mild induced depression. Alternatively, it might be the result of a general slowing effect of depressed mood on memory retrieval counteracting a facilitative effect on retrieval specific to unpleasant experiences. In any case, the results of this experiment certainly suggested differential effects of mood on the *relative* accessibility of pleasant and unpleasant experiences. There were significant correlations between the extent to which subjects differed on measures of self-reported mood between the two occasions on which they retrieved memories, and the extent to which their retrieval times for pleasant experiences differed between the two occasions. These correlations strengthened the suggestion that mood state was indeed an important determinant of relative accessibility. Further evidence from this study suggested that these effects could not be explained in terms of effects of mood on the categorisation of experiences retrieved.

The basic findings of this study, that the Velten happy and depressed mood induction procedures produce differential effects on the times to retrieve pleasant and unpleasant experiences, have subsequently been replicated in a study by Riskind, Rholes, and Eggers (1982, extended version).

The results of the Teasdale and Fogarty study suggested that mood state could indeed bias aspects of the cognitive processing of hedonically toned material. However, effects on retrieval time lacked a direct relevance to the problem that was of most interest: Depressed patients do not complain of the relative times it takes them to retrieve pleasant and unpleasant experiences! Their problem is that, in depressed mood, there is a shift in a negative direction in the relative probability of thoughts with pleasant and unpleasant content "coming to mind". The general notion that mood affects the accessibility of memories, which had been measured by retrieval latencies, obviously implies effects of mood on probability of retrieval as well.

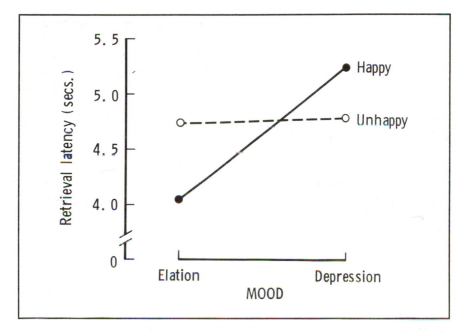

FIG. 2.2. Mean retrieval latencies of happy and unhappy autobiographical memories in elated and depressed moods. Data from Teasdale & Fogarty (1979). Figure reproduced from Teasdale (1983b) with permission.

A study by Teasdale, Taylor, and Fogarty (1980) examined this issue. Again, elated and depressed moods were induced in student subjects on two occasions using a Velten-like procedure, and neutral cue words were presented to which subjects had to retrieve an associated experience. However, in contrast to the procedure of the previous study, subjects were not told whether the experience was to be pleasant or unpleasant. Instead, they were to retrieve the first experience that came to mind, indicate when they had retrieved it, and then say out loud a few words describing the experience to help them recall the incident more fully later. At the end of the session they wrote more complete descriptions of the experiences retrieved to each cue word. On a third occasion, in normal mood, subjects rated the hedonic tone of the experiences they had retrieved, in the two induced moods, using these descriptions as reminders. By having subjects rate the experiences that had been retrieved in elated and depressed moods in the same neutral mood, any effects of mood state on the hedonic tone of the memories retrieved could confidently be interpreted as effects of mood on accessibility, rather than on rating behaviour.

Significantly more experiences for which the subject had rated feeling extremely happy at the time of the original experience were retrieved in elated than in depressed mood, whereas the converse was true for experiences for which subjects had rated feeling extremely unhappy at the time of the original experience. The relative probability of recall of experiences in the elated and depressed moods showed a regular increase as the happiness ratings of the original experience progressed from extremely unhappy to extremely happy (Fig. 2.3). Across subjects, differences on a measure of accessibility (the percentage of happy memories retrieved) between mood conditions were significantly positively related to differences in mood between conditions. As in the earlier study, these findings are consistent with the idea that mood state was the important factor affecting accessibility.

Thus, using a probability rather than a latency measure of accessibility, the findings of the original study were essentially replicated and extended.

FIG. 2.3. Relative probability of recalling autobiographical memories of different happiness ratings in elated and depressed moods: E/D = % of memories in elated mood at that rating /% of memories in depressed mood at that rating. Data from Teasdale, Taylor, and Fogarty (1980).

The basic finding of an effect of induced depressed mood, compared to happy mood, increasing the relative probability of recall of negative autobiographical memories, and decreasing the relative probability of recall of positive autobiographical memories has since been very widely replicated (Bower, 1981; Madigan & Bollenbach, 1982; Natale & Hantas, 1982; Snyder & White, 1982; Teasdale & Taylor, 1981).

One of these studies is worth mentioning in more detail because it neatly avoided one of the nagging doubts that arises, however slightly, in connection with the usual form of investigation of autobiographical memory: The experimenter is not usually present when the to-be-recalled events originally occurred, so how can he be sure that they actually happened, or, indeed, that they were of the hedonic tone that the subject remembers? Bower (1981, p. 132) got round this difficulty by having subjects record in daily diaries details of emotional incidents that happened to them over the course of a week. Subjects returned one week later. They were then hypnotised, half being put in a pleasant mood and half being put in an unpleasant mood, and all were asked to recall every incident they could from those recorded in their diaries the week before. As expected, people in a pleasant mood recalled a greater percentage of their recorded pleasant experiences than of their unpleasant experiences, whereas people in an unpleasant mood recalled a higher percentage of their unpleasant rather than their pleasant memories.

Changes in Clinical Depression and Recall of Autobiographical Memories

Evidence of the kind we have just reviewed points strongly to differential effects of experimentally manipulated mood (happy versus sad) on the relative accessibility of happy and unhappy memories, whether this is measured by latency of retrieval or probability of recall. It is important to know whether these effects of experimentally altered mood can be generalised to the effects of naturally occurring changes in mood in depressed patients. First, it is possible that experimentally induced depressed mood, although sharing many of the attributes of clinically depressed mood, differs from it in other respects. Second, there is always the possibility that the effects observed in the experimental studies are actually the result of the procedures used to induce moods, rather than of the mood states themselves. If similar effects on the accessibility of happy and unhappy memories can be shown for both induced and naturally occurring changes in depressed mood then it will increase our confidence in the relevance of the experimental studies, and support mood state as the important factor determining accessibility. For this purpose it is necessary to study changes in depression that are not themselves the result of other factors, such as environmental events, which might have direct effects on the accessibility of memories.

David M. Clark devised a neat solution to this problem by studying depressed patients with marked regular diurnal variation in mood. Some patients show a consistent pattern of being considerably more depressed in the morning than in the evening, whereas others consistently show the reverse pattern. These changes do not usually appear related to any particular events occurring during the course of the day, and are generally assumed to reflect biological rhythm rather than environmental events. So, if patients with such regular rhythms were studied at their points of minimum and maximum depression during the day and found to show similar effects on accessibility of memories to those of experimentally induced elation and depression we could have some confidence: (1) that the results of the experimental studies could be generalised to clinical depression, and (2) that the effects on accessibility could plausibly be attributed to changes in mood rather than to other factors.

Following this strategy, Clark and Teasdale (1982) studied a group of patients with regular diurnal variation in their depression. For each patient the recall procedure used by Teasdale et al. (1980) and Teasdale and Taylor (1981) was repeated, once at the point of maximum depression in the daily cycle and once at the point of minimum depression. Subjects rated memories from both their low and high depression sessions at the same session to avoid confounding biasing effects of mood on rating with effects on accessibility. As shown in Fig. 2.4, for experiences originally rated as happy, the percentage of memories retrieved was significantly greater in the low depression than in the high depression session. For unhappy experiences the converse was true. The pattern of results was similar to that in previous mood induction studies (e.g. Teasdale & Taylor, 1981), confirming the relevance of the latter and supporting mood as the important factor. As in the earlier studies, Clark and Teasdale (1982) found a significant correlation between differences in depressed mood across the two sessions on which each subject was seen and differences in measures of relative retrieval of unhappy memories.

Patients with marked regular diurnal variation represent only a minority of all depressed patients. In order to examine the generality of the findings of Clark and Teasdale (1982), Clark (1983b) used an essentially similar procedure to study the effects of changes in depression in a more representative sample of depressed patients over an interval averaging five weeks. The evidence from this study also showed that changes in depression were associated with changes in accessibility of memories: For patients whose depression improved there was a significant increase in the mean happiness ratings (of the original experience) of the memories retrieved, whereas for patients whose depression did not improve happiness ratings remained constant.

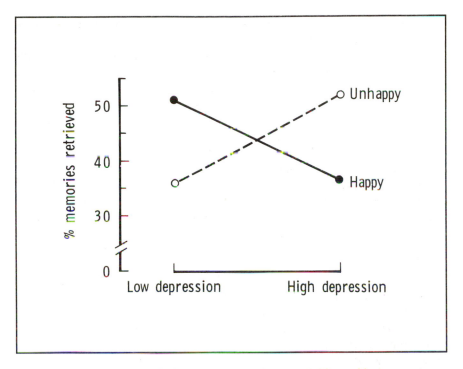

FIG. 2.4. Probability of retrieving happy and unhappy autobiographical memories at the more depressed and less depressed phases of patients' diurnal cycles. Data from Clark and Teasdale (1982). Figure reproduced from Teasdale (1983b) with permission.

Conclusions

Our purpose in looking at investigations of mood effects on memory was to examine the possibility that negative thinking in depression might be a consequence of depressed mood, rather than the antecedent suggested by Beck's cognitive model. The reason for focusing on memory, rather than directly on thinking itself, is that it is more immediately tractable with existing experimental methods.

The conclusions from the studies reviewed are clear. Memories of autobiographical events are recalled better when the hedonic or affective tone of the events matches that of the mood in which memory retrieval occurs than when it does not. Such *mood-congruous memory* has been demonstrated both for experimentally induced and for naturally occurring moods. These findings suggest that at least some aspects of negative thinking may be the result of depressed mood selectively biasing access to memory so that negative material is more likely to be accessed and used, and positive material is less likely to be accessed and used.

Studies of mood-congruous memory provide a convenient focus for our applied science approach to understanding depressive thinking. We can study this phenomenon in the laboratory and, taking advantage of the precision of investigation this affords, we can formulate and evaluate theories to explain mood-congruous memory. We can then examine to what extent these theories also help us to understand negative depressive thinking. So, how is mood-congruous memory to be explained?

Teasdale and Fogarty (1979) suggested that mood-congruous recall could be seen as an example of the more general phenomenon of context-specific encoding and retrieval. In general, material is more likely to be remembered if the context at the time it is retrieved is similar to the context that existed at the time that it was originally encoded (Tulving & Thomson, 1973). Pleasant experiences normally occur in the context of a happy mood state and should therefore be easier to retrieve from memory in a happy mood than in a depressed mood. Conversely, unpleasant experiences normally occur in the context of an unhappy mood and so should be easier to retrieve when mood is depressed rather than happy.

There is good evidence that changes of "state" induced by drugs, such as alcohol, can act as contexts that affect memory. Recall of material is better if the drug state at recall matches that during learning than if the state at recall differs from that at learning. For example, if a subject learns a list of words when drunk, memory for the list will be better if the subject is subsequently tested when drunk rather than sober (Eich, 1977).

Weingartner, Miller, and Murphy (1977) extended application of the concept of state-dependent learning to states resulting from changes in mood. In a group of patients who cycled between states of mania and normality they asked subjects to generate, and subsequently to recall, word associations over a number of occasions differing in mood state. They found that more previously generated word associations could be recalled when the mood state at recall was similar to the mood state existing when the associations were generated. They interpreted their results in terms of context-specific encoding of events and related context-specific retrieval strategies; events may be encoded differently in different mood states, and similarity of mood context at recall to that at encoding may determine ease of retrieval of the events.

Teasdale and Fogarty (1979) proposed that the effects of mood on recall of autobiographical memories could also be accounted for by mood-state-dependent retrieval. Subsequently, Bower (1981) presented a more detailed application of the concept of mood-state-dependent learning to understanding a wide range of phenomena related to the effects of mood and memory. Many of these phenomena are of direct relevance to understanding negative depressive thinking. Bower's theory is presented in the next chapter. This theory has had an extremely influential and formative effect on the field of emotion and cognition. More recently, a number of formidable difficulties with Bower's theory have been recognised: We shall describe the difficulties later. For now, we will follow the actual chronology of developments in this area of research by considering Bower's theory, its initial empirical support, and the way in which it provided useful insights into understanding depression.

CHAPTER THREE

Bower's Associative Network Theory of Mood and Memory and its Application to Depression

The Empirical Background

The fundamental process in Bower's associative network theory is the creation of associative links between representations of material and the mood state in which it is encoded. Mood-state-dependent retrieval, the enhanced recall of material when mood state at retrieval is the same as that at encoding, rather than different, provides the most direct means of demonstrating the possible existence of such associative links.

Mood-state-dependent retrieval was first demonstrated successfully by Bower, Monteiro, and Gilligan (1978). These workers reported three experiments examining mood-dependent effects on memory for verbal material. Hypnotic suggestions were used to induce happy and sad moods in selected hypnotically susceptible subjects.

In the first two experiments subjects learned a single-word list containing happy and sad abstract nouns such as "humour" and "misery". For one group of subjects the word list was presented in induced sad mood, whereas for a second group the list was presented in induced happy mood. Later, half of each group of subjects recalled the list while feeling happy, the other half recalled it while feeling sad. Neither experiment yielded evidence of mood-dependent retrieval. Recall was no better when recall mood matched the mood in which the list had been learned originally than when recall and learning moods were different.

In their third experiment, Bower et al. (1978) used a more complex design to investigate whether mood could be used to enhance or diminish the retroactive interference that normally arises when a person learns two-word lists. Subjects learned List A while in mood state 1, then learned List B while in mood state 2, and then later recalled List A and List B while in mood state 1 or 2. If mood state provides a distinctive context aiding discrimination of the lists then minimal interference in recall of List A should occur when the List A recall mood is the same as the List A learning mood but different from the List B learning mood. Conversely, maximal interference in List A recall should occur when recall mood is different from that in which List A was learned but the same as that in which List B was learned. The increased or decreased interference in these conditions was assessed relative to control groups learning both lists in the same mood, and tested for recall in the same mood as that at learning.

Using this design, subjects were found to show mood-dependent retrieval: When the learning and recall moods were the same, subjects' average recall was 78%, whereas when learning and recall moods were different, recall was only 47%. Average recall in the control groups was 56%. Bower et al. (1978) concluded that mood-dependent retrieval could be demonstrated when interference was high, as in a two-list design. They suggested that the success in demonstrating this phenomenon in a two-list design, compared to the failures to obtain it using single-list designs, was because mood could act as a distinguishing context, but only if the learning context itself was not distinct. In the single-list designs of the first two experiments the list-learning context by itself was sufficiently distinct from common experience to make redundant any additional differentiation provided by the nature of the mood during learning. In the two-list design, however, the mood cue would provide additional differentiation where the target learning list was otherwise easily confused with other learning material encountered in the same overall context.

Given the need to use a complex two-list design to demonstrate mood-state-dependent learning, doubts naturally arise with respect to the generalisability of this phenomenon and to the ecological validity of these findings. Specifically, if it can only be shown in this highly contrived laboratory situation, can it have much relevance to the robust effects of mood on autobiographical memory that were discussed in the previous chapter?

Bower et al. (1978) addressed this issue. They suggested that recall of specific incidents from one's life is probably more similar to the conditions of their two-list experiment than to the conditions of their single-list experiments. A person must remember a configuration of actors, actions, objects, and results at a specific time and place, and distinguish that configuration from other incidents involving similar actors, actions, and outcomes at similar places. An intense emotion aroused by an event may make the item more distinctive in memory from events that are otherwise similar apart from the emotion associated with them. Thus, Bower et al. (1978) argued, the two-list design actually had greater ecological validity than the simpler one-list design.

An Associative Network Theory of Mood and Memory

On the basis of Bower et al.'s (1978) successful demonstration of mood-state-dependent memory, and of a number of clinical anecdotal observations, Bower (1981) proposed an associative network theory of mood and memory phenomena. Independently, Clark and Isen (1982), drawing on their previous ground-breaking work on the effects of mood states on cognition and social behaviour, proposed a closely related account.

The following description of Bower's theory is based on his own account (Bower, 1981, pp. 134–136). The theory suggests that concepts, events, and meanings are represented in memory by nodes, joined together by associative links to form a semantic network. The representation of an event consists of a cluster of descriptive propositions. These propositions are encoded by forming new associative links between nodes corresponding to pre-existing concepts. Propositions constitute the basic unit of thought; the basic process of thought is the activation of the representation of a proposition and its concepts. We are conscious of the concepts and propositions for which the current activation level exceeds some threshold. Retrieval involves the spread of activation through the network; events and concepts are recalled when the activation of related nodes exceeds the threshold value. Thought sequences depend on activation spreading from concept to concept, and proposition to proposition, through associative linkages between the corresponding nodes in the network.

Activation of a node can occur as the result of presentation of the stimulus pattern corresponding to the concept, proposition, or event that the node represents. Alternatively, a node can be activated as the result of activation arriving over the network through connections from associatively linked nodes previously activated in an associated thought.

Figure 3.1 shows the way an event such as "Mary kissed me at a specific time and place" would be represented in memory within the associative network. The links are labelled to denote the subject (S) and the predicate (P) of the proposition. Learning consists of establishing associative links between nodes, and increasing their strength. When later asked "What did Mary do?" the Mary concept will be activated by the question, and activation of this node will transmit activation to the Event 19 node (representing the actual kissing event). Activation will then pass to the

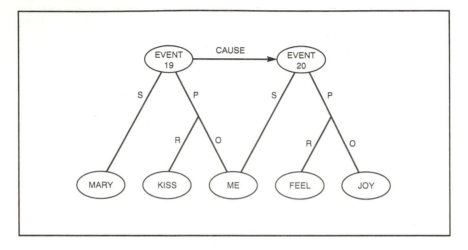

FIG. 3.1. A semantic-network encoding of a proposition ("Mary kissed me") and an emotion it causes. Lower circles, or nodes, represent pre-existing concepts, and lines represent new associations. S = subject; P = predicate; R = relation; and O = object Adapted from Bower (1981) with permission.

branches of this node causing the network to retrieve the other links and so to recall that "Mary kissed me".

Emotion is incorporated into the network model by the proposal that each distinct emotion, such as joy, depression, or fear, has a specific node in the network.

Figure 3.2 illustrates the emotion node corresponding to Emotion 3, which, for concreteness, we shall assume is joy. When activated above a threshold, for example by appropriate evoking appraisals or physiological input, emotion nodes produce their related emotions. Emotion nodes can also be activated by activation arriving through associative links from the semantic network.

Each emotion node is connected to nodes representing events and concepts that have previously been activated concurrently with that emotion node, i.e. that have been encoded or activated in association with experience of the related emotion. So, for example, the node corresponding to the episode represented in Fig. 3.1, "Mary kissed me", would be associatively linked to the emotion node for joy. Similarly, the nodes corresponding to descriptions of events at a friend's funeral would be associatively linked to the emotion node for grief. In this way, each specific emotion node is linked with propositions describing all the events from one's life during which that emotion was aroused.

Activation of an emotion node above a threshold transmits excitation through its links to the units that produce the patterns of autonomic and

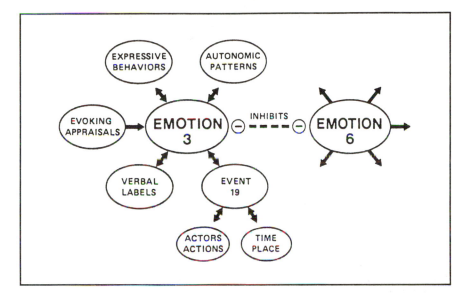

FIG. 3.2. Small fragment of the connections surrounding a specific emotion node or unit. Bidirectional arrows refer to a mutual exchange of activation between nodes. An inhibitory pathway from Emotion 3 to Emotion 6 is also shown. Reproduced from Bower (1981) with permission.

expressive behaviour corresponding to that emotion. In this way, an emotional reaction is produced. Activation of an emotion node also transmits activation through associative linkages to all the memory structures to which it is connected. Consequently, excitation at the nodes of all events that have involved that emotion, or been associated with it, will be increased. According to the network theory, this selective increase in the excitation of nodes previously activated in association with an emotion forms the basis of mood-dependent retrieval and mood-congruous retrieval.

Mood-state-dependent Retrieval

Material encoded in a given emotional state (Emotion 1) in the course of an experiment will be encoded in a context that consists both of Emotion 1 and of the more general experimental context. We can refer to the latter as Context 1. According to the network theory, representations of the material learned become linked both to the node in the memory network corresponding to Context 1, and to the emotion node corresponding to Emotion 1. When, at retrieval, the subject is asked to recall events that occurred in Context 1, the subject is assumed to activate the Context 1 node in memory, and activation spreads from this node as the subject searches for relevant items.

Context 1 will have been associated with many things. For this reason, it is a weak, overloaded cue, so that any one connection from it is subjected to heavy interference. However, if, during recall, the subject is returned to the same distinctive emotional state of Emotion 1 that was present at encoding, the activation from the Emotion 1 node will also spread along associative links to the nodes corresponding to the target items. There, it will summate with the activation spreading from the Context 1 node and cause the target event to become more accessible when retrieval occurs in the same mood as at encoding. By contrast, if mood is altered from Emotion 1 at encoding to Emotion 2 at recall then recall will suffer because the benefits from the intersection of two search cues are lost. Further, the activation from the emotion node corresponding to Emotion 2 will increase the accessibility of interfering associations that will compete with recall of the correct target items.

In this way, the associative network theory offered an appealingly simple explanation for the occurrence of mood-state-dependent retrieval of the type observed in experiments such as that reported by Bower et al. (1978).

Mood-congruous Retrieval of Autobiographical Memories

The associative network theory's explanation of mood-congruous retrieval of autobiographical memories is essentially similar to that just outlined for mood-state-dependent learning (Bower, 1981, p. 136). In a given emotion or mood state, activation of the node corresponding to the prevailing emotion will be greater than that of the nodes for other emotions. It follows that, other things being equal, more activation will spread to nodes associatively linked to the currently active emotion node than to nodes associatively linked to other emotion nodes.

The nodes linked to the currently active emotion node will correspond to representations of concepts and events previously activated in association with that emotion or mood. In general, these representations are more likely to be of events or concepts affectively congruent with encoding mood than of events or concepts incongruent with that mood. In mood-state-dependent retrieval, the activation spreading out from the currently active emotion node selectively increases the chance of retrieving experimental material previously encoded in that mood. In the same way, in mood-congruous retrieval, the verbal stimuli used to prompt retrieval of autobiographical memories are weak, overloaded cues. When these cues are supplemented with the activation from the emotion node corresponding to the emotion prevailing at recall, there will be preferential access to representations of mood-congruent events connected to that emotion node as a result of prior contiguity. Consequently, a pattern of mood-congruent retrieval will be observed.

Bower's theory appeared to offer a satisfying account both of mood-state-dependent retrieval, as demonstrated in the laboratory, and of mood-congruous retrieval of autobiographical memories, as observed in the experiments described in Chapter 2. We have suggested that mood-congruous retrieval may be a useful circumscribed testing arena within which to develop and evaluate theories of mood-dependent thinking more generally. The associative network account appeared to be a particularly attractive candidate to examine in this respect. This theory not only offered a plausible account of mood-congruous retrieval, but, in his 1981 paper, Bower extended application of the theory to explain a range of other aspects of mood-related thinking. Some of these were of obvious relevance to our ultimate goal of understanding negative depressive thinking. For example, Bower (1981) briefly sketched network theory accounts of mood-related biases in the interpretation and evaluation of ambiguous situations, and of the attentional salience of mood-congruent material. These proposals were of great potential relevance to clinical depression where biased expectations in the form, for example, of hopelessness, and biased evaluations in the form of low self-regard, are features of the condition that are actually more striking clinically than biased memory.

We consider and evaluate the network theory's account of mood-related biases in judgement in more detail in Chapter 11. For now, we will focus on applications of network theory directed specifically at achieving a clearer understanding of the phenomena of clinical depression (e.g. Ingram, 1984; Teasdale, 1983b). As we shall see in the next section, application of this experimentally derived theory overcame many of the problems of the clinically derived cognitive model of Beck and his colleagues.

Applications of
Associative Network Theory
to Clinical Depression

The essence of Bower's associative network theory is that in a given mood *now* we are more likely to remember events previously associated with that mood in the *past*. The constructs and concepts previously used to interpret events occurring in association with that mood in the past will also be reactivated, and become more accessible. Consequently, these constructs will be more likely to be used to interpret current events occurring in the mood state. In a depressed mood *now*, all the concepts and constructs previously activated in interpreting the events that made us depressed in the past will be reactivated. These events will tend to be related to themes of loss, failure, self-devaluation, and the like. Consequently, in depressed mood, current experience will be more likely to be interpreted negatively along these themes. Negatively biased thinking in depression is thus accounted for by effects of depressed mood increasing the accessibility of negative interpretative constructs and of memories of unhappy events.

Bower's associative network model, and related experimental work, suggest that depressed mood biases cognitive processing in a negative direction in all of us. We can see the negative thinking of clinical depression as an extreme form of a normal effect of mood on information processing, rather than the result of "matching" environmental events activating related dysfunctional assumptions in vulnerable individuals. The network theory suggests that negative thinking is a *consequence* of depressed mood. It follows that this theory, unlike early versions of Beck's clinical cognitive model, has no difficulty with findings showing that negative thinking reduces as depression improves, even when the improvement results from pharmacotherapy, or from non-cognitive psychological treatments. Similarly, negative thinking in depressions with a primary biological aetiology can be explained: The source of current depressed mood may not matter too much so long as there has been a history of association between depressed mood and activation of negative interpretative constructs and memories in the past.

Network theory differs from the clinical cognitive model in suggesting that negative thinking is a *consequence* of depressed mood. However, network theory also suggests that negative thinking can be an *antecedent* to depression and in this respect is in agreement with Beck's model. As indicated earlier in Fig. 3.2, network theory suggests that emotion nodes can be activated by related cognitive appraisals; negative interpretations can turn on the depression node and so produce depressed affect.

The network theory suggests a reciprocal relationship between negative thinking and depressed mood. Once in depressed mood we are likely to interpret experience negatively. However, the patterns of thinking reactivated are exactly those which will have been involved in the production of depressed mood in the past. Consequently, those same patterns of negative thinking are likely to act to maintain depression in the present. Thus, self-perpetuating vicious cycles of the form shown in Fig. 3.3 can become established. Such cycles can act to maintain and intensify depression: Experiences interpreted in a particular way produce depression, but, once depressed, the cognitive system is biased in a way that will increase the chance that subsequent experiences will be interpreted in just the way that will produce more depression. In this way, application of the network model provides an explanation for the maintenance of depression.

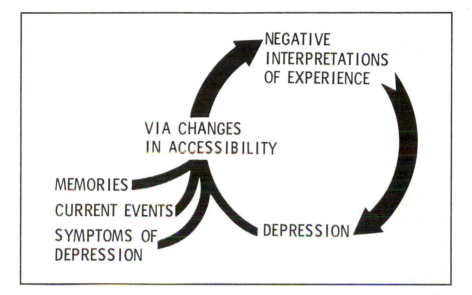

FIG. 3.3. A vicious cycle based on the reciprocal relationship between negative interpretations of experience and depressed mood. Reproduced from Teasdale, (1983b) with permission.

The reciprocal relation between negative thinking and depression suggested by network theory allows it to overcome many of the difficulties of Beck's cognitive model. The vicious cycle model indicated in Fig. 3.3 has provided heuristic insights not only into the maintenance of depression but also into the treatment of depression (Teasdale, 1985) and cognitive vulnerability to depression (Teasdale, 1988). Rather than describing all these applications, we shall focus, as an illustration of the heuristic value of this approach, on the account of cognitive vulnerability derived from network theory.

The Differential Activation Hypothesis of Cognitive Vulnerability

Figure 3.3 illustrates a mechanism that can transform an initial mild depressive reaction, that might otherwise be transient, into a more severe and persistent state. Similar processes can act to maintain depressions of greater severity over extended periods and prevent the natural remission that might otherwise occur.

Application of the network model to depression suggests that vulnerability to severe or persistent depression can be thought of in terms of the likelihood that the vicious cycle shown in Fig. 3.3 will be set up and will continue to rotate. What determines whether this will occur or not? That is, what is the basis of vulnerability to depression on this model? Remember that the negative biasing effects of depressed mood on cognitive processing are not restricted to those vulnerable to clinical depression, but are shown by most of us. Why do we not all get trapped in this vicious cycle?

We can identify a number of factors important here, e.g. the kind of environmental input we are dealing with, the extent of perceived social support, the intensity of the initial depressive reaction, and the presence of relatively enduring cognitive interpretative biases (Teasdale, 1988).

The associative network theory suggests that one further important factor is the type of memories and interpretative concepts and constructs that become reactivated in an initial depressed mood. The network model suggests that the constructs and memories reactivated in current depression are those previously associated with depression in an individual's life experience. Individuals will differ considerably in their learning histories in this respect. For example, some will have happy childhoods in which they sense that they are generally valued and cared for, brief periods of sadness being associated with mild parental criticism or specific failure experiences. Conversely, others will have more persistently unhappy childhoods characterised by rejection, separation, or loss. It follows that individuals may differ considerably in the patterns of cognitive processing reactivated by depressed mood. Although these patterns will tend to be negative in all of us, it may be only certain types of negative cognition that produce sufficient further depression to keep the cycle illustrated in Fig. 3.3 revolving. For example, reactivation of constructs related to a globally negative view of self as worthless, stupid, inadequate, and unloveable, or to a hopeless view of the future, will be more likely to lead to interpretations of experience that produce further depression, than will reactivation of constructs related to less intensely negative constructs.

The differential activation hypothesis (Teasdale, 1983b; 1988) was derived directly from the associative network model. It suggests that vulnerability to intense and persistent depressions may be determined primarily by individual differences in the accessibility of cognitions *once a person has become initially depressed*. On this view the problem is essentially related to the dynamics of the evolution of a depressive episode. Vulnerable individuals may "think" quite functionally in a normal mood state. However, as their mood becomes more depressed, a very dysfunctional set of cognitive biases becomes switched in. This approach contrasts with the more structural view of the clinical cognitive model, which emphasises enduring differences in basic assumptions and attitudes as the core vulnerability factor. The differential activation hypothesis does not deny the possible importance of enduring differences of the latter form.

However, its dynamic emphasis means that it can readily accommodate the failure to find differences on cognitive measures between recovered depressed subjects and normal controls, a finding which presented clear difficulties for the clinical cognitive model (p. 9). The differential activation hypothesis suggests that differences will be more likely to be obtained if measures are taken in mildly depressed mood.

There is encouraging preliminary support for this prediction. Teasdale and Dent (1987) compared performance on a measure reflecting the accessibility of global negative self-constructs in recovered depressed and never-depressed subjects. Accessibility of constructs was assessed both in normal mood and in experimentally induced depressed mood. The measure used required subjects to read a list of positive and negative trait adjectives, including global negative trait adjectives such as *pathetic*, *stupid*, and *worthless*, and to indicate the adjectives that described them and those that did not. Subsequently, they were given a surprise recall test for the adjectives. Within this paradigm, the extent of incidental recall of global negative words, previously rated as self-descriptive, is assumed to reflect the activation of those aspects of the self-concept to which the words refer. It was predicted that in depressed mood recovered-depressed subjects would recall more global negative words rated as self-descriptive than control subjects. The results showed that, in induced mild depressed mood, recovered-depressed subjects differed significantly in the predicted direction from controls on the measure of accessibility of global negative self-constructs. In the absence of depressed mood, scores on the measure of negative self view were identical for the recovered-depressed and never-depressed subjects (Teasdale, 1988, p.259).

Miranda and Persons (1988), and Miranda, Persons, and Byers (1990) have reported comparable findings from two studies of recovered-depressed and never-depressed subjects. Both studies examined the relationship between naturally occurring mild depressed mood (measured by the Multiple Affect Adjective Checklist) and scores on a measure of dysfunctional assumptions, the Dysfunctional Attitude Scale (DAS, Weissman & Beck, 1978). All subjects scored in the nondepressed range of the Beck Depression Inventory at the time of study, indicating that the previously depressed subjects were fully recovered from their episodes of depression.

The pattern of results was similar in both studies. The results from Miranda and Persons (1988) showed that recovered and never-depressed subjects did not differ in DAS score at low levels of depressed mood, replicating the general negative findings of prevous studies that had compared such groups in normal mood (p. 9, this volume). However, with increasing depressed mood, the DAS scores of the recovered-depressed group increased whereas those of the never-depressed group did not.

Consequently, mean DAS scores of the two groups differed substantially for subjects tested in mildly depressed mood, just as the differential activation hypothesis predicts.

Williams (1988) obtained further evidence supporting the differential activation hypothesis from a prospective study of Oxford undergraduates. Scores on the incidental recall measure of global negative self-view used by Teasdale and Dent (1987) were obtained in both normal and experimentally induced mild depressed mood, at Time 1. Subjects were then followed over the course of a year, completing the Beck Depression Inventory every few months. Measures of negative self-view taken in normal mood at Time 1 failed to predict depression at any of these assessments. By contrast, measures of the extent to which, at Time 1, negative self-view increased as subjects moved from normal to induced depressed mood significantly predicted subsequent depression on three out of the four assessment occasions. Again, these findings provide promising initial support for the idea that cognitive vulnerability to depression may not be related so much to enduring differences in dysfunctional attitudes or assumptions as to differences between individuals in the patterns of thinking that become activated once they are in mildly depressed mood.

Conclusions

In Chapter 2 we took mood-congruous retrieval as a starting point for a systematic, experimentally based, enquiry into mood-related cognitive biases. The strategy we adopted aimed to increase understanding of depressive thinking in general by investigating a specific aspect of it in some depth. Chapter 2 concluded that mood-congruous retrieval might profitably be understood in terms of the more general phenomenon of context-specific encoding and retrieval. In other words, mood-congruous retrieval could be seen as an example of mood-state-dependent learning.

This chapter has focused on Bower's associative network model of mood and memory. According to this theory, mood-state-dependent learning is the basic phenomenon underlying mood-congruous retrieval and a wide range of other mood-related biases in information processing. Bower et al. (1978) provided initial experimental evidence for the existence of mood-state-dependent learning.

The associative network model has offered a plausible account of mood-state-dependent learning, mood-congruous retrieval, and a range of effects of mood on cognition. Further, as we saw in the previous section, network theory has fruitfully been applied to understanding a number of aspects of clinical depression. The insight that negative interpretations can be a *consequence* of the depressed state as well as an *antecedent* to depression overcomes one of the major difficulties encountered by Beck's original cognitive model. At the same time, this view retains one of the most important practical implications of the Beck approach: If negative interpretations antecede depression, then it is important to explore further psychological treatments, such as cognitive therapy, that aim to modify negative thinking.

Application of the associative network theory to cognitive vulnerability provided another example of how this experimentally derived approach has given useful insights in an area where existing evidence has caused difficulties for the clinical cognitive model. The suggestion of the differential activation hypothesis, that differences between recovered depressed subjects and controls are likely to be found if measures are taken in mildly depressed, rather than normal mood, has received encouraging preliminary support.

Overall, a preliminary assessment of the associative network model as a candidate theory to explain depressive thinking seems to be "so far so good". One of the virtues of such an experimentally derived theory is that it is open to continuing detailed exploration and test. At the same time, historically, that network theory was being applied fruitfully to understanding clinical depression, back in the laboratory experimentation directly relevant to evaluating and refining the theory continued. In the next chapter we consider the outcome of these investigations.

CHAPTER FOUR

Evaluating the Associative Network Model of Mood and Memory

The associative network theory has been subjected to detailed empirical and theoretical examination. Experimental investigations have focused both on testing predictions derived from the model, and on examining mood-state-dependent learning, the phenomenon assumed to form the basic substrate of mood-related cognitive biases within associative network theory. We begin by considering evidence of the replicability of Bower et al.'s (1978) demonstration of mood-state-dependent retrieval.

Mood-state-dependent Memory: Attempts at Replication

Bower et al. (1978) obtained evidence of mood-state-dependent memory when they used a two-list design, but failed in two studies using single-list designs. Difficulties in demonstrating mood-state-dependent retrieval, using one-list designs, have been reported in a number of other studies. Some (e.g. Isen, Shalker, Clark, & Karp, 1978; Nasby & Yando, 1982, Experiments 1 and 2; Schare, Lisman, & Spear, 1984) found no effects. Others (e.g. Leight & Ellis, 1981, Experiment 2; Macht, Spear, & Levis, 1977) found only partial or asymmetric mood-dependent retrieval. Positive results for mood-dependent retrieval were reported in six studies, most using the two-word list interference design (Bartlett, Burleson, & Santrock, 1982; Bartlett & Santrock, 1977; Goerss & Miller, 1982, cited by Bower & Mayer, 1989; Mecklenbräuker & Hager, 1984; Schare et al., 1984,

Experiment 3; Thompson, cited by Bower, 1981). These studies appeared to offer convincing corroboratory evidence to Bower et al.'s (1978) findings. However, following three failures to obtain mood-dependent retrieval using the two-word list design (Ellis, 1983, and Bayer, 1982, both cited by Bower & Mayer, 1989; Wetzler, 1985), doubts about the replicability of the phenomenon of mood-state-dependent retrieval (MDR) arose. In response, Bower and Mayer (1989) conducted a series of experiments attempting to replicate the earlier positive findings. In their first three studies, the procedure was essentially the same as that used by Bower et al. (1978). Not one of these studies obtained the predicted mood-state-dependent effects. Bower and Mayer (1989, p. 133) concluded that the initial demonstration of mood-dependent retrieval by Bower et al. (1978) was "an unreliable, chance event, possibly due to subtle experimenter demand. Given similar procedures, the MDR effect simply does not replicate".

In all these unsuccessful attempts to demonstrate mood-dependent retrieval, mood was induced before the word list to be learned was presented. In other words, the relationship between the words and the mood was merely one of contiguity or temporal association. An experiment by Thompson (cited by Bower, 1981) produced positive evidence of mood-dependent retrieval when subjects were asked to think of each word as deepening or intensifying their mood. This led Bower and Mayer (1989, p. 136) to suggest that mood-dependent retrieval might require the subject to relate their aroused emotional reaction causally to the material to be learned: "If subjects causally attribute their emotional reactions to the material—if they perceive the two as 'causally belonging' together—then we believed that they should form a strong association in memory between the stimulus event and the emotion it evoked. According to this hypothesis, contiguity alone, without belongingness, produces either no connections or only weak ones". The stress in this "causal belongingness" hypothesis is on the *perception* and *attribution* of causality of the mood to the event. There is no need for the event "really" to have caused the mood. This is an important point, both in relation to the adequacy of the hypothesis, and also in relation to the way the hypothesis might be investigated. According to the causal belongingness hypothesis, if subjects can be persuaded to believe that certain events caused a shift in their mood then this should produce mood-dependent retrieval for those events, whether or not the events actually had a causal role. Bower and Mayer (1989) tested this hypothesis in two experiments. The learning stimuli were brief descriptions of happy or sad episodes. Subjects were asked to imagine themselves experiencing each episode and to imagine it causing an appropriate emotion in them. To assist them, a musical mood induction was first used to get them into the appropriate mood. The music continued to play as they deepened their mood in the direction of increasing happiness or sadness with the presentation of each event description. The presence of mood-dependent retrieval was assessed by comparing recall of items learned in a mood that matched retrieval mood with recall of items learned in a mood that mismatched retrieval mood. In the first experiment (Bower & Mayer, 1989, Experiment 4), average recall was 64% for mood-matching items versus 56% for mismatching items, a difference of only marginal statistical significance. More powerful effects were shown in subjects with more extreme moods. A replication of this "causal belongingness" experiment (Bower & Mayer, 1989, Experiment 5), although essentially identical to Bower and Mayer's Experiment 4, failed to obtain positive results. Bower and Mayer were unable to offer any ready explanation for the ultimate lack of success of their remarkably persistent attempts to demonstrate mood-state-dependent memory, suggesting that the causal belongingness hypothesis should be viewed only as an interesting conjecture that was not confirmed by the particular methods chosen to investigate it. They concluded that their earlier positive findings (Bower et al., 1978, Experiment 3) "were either an unreplicable, chance outcome or possibly due to the experimenter demand produced by an expert hypnotist who had close rapport with his subjects" (Bower & Mayer, 1989, pp. 152-153).

Mood-state-dependent learning represents the central phenomenon assumed to underpin the network model of mood and memory. The failure to replicate Bower et al.'s (1978) original findings, which provided the initial empirical foundation for the network theory, undermines the confidence we can place in this theory. Further difficulties have arisen as the predictions of network theory in relation to a range of mood-related cognitive biases have been examined. We consider this work next.

Absence of Predicted Perceptual Effects

The associative network model suggests that, in a given mood state, extra activation flows out from the currently active emotion node to all nodes representing mood-congruent events, concepts, and constructs. It follows that the perceptual thresholds for words related to mood-congruent concepts should be reduced relative to those for mood-incongruent concepts. As Bower (1985, p. 1) pointed out: "The spreading activation theory in my *American Psychologist* paper of 1981 predicts a perceptual effect, that a pleasant mood would prime and lower the threshold for pleasant words—or, at least, increase the response bias in their favour. And, unpleasant moods should facilitate identification of unpleasant words". In this same paper, Bower reported four experiments failing to find the predicted mood effects on word perception. These negative findings have been corroborated by at least as many studies conducted by Maryanne

Martin, David Clark, and their colleagues in Oxford (e.g. Clark, Teasdale, Broadbent, & Martin, 1983). We have here a situation in which effects strongly predicted by the network model have simply not been obtained. This is obviously a considerable embarrassment to the associative network theory.

The absence of mood effects observed in these studies poses problems for any model that suggests that mood affects the relative activation of concepts closely linked to hedonically valenced words. These findings suggest that we might profitably consider the possibility that moods may have their effects at a higher level of representation than the level of words or concepts (see following).

Effects of Mood on Judgement

The associative network model suggests that effects of mood on evaluative judgements are mediated through the effects of mood on memory. For example, it is argued that in a negative mood the relative accessibility of representations of negative instances related to a person or topic will be increased. This will bias judgements made in the mood in two ways. First, the available database on a topic used to make judgements will be biased in a mood-congruent direction. Second, consistent with Tversky and Kahneman's (1973) availability heuristic, material that is more available or accessible will be given greater weight in the judgemental process. Consequently, in a negative mood, the greater accessibility of negative material in memory will mean that this material is accorded greater weight in judgements. For example, Bower (1981, p. 140) reported a study in which subjects gave "thumb-nail personality sketches" of familiar people in their lives (e.g. cousin, uncle, friend, teacher, etc.) in happy or angry moods. Happy subjects gave happy character descriptions 84% of the time, but angry subjects gave such descriptions only 59% of the time. Bower (1981, p. 140) concluded: "Assuming heterogeneous impressions have been stored about familiar persons, we may suppose that current mood causes retrieval of primarily positive or primarily negative memories of a familiar person. In this way, the summary evaluation is thus biased by the *availability* of the positive versus negative features that come to mind (see Tversky & Kahneman, 1973). This is just an affect-state dependent effect in disguise."

In Chapter 11, the experimental evidence on effects of mood on evaluative judgements is discussed in greater detail. This will reveal difficulties in three areas for the associative network theory's contention that mood effects on judgement are mediated through mood effects on memory: (1) there is often a dissociation between the effects of mood on judgement and on memory; (2) the effects of mood on judgements are often more global than a selective accessibility explanation would predict; and

(3) mood effects on judgement can be eliminated by providing information on the source of the mood. The difficulties of the network theory's account of mood effects on judgement are particularly relevant to our concerns: Negatively biased judgements of self-worth or of the possibilities of future success and happiness are some of the most striking features of depressive thinking that we have to explain.

Nonequivalence of the Effects of Different Moods

The network model proposes a general account of, for example, the way in which a current mood state increases the relative probability of recall of material congruent in hedonic or affective tone with the mood state. It follows that the type of mood-congruous memory biases seen in depression should also be seen, for appropriate content, in anxiety. That is, in the same way that depressed mood increases the recall of memories or material with unhappy or negatively evaluative content, so anxious mood should increase the recall of threat- or danger-related material, as this will previously have been associated with the experience of anxiety. In fact, in contrast to the robust effects of mood-congruous recall in depression, it has often been difficult to demonstrate comparable memory effects for anxiety (e.g. Mogg, Mathews, & Weinman, 1987; Williams, Watts, MacLeod, & Mathews, 1988, pp. 89-90). Conversely, the demonstrated effects of anxiety on measures of selective attention such as the Stroop colour-naming task (Mathews & MacLeod, 1985; Watts, McKenna, Sharrock, & Trezise, 1986) or dot probe technique (MacLeod, Mathews, & Tata, 1986) have not been so readily demonstrable for depression (e.g. MacLeod et al., 1986; and see Williams et al., 1988, pp. 167–168). Such findings of asymmetries between mood states pose considerable difficulties for an unelaborated version of the associative network model.

Theoretical Difficulties

In addition to the difficulties posed by accumulating experimental evidence, problems for the associative network model at the theoretical level have also been increasingly recognised.

The "Fan-out" Problem

Within the associative network model, the central effective mechanism underlying mood effects on cognition is the spread of activation from an emotion node to the nodes corresponding to all the events and concepts previously activated during experiences of that emotion throughout a person's life. The increased activation from an emotion node that occurs in a mood state is assumed to spread out divided among links to all the nodes attached to it. As Simon (1982) has pointed out, this "fan-out" effect creates a considerable problem for the network account because there must be an enormous number of nodes referring to the emotional events associated with each emotion node. It follows that any increment in activation from the emotion node resulting from a change in mood state will be divided and "diluted" many times through these multiple connections. Consequently, the increment in activation at any one node corresponding to a specific event will be extremely small. It is difficult to see how such small effects could be sufficient to produce, for example, mood-congruous recall.

Gilligan and Bower (1984) acknowledged that the fan-out problem is a formidable difficulty for the network theory. Indeed, it seems that it will be a problem for any model that relies on spreading activation and direct links from emotion to representations at the level of specific concepts and events. The problem can be overcome by abandoning the spreading activation metaphor, or by connecting emotion to a higher level of representation, or, of course, by adopting both these moves.

The "fan-out" problem appears to be a central flaw in the theoretical underpinnings of the network model. In addition further, more specific, inadequacies have been recognised. Bower and Cohen (1982) themselves identified the following problematic areas, and proposed amendments to the original model to accommodate them: (1) the role of cognitive appraisals in the generation of affect; (2) the distinction between "hot" versus "cold" use of emotion concepts; (3) the fact that emotional experiences can be remembered with emotion ("hot") or without emotion ("cold"); and (4) the reinterpretation or reappraisal of earlier emotional memories. The second and third of these issues are of particular interest.

"Hot" versus "Cold" Processing and Representations of Emotional Material

The original network model had one node for each emotion, such as "fear", and suggested that reference to or use of that concept would somehow "turn on" that fear node in the network. Bower and Cohen (1982, p. 308) point out that this is also the operation the model identified as "feeling afraid" subjectively, leading to "the absurd implication that people always feel afraid when they refer to the concept". They note that people discourse coolly about emotions many times without feeling the emotion at all. The solution they proposed to this problem was to suggest a distinction between a "cold" node corresponding to the concept of, for example, fear, and a "hot" node corresponding to the experience of fear itself. This is very much an ad hoc solution. It is also one which does not address the more general problem that we can use affect-related concepts (such as *loving*, *worthless*, or *terrifying*) without necessarily experiencing the related emotion. Within the network theory, nodes for these concepts are linked to the emotion nodes by connections through which activation flows in both directions. Consequently, use of these concepts would be expected to increment the activation of related emotion nodes, and so to intensify emotion. Clearly, this does not inevitably occur. This problem could be solved by proposing whole duplicate sets of "hot" and "cold" concept nodes, but this would be a cumbersome solution, particularly as there would then also be a need for mechanisms to select between the types of node.

A related problem is that emotional memories can be remembered either with re-experience of the original feelings ("hot"), or without them ("cold"). In the latter case, a person may be able to remember not only that the emotional event occurred, but also many detailed aspects of it, without experiencing related feelings. Within the original network model only one form of representation of an event was proposed. This makes it difficult for this approach to handle the extremely important distinction between the "hot" and "cold" processing of emotional memories. Such difficulties seem inherent in an approach that (1) proposes only one form of representation of events, consisting of interconnections between nodes for the concepts encoding the event, and that (2) explains emotional effects in terms of activation flowing backwards and forwards through richly interconnected bidirectional links between emotion nodes and event and concept nodes.

General Limitations of Associative Network Models

Semantic network models deal only with representations at the level of concepts and their direct inter-relationships. This representation of all knowledge in a single uniform format has been noted as a general problem for network theories by a number of workers. Rumelhart and Norman (1983, p. 38), for example, have pointed out that semantic network models, in general, cannot represent knowledge at levels of meaning beyond that of the word or sentence. Within mainstream cognitive psychology, this has led to attempts to introduce higher-order levels of representation such as schemas, scripts, and plans (Rumelhart & Norman, 1983). Similarly, Power and Champion (1986, p. 203) suggest that there are many domains of knowledge that require much larger units of organisation than those handled by network theories, e.g. typical sequences of events, actions, and situations for which a more molar level of organisation is more useful. The need for higher levels of representation is particularly relevant to emotion, where the importance of the wider context in determining the emotional impact of an event or item of information is generally recognised (e.g. Brown & Harris, 1978, Chapter 5).

Network models also have a number of weaknesses as accounts of memory, in general (Power & Champion, 1986). Morton, Hammersley, and Bekerian (1985) have argued that network models cannot account for certain failures in memory. For example, it is difficult for such approaches to explain the inability to recall someone's name despite recalling many other details about them (e.g. height, occupation, when you last met them, the fact they owe you £5, etc.). In a network model the spreading activation from these nodes *should* intersect at the required name, yet recall may not occur until later. Morton et al. (1985) argued that such observations should direct us towards models of memory in which, in contrast to network models, concepts may have multiple unconnected representations.

A Working Evaluation of the Associative Network Theory of Mood and Memory

It is clear that closer examination and investigation of Bower's associative network theory of mood and memory has revealed a number of formidable difficulties at both the empirical and theoretical level. Before considering the implications of these difficulties for the usefulness of the network approach to our goal of understanding depressive thinking, it is necessary to consider briefly how, in general, we should approach the task of evaluating such conceptual frameworks.

A general conceptual framework, such as the associative network model of mood and memory, has to be judged on the extent to which it is useful or not, rather than whether it is "true". Unlike a specific hypothesis, a conceptual framework is not amenable to falsification by experimental results that run counter to prediction. A framework can accommodate such results by making suitable adjustments in the light of the new data. This can either lead to an improved framework or one which has so many ad hoc patches and fresh assumptions added to it that it becomes less useful. In this latter situation, it may be judged that, overall, the existing framework has done a good job but that it is now more useful to look to alternative frameworks. This decision is, ultimately, a matter of personal judgement.

Our own view is that the difficulties of the network model reviewed in this chapter force us to a re-evaluation of this approach. Although initially attractive and useful as a candidate theory for understanding negative depressive thinking, the associative network approach must now be regarded as having so many problems that consideration of alternative theoretical approaches is justified. A strength of experimentally derived theories such as the associative network model is that the clarity with which they are expressed allows derivation of hypotheses that make specific, testable, predictions. As a result, we have been able to assess the strengths and weaknesses of the network theory with some precision. The detail with which we can pinpoint the deficiencies of the network model allows us to produce an outline "prescription" for alternative theories if they are to avoid the problems encountered by network theory. We present our "prescription" next.

A "Prescription" for Alternatives to the Associative Network Theory of Mood and Memory

The effects of mood on information processing are unlikely to be explained adequately by simple models in which concepts and events are represented in a single representational format and these representations are "automatically" and directly primed or activated by moods. Rather, in order to account adequately for cognitive-affective relationships, models are likely to need to include qualitatively different types of representations (1) to accommodate the distinction between "hot" and "cold" memories and knowledge; (2) to allow for multiple, functionally independent, representations of related material in memory; and (3) to capture the need for representations at levels of abstraction more generic than those of the word, concept, or sentence.

In Part II of this book we outline an alternative conceptual framework for understanding mood effects on information processing and affect-cognition relations in general. This framework will then be assessed against the criteria stated, and its account of specific experimentally demonstrated mood effects on cognition compared with that offered by the associative network account. Before proceeding to Part II we summarise the broad conclusions emerging from Part I.

Part I: Conclusions

We have seen that Beck's original cognitive model of depression, derived from acute clinical observation and inspiration, has been of fundamental importance in drawing attention to the possible role of negatively distorted thinking in the origins, maintenance, and treatment of depression. Essentially a clinical theory, it has had enormous heuristic value but has encountered increasing difficulties as an explanatory account. Particularly problematic has been evidence suggesting that negative thinking may be a consequence of depression, and also the difficulty in demonstrating the predicted persisting cognitive vulnerabilities in those who have been depressed. The rigour with which negative depressive thinking could be examined was increased considerably by taking it into the laboratory and focusing on the specific phenomenon of mood-congruous retrieval of autobiographical memories. Investigations of this phenomenon in normal and clinical populations provided the precise evidence from which more detailed experimentally derived explanatory accounts could be generated.

The most influential of these accounts, the associative network model of mood and memory, had an initial attraction and plausibility. Taking this theory out of the laboratory and applying it back to clinical depression provided us with a view of negative thinking that overcame the difficulties of the Beck model. The network view accounted satisfactorily for evidence of negative thinking as a consequence of depression, and provided a more firmly supported view of cognitive vulnerability than did the clinical cognitive model. Furthermore, it did so while retaining, through the suggestion of a reciprocal relationship between negative thinking and depression, the essential postulate of Beck's model that negative cognition can play an important role in the maintenance and treatment of depression.

Reflecting the continuing iterative interaction between experiment, theory, and application, characteristic of the applied science approach, the next stage was to reconsider the adequacy of the associative network theory in relation to further experimental and theoretical scrutiny. As we have seen in the present chapter, this scrutiny revealed enough problems to suggest that it would be useful to consider alternative theoretical approaches. Recognition of only a single level of semantic representation, or meaning, appeared to be a central source of difficulty for network theory. Interestingly, the clinical cognitive model shared the same weakness. Like network theory, the clinical model has particular difficulties with the contrast between "hot" and "cold" processing, and between knowing "with the head" versus "with the heart". Both of these contrasts are of particular importance in understanding clinically significant cognitive-affective phenomena. A virtue of the experimental-theoretical component of the total applied science strategy is that the precision with which the deficiencies of existing theories can be identified provides guidance for the development and recognition of improved theories.

In Part II we describe an alternative candidate theory, Interacting Cognitive Subsystems. From our discussion of the inadequacies of network theory, and of the desirable features to be included in alternative approaches, it should come as no surprise that this theory is more complex than Bower's associative network model of mood and memory.

PART II

The Interacting Cognitive
Subsystems (ICS) Approach

CHAPTER FIVE

The Interacting Cognitive Subsystems Framework

Introduction

We need an explanatory account that (1) recognises qualitatively different types of information; (2) includes emotion; and (3) allows accounts of cognitive-affective interaction to be incorporated into a more general, comprehensive, account of information processing. The Interacting Cognitive Subsystems (ICS) framework aims to provide such an account.

First described by Barnard (1985), ICS claims to offer a conceptual scheme within which, in principle, accounts of any aspect of information processing can be developed. ICS was originally applied to the explanation of performance on short-term verbal memory tasks (Barnard, 1985). Subsequently, it has found fruitful application in the field of human-computer interaction (e.g. Barnard, 1987; Duff, 1992). ICS has only recently been extended and applied to the interaction of cognition and emotion (Barnard & Teasdale, 1991).

Given the ambitious aim of providing a comprehensive information-processing framework, it will come as no surprise that the full richness of the ICS approach cannot be conveyed in a few paragraphs. Our strategy for presenting ICS is to reveal, progressively, aspects of the total approach on a "need-to-know" basis. We begin with a brief statement of the essential features of this framework. The remainder of the chapter discusses each of these aspects in considerably more detail.

ICS—The Essence

ICS explicitly recognises qualitatively different kinds of information, or mental codes, each corresponding to a different aspect of experience. Information processing within ICS consists of two basic processes: the storage of patterns of information, and the transformation of patterns of one kind of information into patterns of other qualitatively different kinds of information. The operations of these two basic processes are constrained by a set of seven principles, e.g. any given transformation process can only handle one coherent stream of information at a time (Barnard, 1985).

Each different kind of information is transformed and stored by processes that are specialised for dealing with that particular kind of mental code and no other. These specialised processes are arranged in distinct subsystems, each subsystem storing and transforming only one kind of information.

Information processing depends on information flowing from one subsystem to another. Each subsystem generates, from the patterns in the single information code that it takes as input, new patterns in the information codes that it creates as output.

A subsystem can perform several simultaneous and parallel transformation operations on the patterns of information it receives as input. The output from a given subsystem can be fed to several other subsystems, where further processing of related information can occur in parallel. The outputs from these subsystems can feed back, in turn, to the original subsystem. As a result of such sequential, parallel, and distributed processing, complex, mutually interacting patterns of information processing can evolve over time. The nature of such processing will depend on the total configuration of processing resources involved and the kind of information that is flowing round the system and being accessed from memory stores.

Development of the processes that transform information, and development of most of the mental codes, depend on the accumulated experience of the system. Recurring regularities and co-occurrences in the patterns of different kinds of information are extracted to form the basis of transformation processes, and of new patterns in higher-order codes.

Information related to a given topic may be represented in patterns of several different mental codes. The representations related to a given topic in one code can have functional relationships that are quite different to those of related representations in other codes. A very important example of this aspect of the ICS approach is the proposal that only patterns in one particular form of information are directly related to affect.

ICS is explicit about the relationship between aspects of information processing and aspects of subjective experience. Each of the different information codes corresponds to a distinct quality of subjective experience. Within each of those distinct types of experience, diffuse and focal subjective experience correspond to different underlying information-processing configurations.

Having baldly described certain key features of the ICS approach in this way, we will now consider each of them in more detail.

Qualitatively Distinct Types of Information

ICS recognises a distinction between qualitatively different types of information, encoded in separate mental codes. Three of these codes encode sensory information; two encode intermediate stuctural level descriptions, capturing recurring regularities in the sensory code patterns encountered; two encode specific and generic levels of meaning; and the remaining codes encode the information required for effector action. The codes are summarised in Table 5.1, and the relationships between sensory, structural description, and meaning codes are illustrated in Fig. 5.1.

The three sensory codes (Acoustic, Visual, and Body-state) represent the information delivered by the first stage analysis of raw sensory input. The Acoustic code (AC) captures features such as the pitch, intensity, and timbre extracted from patterns of sound waves . The contents of Visual code (VIS) represent features extracted from patterns of light, for example, hue and variations in brightness over spatial location. Patterns of Body-state code (BS) reflect features extracted from the analysis of sensory input from internal receptors, related to taste, smell, touch, proprioception, and pain.

At the intermediate level of structural description, patterns of Morphonolexical (MPL) code represent recurring regularities, such as the sounds of words, that have been detected in the patterns of Acoustic code encountered. This code will vary from one speech community to another: for example, the regularities encoded in the Morphonolexical code derived by a person surrounded by Japanese speakers will differ from the regularities encoded in the Morphonolexical code of a person growing up in the company of English speakers.

In parallel fashion, patterns of Object (OBJ) code represent recurring regularities and co-occurrences extracted from the total data set of Visual codes encountered by an individual. Such regularities will include structurally integrated visual objects, such as tables or balls; spatial relations, such as above or behind; and dynamic characteristics, such as moving in a falling arc.

Patterns of Propositional (PROP) and Implicational (IMPLIC) code capture recurring regularities at even higher levels of abstraction. The relationships between entities encoded at these levels represent meaning. ICS recognises two levels of meaning reflected in patterns of, respectively,

TABLE 5.1
The Principal Information Codes of the ICS Framework

Sensory & Proprioceptive Codes

Acoustic (AC): encodes dimensions such as sound frequency (pitch), timbre, intensity, etc. Subjectively, this is what we "hear in the world".

Visual (VIS): encodes dimensions of light such as its wavelength (hue), brightness over visual space, etc. Subjectively, this is what we "see in the world" as patterns of shapes and colours.

Body-state (BS): encodes dimensions of internal sensory input such as type of stimulation (e.g. cutaneous pressure, temperature, olfactory, muscle tension), its location, intensity, etc. Subjectively, this code corresponds to bodily sensations of pressure or pain, positions of parts of the body, as well as tastes and smells.

Intermediate Structural Description Codes

Morphonolexical (MPL): encodes an abstract structural description of entities and relationships in sound space. Dominated by speech forms, where the principal dimensions encompass a surface structure description of the identity of words, their status, order, and the form of boundaries between them. Subjectively, and when uncorrelated either with real-world acoustic events or with articulatory information, this code corresponds to what we "hear in the head".

Object (OBJ): encodes an abstract structural description of entities and relationships in visual space. The principal dimensions encompass the attributes and identity of structurally integrated visual objects, their relative positions, and dynamic characteristics. Subjectively, and when uncorrelated with real-world visual events, this code corresponds to what is actively produced in "visual imagery".

Meaning Codes

Propositional (PROP): encodes a description of entities and relationships in semantic space. The principal dimensions encompass the attributes and identities of underlying referents and the nature of relationships among them. Subjectively, this code corresponds to being aware of specific semantic relationships ("knowing that").

Implicational (IMPLIC): encodes an abstract description of human existential space itself. This space is abstracted over both sensory/proprioceptive and propositional input. The principal dimensions encompass both ideational and affective content. Very high-level regularities in the world, the body, and the "mind" are captured at this level. The mental entities constructed can be seen as schematic models of experience. Subjectively, this code is associated with holistic "senses" of knowing (e.g. of "familiarity" or "causal relatedness" of ideas) or of affect (e.g. apprehension, confidence).

Effector Codes

Articulatory (ART): encodes dimensions such as the force, the target positions, and timing of articulatory musculatures (e.g. place of articulation). Subjectively, this code corresponds to our experience of subvocal speech output.

Limb (LIM): encodes dimensions such as the force, the target positions, and timing of skeletal musculatures. Subjectively, this code corresponds to "mental" physical movement.

Propositional and Implicational code. This distinction is central to many of the applications of the ICS framework. We indicate it briefly here and return to consider it in more detail later.

Patterns of Propositional code represent semantic entities (concepts) and the relationships between them. The representation of such

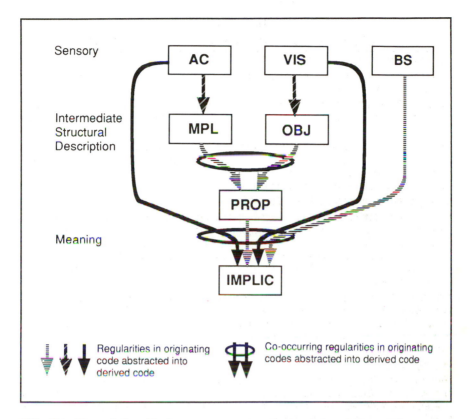

FIG. 5.1. The relationship between sensory, structural description, and meaning codes.

propositional statements has been the focus of, for example, semantic networks that encode relations such as "birds have wings" or "James is taller than William". Meaning at this level is relatively easy to grasp as it corresponds fairly closely to the kind of meanings conveyed by the sentences of language. Patterns of Propositional code capture meanings at the level of statements that assert specific relations that have a truth value, and can be assessed as true or false.

Codes representing meaning develop from the detection and extraction of patterns co-occurring and recurring across more than one lower-level code. Propositional meanings arise principally from the extraction of co-occurrences across patterns in Morphonolexical speech code and patterns of Object code, corresponding to visual objects and their relations. So, for example, the relational concept "above" will be derived from repeated experiences of seeing a certain spatial relationship between two objects in conjunction with speech code patterns such as "above" or "over" or "on top of".

This integration across lower codes is taken a step further at the Implicational level. Patterns of Implicational code constitute the most generic level of representation of all the ICS codes. Implicational codes capture recurring co-occurrences in the patterns across all other representational and sensory codes. Implicational code patterns integrate elements directly derived from low-level sensory codes together with elements derived from recurring higher-order patterns in Propositional code. These latter correspond to complexes of propositional meaning that have regularly co-occurred with those sensory elements in the person's experience. Prototypical patterns recurring across all other codes are extracted, integrated, and represented as patterns of Implicational code. Implicational code captures very high-level regularities in the world, the body, and "the mind". The mental entities constructed at this level can be seen as *schematic* models of experience.

These schematic models represent an holistic level of meaning. It is difficult to convey this sense of meaning adequately by language since the fairly direct relationship between words and related semantic entities and relations that exists at the propositional level no longer holds at the level of Implicational meaning. We discuss this type of meaning in more detail later. For now, we will consider a single example of the contrast between Propositional and Implicational meaning.

Consider a situation where A says to B "Try again". The propositional meaning of this statement ("I want you to try again"), considered in isolation, is fairly clear. We can add further Propositional level information to fill out the wider context to create different higher-order meanings. For example, in one case, we learn that A is a four-year old child asking B, her father, to rescue a beloved pet that has fallen down a well, that the water level in the well is rising, that night is falling, and that a severely cold night is forecast. In another case, we learn that A is B's boss, that B has been trying to get the books to balance, and that he has just failed in this objective for the tenth time. Clearly, the wider contexts give us two quite different higher-order views of these situations, that we can talk of as different "holistic" meanings. Such meanings cannot adequately be represented by a single Propositional statement that can be assessed for its truth value.

Let us now, in addition to the wider Propositional context, also bring in the contribution of sensory elements to create further variations of Implicational meaning. In one case, let us imagine A (the boss) uttering the statement in a soft, gentle voice tone, while smiling, and that B hears this while, at the bodily level, he feels alert and refreshed following a good night's sleep. In another case, A utters the statement in a strained, tense, exasperated voice tone, through gritted teeth, and B hears this at a point where he is already feeling exhausted at the bodily level. We are dealing here with considerably different "meanings" of the total situation to B in the two cases. The concept of "Implicational" meaning asserts that this totality of meaning can be captured "whole" (at an holistic level), in a way that is qualitatively different from the collection of propositional meanings and sensory information that may contribute to it. In the present example, the schematic models encoding the contrasting holistic meanings could be (albeit inadequately) tagged as ["What an understanding supervisor and how glad I am to be working here"] versus ["I have done it again and am for the chop, in this driving and uncaring organisation"].

We complete our survey of the information codes by noting two effector codes. Patterns of Articulatory (ART) code encode the information required for the control of motor speech output. Patterns of Limb (LIM) code encode the information required for the control of all other overt motor action.

Information Processing—Two Basic Operations

Within the ICS framework, all the "work" is done by two types of basic operations. The first of these are processes that transform the information encoded in one of the mental codes to information encoded in another mental code. We use the convention of representing such transformations by an arrow with the abbreviation for the mental code input to the process to the left of the arrow, and the abbreviation for the mental code output from the process to the right of the arrow. So, MPL $\rightarrow$ PROP represents the process which transforms the information encoded in Morphonolexical (speech level) code to information encoded in Propositional code (corresponding to derived propositional meaning).

Information processing occurs through a succession of such transformations. For example, the comprehension of spoken speech followed by the production of a vocal response would depend on the sequence: AC$\rightarrow$MPL; MPL$\rightarrow$PROP; PROP$\rightarrow$IMPLIC; IMPLIC$\rightarrow$PROP; PROP$\rightarrow$MPL; MPL$\rightarrow$ART. Processes are arranged within a cognitive architecture that allows for both serial and parallel processing of information (see following). As we shall see, this enables ICS to offer a framework with considerable explanatory power that can do justice to the complexities of human information processing.

ICS does not specify the precise form in which the actual operations of recoding transformations are realised. A connectionist network (Rumelhart & McClelland, 1986) taking one form of code as input and producing another form of code as output would be a wholly appropriate way in which to think of transformation operations being implemented. This approach captures features of transformation processes well: (1) they "learn" the appropriate recodings from one code to another on the basis of repeated experiences of co-occurrences between input patterns and output patterns; (2) they can be viewed as embodying "procedural knowledge" in that they "know" what output pattern to produce given a particular input pattern; (3) they are sensitive to the total pattern of input code so that a few discrepant elements in the total pattern can have profound effects on the output; but (4) they can operate on partial or degraded input patterns so long as these do not contain discrepant elements.

The second type of basic operation within ICS is the COPY process. This creates an exact copy of all the information in a given mental code entering the subsystem that handles that code, and stores it in a memory record specialised for information in only that code. As there are nine different types of information code, there are nine separate and distinct memory stores, each containing records of patterns in only one code. Within ICS, multiple representations of the same event can be stored, each representation reflecting the features of the event captured by a particular information code. So, for example, an upsetting interpersonal encounter could be encoded and stored in parallel (1) in separate sensory codes describing the scene in terms of, respectively, the qualities of sound (AC), light (VIS), and proprioceptive (BS) patterns involved; (2) in more perceptual codes that encode the scene in terms of the visual objects (OBJ) and speech components (MPL) present; (3) in a semantic code (PROP), which captures the meaning of the situation in the form of sequences of propositional statements; and (4) in an integrative schematic code (IMPLIC), which captures prototypical features of the situation corresponding to generic aspects of experience extracted from previous episodes. IMPLIC code might represent, for example, the schematic model related to the prototypical "argument with person I care for but who does not understand me" theme.

As well as providing an "episodic" record of all the patterns encountered in a given code, the code-specific memory stores provide the database from which code patterns that recur regularly can be detected and extracted.

Within ICS all "learning" occurs at the level of individual transformation processes. These processes "learn" to map inputs onto outputs on the basis of regular co-occurrences in the patterns of information stored in the episodic memory records of subsystems.

Stored representations play an equally important role in processing activity in general. We rely on such representations to remember where we have put things, what we were told, and so on. As will become more evident later, individual transformation processes (such as MPL → PROP) can use either direct input or stored representations of past inputs as the basis on which to generate outputs. In this way, use of memory records is an integral part of much processing activity.

Subjective Experience

The COPY processes described in the previous section form the basis of conscious experience. Subjective experience is seen as reflecting the nature of the code patterns that are being copied within particular subsystems at any given moment. Each of the different information codes is associated with a different aspect of phenomenal experience, as summarised in Table 5.1.

ICS suggests that we can use subjective experience as an indicator of the processing of specific types of information. In this way, both our own introspections and subjects' reports of their subjective experience can contribute usefully to the development of explanatory accounts. In contrast to the discredited procedures of the introspectionists, subjective experience is not assumed to give direct access to the underlying nature of cognitive operations.

This outline account of subjective awareness will be expanded, as the need arises, at later points in the book.

The Cognitive Architecture

Within ICS, the transformation and COPY processes are arranged in a cognitive architecture consisting of nine subsystems. Each cognitive subsystem is based on the same design, shown in Fig. 5.2, and each is specialised for processing input in only one information code. All the transformation processes that take a given mental code as input are arranged in parallel within the same subsystem. For example, the Acoustic subsystem contains both the AC→MPL and AC→IMPLIC transformation processes arranged in parallel. So, the AC→MPL process can convert patterns of Acoustic code sound information into elements of Morphonolexical speech code at the same time that the AC→IMPLIC process is analysing the Acoustic input to detect any patterns characteristic of, for example, angry voice tone. Outputs of these two transformation processes will then be fed to, respectively, the Morphonolexical and Implicational subsystems, for further processing.

The parallel arrangement of transformation processes within subsystems, coupled with the fact that all four "central" codes (OBJ, MPL, PROP, and IMPLIC) have transformation processes for reciprocal conversions of mental code (e.g. PROP→IMPLIC, IMPLIC→PROP; OBJ →PROP, PROP→OBJ), allows the development of complex, dynamic, reciprocal interactions between subsystems. For example, Fig. 5.3 shows, in outline, the patterns of reciprocal interaction between subsystems that are of most importance in the maintenance of emotional states such as depression (see Chapter 12).

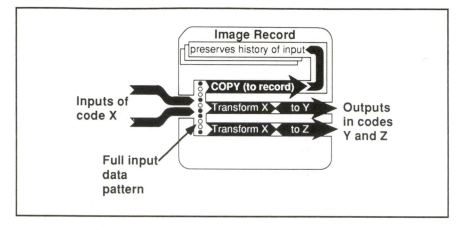

FIG. 5.2. The basic structure of a cognitive subsystem, illustrating the parallel organisation of transformation processes, the COPY process, and the memory store (image record)

Figure 5.4 illustrates, in greater detail, the total cognitive architecture of ICS, showing the more important of the recoding processes within each subsystem. In addition to the nine mental codes introduced earlier, Fig. 5.4 refers to two other outputs of Implicational processes (SOM and VISC). These, and certain other outputs (e.g. Motor, MOT) are "codes" that directly control effectors of one sort or another. Unlike their sensory counterparts, these particular codes are neither stored nor transformed. As such they were not included in our discussion of the nine principal codes, each of which is associated with its own subsystem. The Somatic (SOM) and Visceral (VISC) outputs of the Implicational subsystem play a key role in cognitive-affective processing, as we shall see later.

Dynamic Control

Within ICS, the combination of parallel and serial processing, together with the presence of reciprocal transformation processes (e.g. PROP→ IMPLIC; IMPLIC→PROP), allows the development of complex, dynamically evolving patterns of processing such as those illustrated in Fig. 5.3. How are these patterns of information flow and processing controlled?

Within ICS, control and co-ordination arise from the mutual interaction between semi-autonomous subsystems. The interacting cognitive subsystems operate very much as a "community", engaging in continuing interplay, exchange, and mutual influence to get the work of processing information done. We provide a number of detailed illustrations of such

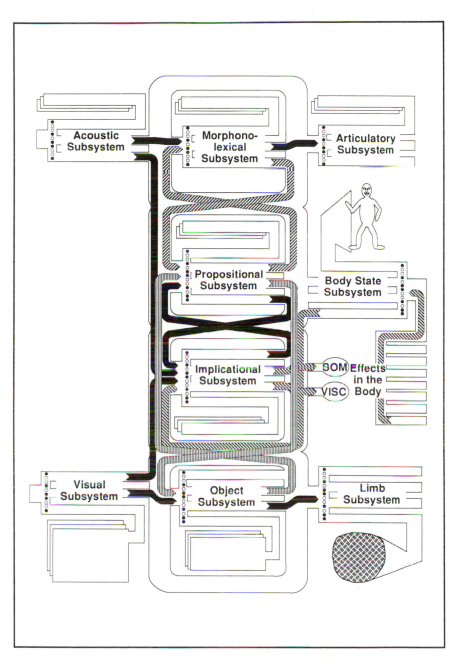

FIG. 5.3. The nine subsystems of the Interacting Cognitive Subsystems framework. The figure illustrates, in outline, the patterns of interaction that are of most importance in the production of emotion.

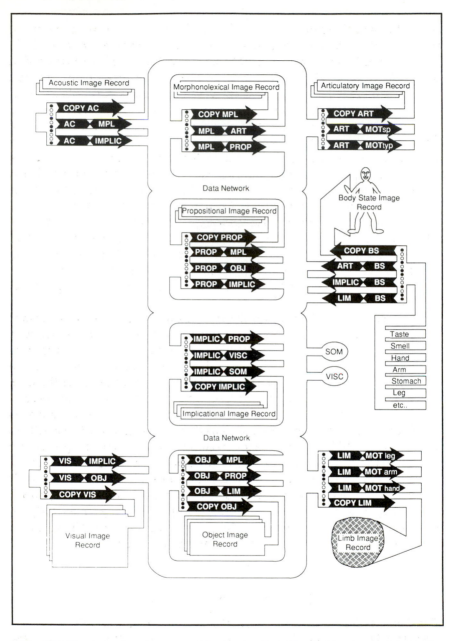

FIG. 5.4. The overall architecture of Interacting Cognitive Subsystems, showing the processes within subsystems that determine how information flows around the system. The data network is a means of depicting the rich interconnectivity between the processes of different subsystems while avoiding many overlapping arrows.

mutual interaction later in this book. For the moment, we note two of the most important factors that underlie control and co-ordination within ICS.

One factor is selection. The first basic principle governing the operation of ICS (Barnard, 1985, p. 216) is that any given transformation process can only recode (transform) one coherent data stream at a time. This means that, at the level of the individual transformation process, there has to be selection between the data streams arriving at a subsystem: At any one time only one of those data streams can be operated on by the transformation process. So, for example, if two people are speaking at the same time, the AC→MPL process will only be able to generate an MPL output for one of the two speakers. It follows that information from only one of the voice streams will be processed further. For example, extraction of the propositional meaning of the speech (by the MPL → PROP process) will only be possible for the speech stream that has already been subjected to AC→MPL processing. The basis of the selection made by an individual transformation process is inherent in the "procedural knowledge" of the process, and is based on its previous "learning history".

The second general factor influencing the direction in which patterns of information processing evolve is the existence of discrepancies between related pieces of information within the system. A range of cognitive modelling approaches use discrepancies in important ways to drive learning. For example, connectionist modelling techniques use differences between the actual and desired outputs as a basis for changing the relative strengths of the connections within the network (e.g. Rumelhart & McClelland, 1986). In a symbolic model like SOAR (Laird, Newell, & Rosenbloom, 1987), discrepancies between the information-processing requirements of a task and the information-processing repertoire already available are also a potent driving force for the expansion of the system's repertoire. In the same way, ICS assumes that informational discrepancies are a major force for developmental change and acquire priority in controlling the dynamics of interactions between processess. We expand on these assertions at appropriate points later in the book.

Theoretical Complexity in ICS

The basic building blocks of the ICS framework are simple and their operation is constrained in a principled way (Barnard, 1985). However, the possibility of mutual interactions between subsystems, developing dynamically over time, allows these simple basic elements to combine in ways that match the complexity and richness apparent in cognitive-affective interaction in human experience.

ICS claims to provide a comprehensive conceptual scheme within which, in principle, accounts of all aspects of information processing can be developed. Given such an ambitious aim, it should not be surprising that the framework will appear complex. This seems inevitable in an approach that attempts to use the same conceptual apparatus to account for an extended range of experimental and real-world phenomena. In reality, if one wants to understand a wide variety of phenomena, the alternative approach of developing a large number of separate "customised" explanatory accounts for specific domains will, ultimately, prove more complex and less heuristic.

Howard Leventhal has presented a comparably complex approach in his perceptual-motor theory of emotion (Leventhal, 1979, 1984; Leventhal & Scherer, 1987). (This theory, incidentally, has been a most helpful influence in our attempts to incorporate emotion into ICS.) We take heart from Leventhal's (1979, pp. 39–40) comments on his own approach:

> The theory I have elaborated is complex rather than simple, difficult to assimilate and remember, but I believe it comes closer to providing us with a workable model of affective reactions than the simpler theories ... I see no way of dealing with the more complex problems of social and emotional behaviour without theoretical analyses of the kind here proposed. The prior alternatives have been separate hypotheses ... and empirical generalisations. Empirical generalisation leads to endless bickering and attempts to settle arguments by counting how many studies come out one way or another. Theories based on single hypotheses lack the power needed for analysis of the problem. What is essential is a theory of the underlying mechanisms of emotion which allows us to anticipate and account for alternative and apparently conflicting outcomes.

We shall return to a fuller discussion of the issue of theoretical complexity in the final chapter of the book. For now, we continue our description of the ICS framework by considering, in more detail, in the next chapter, the two types of meaning recognised by ICS, and their interaction.

Summary

1. ICS is an apparently complex approach. Such complexity is unavoidable in any attempt to provide a comprehensive conceptual framework of the kind that understanding cognitive-affective interaction requires.
2. ICS recognises nine different forms of information, or mental codes. Of particular importance, both a specific (Propositional) and holistic (Implicational) level of meaning are recognised.

3. Each of the nine forms of information is processed by its own specialised subsystem. Each subsystem has its own memory records, so that there are nine distinct memory stores, each storing representations in only one information code.
4. All information processing consists of the storage of information or its transformation from one form to another. Such transformations are effected by individual processes, arranged in parallel within subsystems.
5. Transformation processes are "learned" and develop on the basis of detecting recurring regularities in input and output code patterns.
6. Subjective experience corresponds to the activity of COPY processes, is different for each information code, and can be used as a guide to the products of transformation processes.
7. The combination of serial and parallel processing, and the presence of reciprocal transformations (e.g. PROP→IMPLIC; IMPLIC→PROP) allow the evolution of complex, dynamically evolving patterns of information processing.
8. There is no "central executive" controlling the activity of subsystems. Rather, control is by mutual interaction between semi-autonomous subsystems. The selection of data streams by transformation processes and the existence of discrepancies between related aspects of information are particularly important influences affecting these interactions.

CHAPTER SIX

Two Levels of Meaning and their Interaction

We do not propose to grapple with the problem of specifying what we mean by meaning. Rather, our aim here is to focus on the contrast between the two levels of meaning represented by patterns of Propositional and Implicational code. We shall concentrate on meaning at the Implicational level, as meanings at the Propositional level can be conveyed relatively directly by language, and are therefore not difficult to grasp intuitively. We shall also discuss the central role played by the interaction between specific Propositional and generic Implicational meanings (the "central engine" of cognition) in a wide variety of tasks.

Implicational Meaning

There are three important aspects of Implicational meaning to be grasped: (1) the very high level of abstraction represented; (2) the nature of "schematic models"—what are they and how are they used? and (3) the contribution of both sensory-derived and meaning-derived elements to patterns of Implicational code.

We can use a parallel with the more familiar specific meanings represented by sentences to convey something of the very high level of abstraction represented in Implicational meanings. The specific meanings of sentences depend on binding together particular sequences of lower-order constituents such as letters, phonemes, or morphemes. In sentence interpretation the MPL→PROP process effectively discards the details of the surface structure of a sentence and replaces it with a more abstract encoding of referents, their properties, and semantic relationships. This more abstract representation encodes the specific, Propositional meaning of the sentence. In much the same way the construction of an Implicational representation from Propositional content (PROP→IMPLIC) replaces the details of many individual propositions with a yet more abstract and holistic representation of their content. This holistic representation, which may also include sensorily derived elements, encodes Implicational meaning.

In a sentence, the specific meaning conveyed by the total pattern of constituent elements is greater than the sum of the individual letters, phonemes, etc. In the same way, the generic Implicational meaning derived from configurations of specific meanings and coherent sensory patterns is qualitatively different from the sum of its constituent parts. This is why Implicational meanings cannot be conveyed adequately by language at the level of single sentences. Traditionally, attempts to convey meanings at this level by language have relied on parables, stories, and poems.

Our solution to the problem of communicating Implicational meaning is to refer to Implicational schematic models by verbal tags such as ["self as failure"] or ["argument with someone I care about but who does not understand me"]. These convey, very partially, the *topic* of the Implicational schematic model, but obviously not its constituent breakdown.

Implicational schematic models include constituents derived from the external world (via AC→IMPLIC and VIS→IMPLIC), the internal world of the body (via BS→IMPLIC) and the conceptual world of meaning (via PROP→IMPLIC). The specific meaning of a sentence can be altered radically by changing the sequence or value of individual constituent elements ("The man said go on" versus "The man said no go"). In the same way, generic Implicational meaning can be altered either by changing the value of elements related to specific meanings or of elements related to sensory elements. So, for example, the tendency to synthesise the schematic model ["myself as a total failure"] on hearing that one has failed on a particular task will be affected both by the wider context of specific meanings (how many other people failed at the same time) and by sensory state at the time of hearing the news (a smiling facial expression and alert, erect posture versus a frowning, downcast expression and slouched, beaten posture).

Schematic Models and Implicit Knowledge

The implicit knowledge encoded in coherent patterns of Implicational code can be thought of in terms of schematic models of experience. Just as mental models, in general, represent the inter-relationships between semantic elements (Johnson-Laird, 1983), so these schematic models represent inter-relationships between generic features of experience.

The essence of a model is that it represents aspects of the phenomenon modelled, especially the relationships between important features. So, a mechanical model of the solar system (Fig. 6.1) uses rotating metal spheres to represent the Sun and planets, their spatial relationships, the fact that planets revolve around the Sun, the fact that moons revolve around planets, and the relative speed of movement of the constituents. From observing the operation of the model it is possible not only to deduce that eclipses and conjunctions will occur, but also, in principle, to work out when they will occur.

In what ways is a coherent pattern of Implicational code analogous to such a model? The Implicational model is composed of informational elements, rather than metal spheres. These elements correspond to generic aspects, or dimensions, of the "external" and "internal" worlds extracted as "important" on the basis of previous experience. Each element can take different values, representing the current state of affairs with respect to the contrasts and dimensions related to that element. Let us consider a specific schematic model, for example, that related to ["dangerous domestic environment for a young child (self-present)"]. This model might include

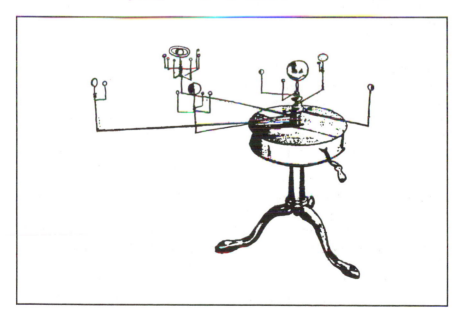

FIG. 6.1. A mechanical model of the solar system. As in schematic models, the key features represented involve the inter-relationships between elements.

elements related to the following dimensions of the "external world": "sharpness", derived from visual input indicating nonrounded corners and edges of surfaces such as tables or bookcases, moderated by the height of the surface in relation to the child's height; "breakability-cuttability" related to the presence of breakable objects, such as glass vases, their ability to cut if broken, their height in relation to the child's reach; "presence of young child" (obviously!), moderated by assessment of its degree of boisterousness and hyperactivity, state of consciousness (asleep-awake); "presence of parent and distance from child"—is the child sitting on the parent's knee under close control (or asleep) or wandering unnoticed while the parent is engrossed in conversation?; "parenting style of parent"—permissive-uncontrolling versus firm-and-responsible; "presence of other adults"—how many, who, how close to the child?; "presence of other immature beings"—such as other boisterous young children, or large, playful dogs, etc.

In addition to these elements reflecting the state of the "external" world, there will also be elements reflecting the "internal" world of the body and mind. So, Body-state derived elements will reflect the state of proprioceptive feedback from the face (relaxed smile versus worried frown), from the general somatic musculature (relaxed versus tense), and from autonomic arousal (low versus high), etc. Propositionally derived elements will reflect the content of recent thoughts (e.g. does the content include predictions of potential accidents, or not?, etc.).

We can think of these, and many further, dimensions of contrast as elements contributing to a total pattern of Implicational code such as [O●●O●●O]. For convenience, we can think of present status on each of the dimensions as represented by values of O or ● for each element. Each of these elements can be thought of as analogous to a letter in a sentence. Extraction of the patterns that correspond to letters (and words) from a visual input depends on an extensive learning history in which we have learned to parse complex visual arrays into letters (and words) as consistent recurring features. In the same way, extraction of the features related to the dimensions encoded in elements of Implicational code involves selection of information from the potentially vast array of information being processed by all subsystems. As in learning to extract letters, the extraction of features, and which features are extracted, will be a function of learning history. An individual brought up in a culture using Roman letters is unlikely to parse Arabic script in the same way as someone who has learned to read using Arabic characters. The first individual will perceive Arabic script primarily as complicated squiggles with few recurring features. Analogously, at the more generic Implicational level, someone brought up in a family where performance evaluation was accorded high salience will parse experience into Implicational elements that will be quite different from someone brought up in a much more laissez-faire family or culture.

The particular set of elements involved in a given Implicational model are an important characteristic of the model. This particular set of contrast dimensions is only a subset of an enormous potential set. The values (O or ●, in our simplified convention) on each of its constituent elements define the current state of the model. The inter-relationship between the values on different elements of the model is especially important. In a sentence, O followed by N has very different implications from N followed by O. In the same way, in an Implicational model, a pattern of Os and ●s reflecting the state of the elements related to presence of a young child, a large dog, and a priceless glass vase has very different implications depending whether or not the patterns of Os and ●s on other elements indicates that the child is on its parent's knee, the dog is at its master's feet, and the vase is in a display cupboard.

We have the elements of our schematic model assembled, but how does it work? How does it tell us anything, make predictions, or know when to produce an emotional reaction? Let us return to our model of the solar system for a moment. We suggested that operation of this model, suitably observed, would reveal the presence of eclipses, conjunctions, and the like, and allow us to predict their occurrence. Knowledge of the existence of such phenomena and when they will occur is "implicit" in the model. This "implicit" knowledge could be translated into a usable, explicit form by arranging a suitable optical or mechanical device to detect when, for example, the centres of the Sun, Earth, and Moon are aligned, and, at that point, to pass a message to a printer to print "ECLIPSE".

In the case of the Implicational schematic model related to ["dangerous domestic environment for a young child (self-present)"], there is "implicit" knowledge in the model related to predictions concerning the likelihood of harm, the need for preventive or interventive action, and the conditions for producing emotional and bodily reactions. The basis for this knowledge is two-fold. On the one hand, there is the experience accumulated over a lifetime of co-occurrences of related informational elements derived both from direct experiences, when one has been involved personally in related situations, and from indirect experiences, when one has heard, read about, or seen on television related experiences, of others. This knowledge is about "what goes with what" and what are the salient dimensions to be incorporated into the elements of the Implicational model. In other words, this knowledge is about how the complex arrays of information passing through the system are to be parsed into usable elements. These elements constitute the database built into the model, just as the orbits and relative sizes of planets are built into the clockwork model of the solar system.

The second aspect of the implicit knowledge of schematic models concerns the likely consequences, related actions, and emotions when the pattern of values on the elements of the model conforms to a critical pattern. This knowledge will be embodied in the procedural knowledge of the transformation processes in the Implicational subsystem that operate on patterns of Implicational code to produce further outputs. These transformation processes are analogous to the optical or mechanical devices that register an alignment of bodies in the solar system model and trigger the printer to print "ECLIPSE". In the case of ICS, the procedural knowledge will again be based on the accumulated experience of co-occurrences between informational elements; in this case, between specific patterns of Implicational code and the informational consequences. So, for example, the IMPLIC→PROP process will generate Propositional representations related to expectations of damage/harm when the pattern of Implicational code on the input side matches that which, in past experience, has subsequently been followed by Propositional representations of actual or possible harm. Similarly, the IMPLIC→VISC and IMPLIC→SOM processes will generate emotional reactions when the input pattern of Implicational code matches those previously occurring in situations in which those patterns have been followed by production of emotion (see Chapter 7). The production of appropriate action, if the Implicational pattern signals imminent disaster, is the result of IMPLIC→PROP producing appropriate Propositional "commands" on the basis of those that have previously occurred in the presence of that Implicational pattern.

We can see how the schematic model works, and the way implicit knowledge is realised, by considering a specific situation in detail. Imagine you are sitting in a room with a tall cut-glass vase full of gladioli on a low coffee table made of plate glass in an aluminium frame with very definite edges and corners. A three-year old child is asleep on his mother's knee, and a large Old English Sheepdog puppy is snoozing at its master's feet as you chat quietly to the two adults present. At this point, the pattern of Implicational code being delivered to your Implicational subsystem, although containing potentially threat-related values on the elements for young child present, other immature creature present, unstable breakable-cutting object present, and "sharpness", has threat-absent values on the elements related to "mobility of immature participants" and "proximity to/controllability by" elements. So, the total configuration of Implicational elements could be characterised as ["nonthreat, but potential elements of threat present"] and the Propositional output from the IMPLIC→PROP transformation carries the meaning "no action required but stay vigilant".

In the distance, the sound of rattling teacups and plates is heard from the kitchen. The dog pricks up her ears, stands up, stretches and looks expectantly towards the door. The value of the related element of Implicational code ("mobility of immature participants") changes, so that the total pattern now conforms to [potential threat—low risk]. The IMPLIC→PROP process, processing the revised pattern, produces output meaning "be prepared for action". This Propositional output produces, via the PROP→IMPLIC process, a shift in the pattern of thought-derived Implicational elements so that the total pattern now conforms to ["potential threat—low risk—more imminent"].

Suddenly the door opens, and the man of the house enters carrying a tray of drinks, cakes, and cookies. The child wakes up and rushes over to the door. The dog does the same on a course in which she is bound to collide with the child and knock him into the table. The values of Implicational elements are rapidly updated to produce a total pattern conforming to the schematic model ["imminent child-centred disaster—high risk"]. The transformation processes of the Implicational subsystem process this to produce a surge of adrenalin, predictions of injury, and instructions for motor action, just as, when the spheres for Earth, Sun, and Moon were in alignment, the solar system model produced instructions to print "ECLIPSE". You leap to your feet, and pick up the child as he is about to crash into the table and vase. The values on Implicational elements are updated and now approximate the pattern characteristic of the schematic model ["local hero does good"], and you return to your seat while the crowd cheers.

This account, in particular the notion of patterns of values (○ and ●) across a wide range of elements, may remind some readers of Rumelhart, Smolensky, McClelland, and Hinton's (1986) speculative extension of Parallel-distributed Processing (PDP) to schematic processing. Rumelhart et al.'s (1986) PDP account of schemas is a good way to get a further "flavour" of an approach similar in spirit to that of ICS in this respect, but presented in a way that is more computationally explicit than we have attempted.

As with PDP, the transformation processes in ICS can perform "pattern completion" on partial fragments of sentences and schematic models so that they are treated in the same way as more complete patterns. Pattern completion can result from repeated previous experiences with the total pattern that may have occurred a considerable time in the past. So, given many previous encounters with the total sentence, most people reading or hearing "the cat sat on the ..." would complete it with "mat". Similarly, if in the past one has repeatedly formed schematic models related to ["myself as a total failure"], a fragmentary pattern consisting of elements derived from currently processed depressive Body-state feedback (sad, frowning facial expression, stooped posture, low autonomic arousal, etc.) and Propositionally derived elements related to a single specific failure, may be completed to produce the ["myself as a total failure"] pattern.

The extent to which patterns of information from different sources are treated as coherent wholes depends on the procedural knowledge of the transformation process dealing with them. This, in turn, will reflect the previous history of co-occurrences of elements of information in coherent patterns. So, for example, if the MPL→PROP transformation process is presented with "The cat sat on the mat zzzzz", the zzzzz cannot be integrated with the otherwise coherent data stream, and will, most likely, not be subjected to further processing. Similarly, at the schematic model level, elements that do not cohere with the pattern that integrates the remainder of the elements may not be processed further. So, for example, if the majority of the elements conform to a schematic model ["myself as worthless, useless, pathetic, incompetent, unlovable"], elements that do not cohere with this pattern, such as evidence of a recent success, will not be processed further.

On the other hand, elements that have, in the system's processing history, consistently acted as discriminative markers of the coherence or lack of coherence of other patterns of elements may have profound influences on the way patterns of elements are bound together as they are processed. So, at the sentence level, addition of "snoring:" to the earlier sentence makes a coherent data pattern: "The cat sat on the mat snoring: zzzzz". Similarly, at the schematic model level, elements related to "While I may not be very good at many things and often fail, on this occasion I did actually succeed" may enable the evidence of successful achievement to be bound in with the remaining elements to create a modified schematic model.

The attributes of schematic models that we have just described will be of considerable importance in applications of ICS described later in the book.

Further Examples of
Implicational Meaning

The schematic model that is constructed on hearing a well-written, well-performed poem provides a good example of Implicational meaning. A poem communicates an "holistic" meaning that cannot adequately be conveyed by a single propositional statement, or by a group of propositional statements (i.e prose). The impact of a poem depends on the combined, integrated effect of a complex of propositional meanings together with sensory contributions from the actual sounds of the words, the rhymes and meters with which they are spoken, and the visual imagery evoked. The imagery also facilitates simultaneous "parallel" communication of clusters of specific meanings more readily than the normal "serial" presentation of linear sequences of specific meanings in the sentences of prose.

Subjectively, the synthesis of the generic meaning conveyed by a poem is marked by a particular holistic "sense" or "feeling".

Table 6.1 illustrates the way in which the generic meaning conveyed by a poem is greater than the sum of the specific meanings, and how this meaning is crucially dependent on the contribution from sensory elements. The Table gives an excerpt from a poem, together with a prose version that retains the same sequence of propositional meanings but that is without the evocative sound and visual imagery qualities of the poem. The Implicational meaning, or "sense" conveyed by the two versions is very different. The poetic form conveys a sense of melancholy, emptiness, and abandonment that is largely lost in the much more "matter-of-fact" tone of the prose version.

It is useful to regard the information in a schematic model as conveying high-level Implicational meaning, even though this is a different quality of meaning than that conveyed by sentences with which we are more familiar. One way to get a sense of the higher-level meaning conveyed by a schematic model is to read again the extract of poetry in Table 6.1. When you have a "sense" of the feeling engendered by the poem, ask yourself the question "would he be fun to meet at a party?" The implicit meaning inherent in the schematic model created by the poem will enable you to "know" very directly and immediately that the answer to the question is an emphatic "no". There is a considerable contrast if you repeat this experiment having read the prose version of the poem. In this case, the "disconnected" elements of propositional information do not naturally lead to the synthesis of a coherent schematic model with a high-level meaning that can be used to answer the question from such an immediate sense of

TABLE 6.1
Poetry as Implicational Meaning

'O what can ail thee, knight-at-arms,
Alone and palely loitering?
The sedge has wither'd from the lake,
And no birds sing.'

*'What is the matter, armed old-fashioned soldier,
Standing by yourself and doing nothing with a pallid expression?
The reed-like plants have decomposed by the lake
And there are not any birds singing.'*

The original poem in the upper part of the table and the alternative version in the lower part have the same sequence of propositional meanings. However, only the original version conveys a coherent Implicational "sense". (Original from *La Belle Dame Sans Merci*, by Keats).

knowing. Rather, in this situation, the separate aspects of Propositional information conveyed have to be "deliberately" integrated, together with the content of the question, to create an ad hoc schematic model from which the question can be answered. The process takes longer and the subjective experience is more one of "working things out" compared to the "direct knowing" that is experienced when the meaning of the schematic model of the poem is already available for use.

Poetry provides an example of the way in which creative art forms, literary, visual, musical, and dramatic, can be viewed as means for communicating Implicational meaning.

As well as being the focus of much creative art, the perception and communication of Implicational-level meanings has also been a central concern of many spiritual traditions. The following Zen story (from Reps, 1971, p. 52) illustrates nicely the "direct perceptual" quality of Implicational knowledge. A tea-master, Sen no Rikyu, wished to hang a flower basket on a column. He asked a carpenter to help him, telling the man to place it a little higher or lower, to the left or to the right, until he had found exactly the right spot. "That's the place", said Sen no Rikyu finally. To test the master, the carpenter marked the spot and then pretended he had forgotten. The whole procedure then had to be repeated, the carpenter pointing to different places on the column and asking whether each was the right place. Only when the carpenter reached the identical spot again did the master approve its location.

In ICS terms, the judgement of the correct location was based on a sensitivity to Implicational processing, marked subjectively by an holistic "sense". Only when an Implicational schematic model equivalent to ["everything conforming to an harmonious whole"] was being processed would the holistic "sense of proportion" feel right. The story nicely illustrates the potential precision of Implicational meaning and knowing: Only when the elements contributing to the total Implicational pattern again matched the previous pattern exactly was the sense of the same schematic model experienced.

A Sufi story (Shah, 1974, p. 122) can be used to illustrate the contrast between Propositional knowledge and Implicational knowledge. The Sufi master, Uwais, was asked: "How do you feel?" He said: "Like one who has risen in the morning and does not know whether he will be dead in the evening." The other man said: "But this is the situation of all men." Uwais said: "Yes, but how many of them feel it?"

The story points a contrast between Propositional-level "factual" knowledge to the effect that we may all die at any time, and the Implicational-level knowledge related to knowing this, and all its implications, "in our bones". The former, even if frequently repeated, can remain isolated "cold" factual knowledge that may not impinge further on

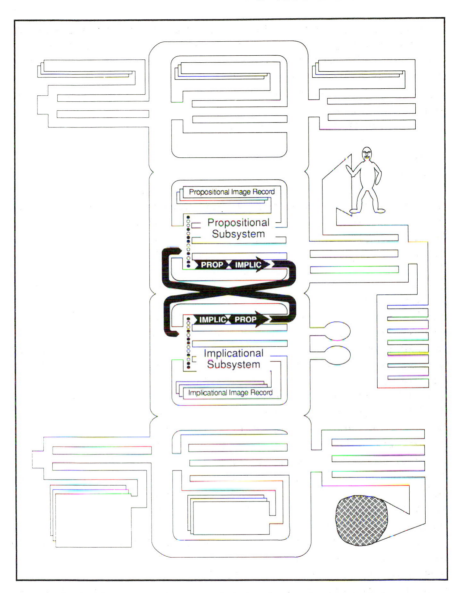

FIG. 6.2. The "central engine" of human cognition: The [IMPLIC→PROP; PROP→IMPLIC] cycle.

information processing; the latter affects our "view" of everything and can radically alter the way we live from moment to moment. When Uwais asks "how many of them *feel* it?" he is referring to the processing of an Implicational schematic model of which elements derived from the

Propositional knowledge that we may all die at any time are only part of a much wider pattern.

The Interaction of Two Levels of Meaning within the Central Engine of Cognition

As we noted in Chapter 5 control and co-ordination of information processing within ICS arises from mutual interactions within the "community" of subsystems. Among these interactions, reciprocal transformations between the Propositional and Implicational subsystems [IMPLIC→PROP; PROP→IMPLIC] (Fig. 6.2) play a key role. In this reciprocal exchange schematic models are used to compute propositional meanings [IMPLIC→PROP] which can, in turn, be sent back [PROP→IMPLIC] to feed further model-based processing. In many important respects this cycle is the "central engine" of human cognition.

This central engine will form the cornerstone of our accounts of many of the phenomena associated with cognition and affect, e.g. the maintenance of moods and clinical depression, extended memory retrieval operations, the production of thought streams, the realisation of intentions, etc. Here we focus briefly on text comprehension and "controlled" processing in the management of nonproceduralised tasks. These will provide initial illustrations of the way that interactions between the Propositional and Implicational subsytems play a central role in developing and elaborating the interpretation of experience, and in the control of behaviour.

Text Comprehension

In the comprehension of text, the essential job of the central engine is to elaborate the information in both text and context. Suppose that a person has just read "John knocked the glass off the table. Mary went to the kitchen to fetch the broom". The reader will infer, although it is stated nowhere, that the glass was broken, and this inference will inform comprehension of the rest of the text. The information processing involved can be described within the ICS framework as follows (Fig. 6.3). From the printed characters on the page being read, Propositional level meanings will be extracted via a series of information transformation processes: VIS→OBJ(1); OBJ→MPL(2); MPL→PROP(3). These Propositional meanings (that John knocked the glass off the table, and Mary went for a broom) will be represented as patterns of Propositional code. These will then be taken as input by the PROP→IMPLIC(4) transformation process to produce patterns of Implicational code. The pattern of Implicational elements produced will reflect the generic content of the specific Propositional meanings, discarding reference to specific agents and objects.

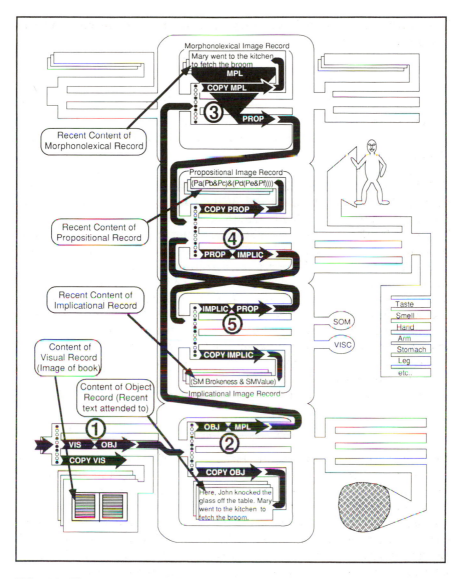

FIG. 6.3. The "central engine" in text comprehension (see text p.76)

We might represent these aspects, loosely, as "something fragile broken" "remedial action implemented". In the person's previous experience, these Implicational elements will have co-occurred with other Implicational elements within a total schematic model that could be tagged as ["brokenness"]. The recently arrived input will only provide partial fragments of the total patterns of Implicational code characteristic of this model. "Pattern completion" can occur to fill out the partial pattern provided by these fragments.

In past experience, synthesis of the schematic model with the high-level meaning "brokenness" will have co-occurred with Propositional information reflecting low-level meanings indicating "something is broken". These co-occurrences will be reflected in the procedural knowledge of the IMPLIC→PROP(5) transformation process. This process, operating on the currently constructed "brokenness" schematic model, will now deliver Propositional meanings to the effect that "something is broken". Further processing, using the specific information from the text stored in the Propositional memory record, will furnish specific content to this meaning; the reader will infer that "the glass was broken". The Propositional representation of this information is then available to contribute, with further Propositional meanings derived from reading subsequent sentences of text, to the synthesis of a further Implicational schematic model. This model will reflect the currently updated higher-level meaning derived from the text. This might, for example, relate to "blameworthiness—punishment". In this way, by a continuing interaction between the Propositional and Implicational subsystems (Fig. 6.2), specific and generic levels of meaning can be derived, inter-related, and developed to provide an understanding of the text.

"Controlled" Processing

In Chapter 5 we indicated that, in ICS, control and co-ordination of processing arise as the result of mutually controlling interactions between subsystems. In this framework there is no separate, general-purpose central executive stucture of the type assumed within much information processing theory. We now consider two inter-related questions that arise from this aspect of ICS: How is the function equivalent to a central executive fulfilled, and how is this related to the contrast between "controlled" and "automatic" processing activity (Hasher & Zacks, 1979; Shiffrin & Schneider, 1977)? More concretely, what happens within ICS during the management of a task that would normally be understood to be heavily demanding of "central executive" or "controlled processing" resources?

Within ICS, the "control" of sequences of information processing, in general, is "data-driven". That is, the output of any given transformation process is determined entirely by its input. This mapping of inputs to outputs reflects the procedural knowledge embodied within the transformation process. The input that "controls" the operation of a transformation process derives from one of three sources.

First, the input may be derived directly from sensory sources. For example, in text comprehension, when the gaze is directed at the printed page, the output of the VIS→OBJ transformation process is entirely determined by the visual stimuli corresponding to the characters printed on the page. In this situation, the "control" of the VIS→OBJ transformation process resides entirely "in the world".

Second, the input may be derived from the output of the immediately preceding transformation process in an extended sequence of information transformations. For example, in text comprehension, the output of the OBJ→MPL transformation will be determined by the input it receives from the VIS→OBJ transformation process. Similarly, the output of the MPL→PROP transformation will be determined by the input that it receives from (among other sources) the OBJ→MPL transformation. In this situation, "control" of a transformation process resides in the other transformation processes from which it takes input. These transformation processes will be in the subsystems that "feed" the subsystem under consideration and that immediately precede it in a sequence of information-processing operations.

Third, the input may be derived from the memory records of the subsystem of which the transformation process is a part. In the example of text comprehension considered in the previous section, input to the Propositional subsystem from the IMPLIC→PROP process indicating that "something fragile is broken" acts as a "description" (see p.108) to access the information recently stored in that subsystem's memory records indicating that a glass (fragile object) is present. Subsequent input to the PROP→IMPLIC process of that stored information, together with the recently arrived information that "something fragile is broken" will ultimately lead to the inference that the glass was broken.

It will be apparent that one subsystem can "control" another by the information that it sends to it, both directly and by the influence that it has in determining both what is stored in memory records and what is accessed from those records. In the case of the four "central" subsystems (OBJ, MPL, PROP, and IMPLIC), reciprocal transformation processes exist, e.g. OBJ→PROP and PROP→OBJ; PROP→IMPLIC and IMPLIC→PROP. As a result, direct mutual control can exist between these central subsystems; the output of one subsystem becomes the input to another subsytem, thereby influencing the output of the latter, which, in turn, may be fed back as input to the originating subsytem, and so exert continuing reciprocal influence. In this way, for example, a transformation process can be controlled by inputs that, effectively, "monitor" its own earlier outputs.

The general idea of parts of a wider system exerting reciprocal influence over each other is not restricted to our own approach. For example, there are illustrations within the connectionist tradition of how mental simulations of a game like noughts and crosses (or tic-tac-toe) can be accomplished by having the output of one network (an "interpretation network") form the input to another network processing what effectively amounts to a mental model of the state of the game (Rumelhart et al.,1986). Cycles of input and output between two related networks would be sub-symbolic equivalents of reciprocal exchanges between subsystems.

Unlike most current connectionist systems, subsystems within ICS incorporate explicit memory representations that can also assist in the generation of an output. Differences in the patterns of transformation processes involved and the use made of memory records allows us to understand, from the ICS perspective, the differences between "automatic" or "proceduralised" tasks, on the one hand, and "nonautomatic", "nonproceduralised", or "controlled tasks" on the other. The performance of nonprocedularised tasks is generally characterised by heavy use of memory records, and/or many exchanges of information between the "central" subsystems.

Among these exchanges, the reciprocal interaction between the Propositional and Implicational subsystems, the "central engine" of cognition [IMPLIC→PROP; PROP→IMPLIC], is particularly important. In this reciprocal exchange schematic models are used to compute propositional meanings [IMPLIC→PROP], which can, in turn, be sent back [PROP→IMPLIC] to feed further model-based processing. For example, co-ordination of a novel task depends on using specific (Propositional) information related to the current task (e.g. the goal to be achieved, the last action completed, and the outcome of that action) in conjunction with generic (Implicational) knowledge distilled from the performance of related tasks in the past.

Such processing cycles can be "goal-directed" either on the basis of previous "reinforcement history", represented in the procedural knowledge of transformation processes, or "intention-driven" towards a goal state represented in terms of specific Propositional descriptions. In the latter case, elements reflecting the discrepancy between Propositional representations of the current and goal states exert a directional influence on the evolution of processing cycles by their continuing contribution to the synthesis of schematic models.

In the ICS view, the distinction between "automatic" and "controlled" processing is more of a continuum than a simple contrast. The co-ordination and control of subsystem activity can increase in complexity as a function of the number of demands for subsystems to exchange information or access memory records. At one end of this dimension, highly automated tasks, such as an experienced motorist driving along a familiar, quiet route, can be sustained by simple "linear" sequences of transformation processes involving no reciprocal transformations or access to memory records. At the other end of the dimension are complex, novel, tasks, such as solving a difficult academic problem, that require many "internal" processing cycles involving many inferential exchanges and much access to memory records.

On this overall view, perfomance of tasks can be nonproceduralised, and centrally demanding, because performance is at an early stage of learning, so that proceduralisation of the routines within a process has not had time to occur. Typically, this will increase reliance on memory records or demand inferential activity in the central engine of cognition. Alternatively, information "in the world", or the tasks to be accomplished, may be so inherently complex that, even with practise, processing cannot be fully "automated" at all levels.

As we have already noted, reciprocal information exchange between the Propositional and Implicational subsystems is a central essential feature of many types of "controlled processing" tasks. ICS's first principle of operation (Barnard, 1985, p. 216) asserts that any one transformation process, such as PROP→IMPLIC or IMPLIC→PROP, can only handle one coherent data stream at a time. We can thus anticipate mutual interference between different aspects of "controlled" processing that compete to use the PROP→IMPLIC and IMPLIC→PROP processes of the central engine of cognition.

The essential feature of the ICS approach to the functions fulfilled by "central executive" structures in other approaches is that the "central" subsystems (OBJ, MPL, PROP, and IMPLIC), by continuing reciprocal exchange of information, and mutual influence, operate as a "community" of information processors. Through their interaction, the control and co-ordination on which "controlled" processing depends is achieved.

In the next chapter, we consider the ICS approach to emotion.

Summary

1. Generic Implicational meanings differ from the more familiar specific Propositional meanings: (a) they are at a very high level of abstraction; (b) they encode schematic models of experience; (c) they include elements directly derived from sensory sources, as well as elements derived from complexes of lower-level meanings; (d) their meaning cannot adequately be conveyed by single sentences.

2. Implicational schematic models encode implicit knowledge. Such models can be thought of in terms of patterns of values across informational elements. The elements represent high-order dimensions in terms of which individuals have learned to "parse"

their experience. A given schematic model is defined by a particular set of values across a particular set of elements. For presentational purposes, we can represent models in terms of patterns of ○s and ●s across defined elements. Schematic models can change rapidly and dynamically as the values on their elements are updated in response to new input arriving at the Implicational subsystem.

3. The ICS concept of Implicational schematic models is similar to the Parallel Distributed Processing (PDP) approach to schemas. As with PDP, schematic models can show "pattern completion" but are also very sensitive to elements that discriminatively mark shifts in the relationships between patterns of elements.

4. Poetry, and other creative arts, can be viewed as a means of communicating Implicational meanings. Such meanings have also been a central concern of spiritual traditions.

5. Reciprocal interaction between the specific information handled by the Propositional subsystem and model-level information handled by the Implicational subsystem constitutes the "central engine" of cognition. This interaction fulfills the role played by the central executive in other cognitive architectures and is central to many of the phenomena discussed in this book. Its action is illustrated with reference to text comprehension and the control of novel or complex tasks. Mutual interference between tasks competing for "central engine" transformation processes can be expected.

CHAPTER SEVEN

ICS and Emotion

We begin by considering the production of emotion in the adult human. ICS proposes that emotion production depends on the Implicational subsystem processing affect-related schematic models. These models encode the regular co-occurrences in sensory and representational codes that have been prototypical of previous affect-eliciting situations.

An interesting feature of this proposal is that emotional responses to very basic sensory input (e.g. a response to a blood-curdling shriek) and emotions reflecting complex, subtle patterns of meaning (e.g. embarrassment) are mediated through the same point in the system. To help understand this feature of the ICS approach to emotion, and to illustrate the reasoning behind allocating the Implicational level a pivotal status in emotion production, we will describe a speculative account of emotional development.

We will conclude the chapter with a preliminary general assessment of the ICS framework, and a brief consideration of ICS in relation to other approaches.

Emotion Production in the Adult

The Implicational subsystem plays a crucial role in the production of emotion. For a given emotion, recurring features in the patterns of information codes created in situations that have previously elicited that emotion are extracted and integrated to produce Implicational schematic models. These models represent the core "themes" characteristic of the emotion. When the Implicational subsystem processes patterns of Implicational code corresponding to these affect-related schematic models, the corresponding emotion is produced. This emotional reaction will be a distributed phenomenon, with subjective, physiological, and action and expressive components.

Within ICS, subjective experience is associated with activity of COPY processes. Qualitatively distinct aspects of subjective experience mark the activity of the COPY processes of each of the different subsystems. Subjective emotional experience is distributed over the COPY processes of several subsystems, primarily those handling Implicational and Body-state information codes.

Emotional experience often includes feelings which have an implicit information content. For example, it is implicit in a sense of apprehension that something awful is about to happen, a feeling of hopelessness implies that my efforts to get what I want will be doomed to failure, and it is implicit in feeling confident that I will be able to cope and things are likely to turn out well. Such subjective feelings with implicit information content mark the processing of related Implicational code patterns by the COPY process of the Implicational subsystem. Holistic "senses" or feelings of this type are the phenomenal experience corresponding to activity in the Implicational subsystem, just as phenomenal experiences of pitch or timbre mark activity in the Acoustic subsystem

Subjective emotional experience also includes sensations that have a much more "physical" quality, devoid of any implicit information content. For example, we may feel tense when anxious, we may experience pangs of grief, or we may feel we are shaking with fury. These subjective feelings correspond to activity of the COPY process in the Body-state subsystem. These more "physical" subjective phenomena are experienced as this process handles the proprioceptive feedback resulting from emotional effector action. This might arise, for example, from increased muscle tone or heart rate, or from the patterned muscular activity corresponding to a particular facial expression or bodily posture.

Within ICS, the autonomic and physiological components of emotional response depend on the IMPLIC →VISC transformation process within the Implicational subsystem. Given an appropriate input pattern of Implicational code, this process produces instructions for a co-ordinated pattern of autonomic response.

Motor-expressive (facial and postural) and more automatic action-disposition components of emotional reaction depend on the IMPLIC→ SOM transformation process within the Implicational subsystem. Given an appropriate input pattern of Implicational code, this process produces instructions for a co-ordinated pattern of response of the somatic musculature.

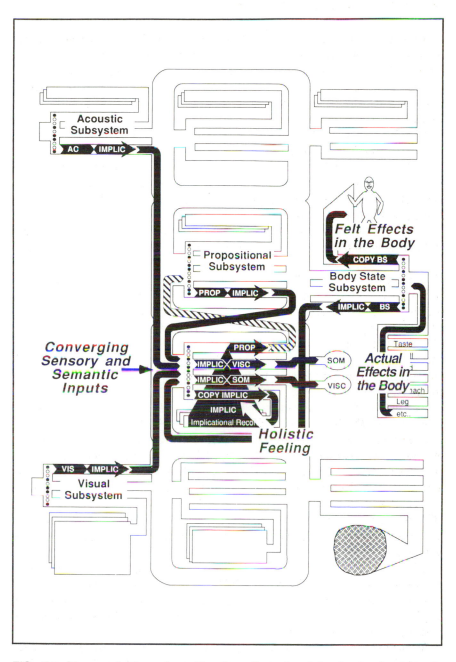

FIG. 7.1. The production of emotion by affect-related Implicational schematic models. Contributions from sensory and meaning sources converge to synthesise schematic models that produce a distributed emotional response.

Figure 7.1 illustrates the contribution of both sensory and meaning-derived elements to the synthesis of emotion-related schematic models, and the distributed emotional response produced by such models.

Figure 7.2 represents an emotion-eliciting Implicational schematic model, and the outputs resulting from its synthesis. This figure uses the convention of representing a schematic model as a pattern of values (arbitarily ○ and ●) across a range of variables. Each variable represents a high-order dimension into which experience is "parsed".

In our discussion of text comprehension in the previous chapter, we saw how Implicational schematic models could generate (via the IMPLIC→PROP transformation process) patterns of Propositional code corresponding to derived, specific meanings. Emotion-related Implicational schematic models may also produce affect-related Propositional representations corresponding, for example, to expectations, attributions, and instructions. These "cognitive" outputs of the Implicational subsystem can play a crucial role in the further course of development of an emotional reaction over time. We discuss this issue at several points later in the book. However, for now, following the conventional course of separating "cognition" and "affect", we do not discuss these outputs as part of the emotional response. For this reason, they are shown dotted in Figs. 7.1 and 7.2.

We have suggested that, in the adult, emotion is produced by Implicational schematic models that encode core features extracted from previous emotion-eliciting situations. We now consider how those situations initially acquired the ability to elicit emotion, and how affect-related schematic models develop.

ICS and the Development of Emotion— A Speculative Account

The new-born infant arrives in this world with a set of innately prepared emotional reactions. Our task is to describe how these reactions develop into the wider, more sophisticated emotional repertoire of the adult. This development includes changes both in the range of situations that will elicit emotions, and in the form of the emotional response.

In Chapter 5, we introduced two key ideas concerning the development of information-processing capability in general. The first was that all "learning" occurs at the level of the individual transformation process. The second was that this learning depends on the storage of patterns of information in the episodic memory records of subsystems. Such stored information supports the extraction of regularities in input codes and the development of appropriate input-output mappings (procedural know-ledge). These two ideas are central to our account of emotional development.

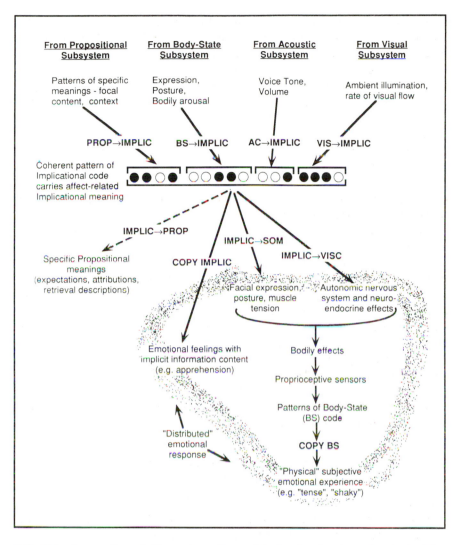

FIG. 7.2. An emotion-eliciting schematic model showing inputs and outputs. The pattern of Implicational code corresponding to the model is represented as a pattern of values (○ or ●) across a range of variables.

In the neonate, certain patterns of sensory code elicit emotional responses on the basis of prepared "pre-wired" procedures. For example, terminating the supply of sweet-tasting fluids while a child is still hungry will elicit a protest-frustration reaction; rapidly looming shapes will elicit alarm and withdrawal; and rocking, cuddling, and fondling will evoke a positive response.

Changes in the Situations that Evoke Emotion

The sensory code patterns eliciting prepared emotional responses will occur in situations that, within a given family and culture, regularly contain co-occurrences of other sensory features. These might involve, for example, distinctive sights and sounds related to actions of care givers. Key global features of the arriving sights and sounds will be transmitted to the Implicational subsystem via VIS→IMPLIC and AC→IMPLIC. Similarly, key aspects of internal sensory input associated with the elicitation of emotion will be transmitted to the Implicational subsystem via BS→IMPLIC.

Regular co-occurrences in the sensory code patterns associated with emotion-provoking situations will be extracted within the Implicational subsystem. In this way, prototypical features characteristic of situations eliciting given emotions will become represented in related patterns of Implicational code. According to ICS, these code patterns "inherit" the emotion-eliciting capacities originally restricted to the prepared sensory codes.

Initially, recurring sensory/perceptual features of sights, sounds, and body states will contribute the main elements of the Implicational code patterns extracted from emotion-eliciting situations. Subsequently, as the representational subsystems develop, elements derived from recurring regularities in representational codes will make increasing contributions. The most important of these representational Implicational elements will be derived from complexes of Propositional code that reflect the underlying interpretations, or meanings, of situations that elicit a given emotional response. These meanings reflect the "thematic content" of situations that elicit a given emotion. Such complexes allow communalities to be extracted across situations that share the same affective theme, although they may differ considerably in superficial sensory features. In this way the "inheritance" of emotion-eliciting capacity can be passed on to situations that may contain none of the sensory features for which there are innately prepared responses. Such situations may be only "symbolically" connected to the situations that initially elicited the prepared emotional response.

In the case of the protest-frustration reaction, for example, development of this emotional reaction would involve elaboration of the sensorily derived Implicational pattern to include Propositionally derived elements reflecting "removal/nonarrival of a desired goal". At this point the Implicational code pattern could be characterised as encoding the affective theme "frustration-disappointment". Processing of this code pattern will be associated with the subjective feeling of "being frustrated" and with the production of characteristic patterns of peripheral autonomic, motor, and action-disposition components. The total Implicational code pattern, and emotion production, will still be sensitive to contributions from sensory-based elements. However, it can now be instantiated by purely representational input derived from situations sharing no sensory features with those that originally elicited the emotional response, e.g. as an adolescent, having one's favourite football team lose a national final.

This example illustrates how developmental changes can "liberate" the production of emotion from dependence on prepared responses to particular sensory complexes. The inclusion of Propositionally derived meanings into patterns of Implicational code leads to an enormous increase in the range of situations that can elicit emotion. This process is obviously of great potential importance in emotional development.

As well as extending the range of situations that elicit emotion, the inclusion of Propositionally derived meanings into the total pattern of Implicational code synthesised in a situation can radically modify or eliminate the emotional response that would occur to the sensory features alone. For example, a high-pitched shriek is initially likely to elicit a prepared defensive reaction. However, following repeated experiences of the same sensory input in the context of play, or of watching television, Implicational codes integrating shriek-based sensory elements with Propositionally based elements indicating basic safety will be developed. Consequently, the response to a shriek in these contexts will be excitement rather than fear. Nonetheless, the prepared response can still emerge in other contexts, e.g. when one is alone in a strange place in the dark. In such situations, according to ICS, an initial, rapid, "automatic", sensory-driven emotional reaction, closely based on the prepared response, is mediated by Implicational elements directly derived by processes such as AC→IMPLIC.

Changes in the Form of Emotional Response

Changes in the form of emotional response can occur as a result of repeatedly experiencing situations that include stimuli that elicit more than one prepared emotional response. For example, the fear and withdrawal response normally elicited by rapidly looming visual objects may be attenuated and modified if a child is, at the same time, held closely and cuddled by its mother. This is because the comforting physical contact elicits prepared "relaxation" responses. Repeated experiences of situations involving the triggering of stimulus complexes of several prepared emotional responses will lead to derivation of affect-related Implicational codes that "inherit" contributions from the effector components of a number of prepared reactions. In this way new forms of emotional effector response can develop, possibly quite different from any single prepared response.

Emotional response can also be modified by controlling emotional expression (Izard, 1990). The presence of Body-state-derived elements in many affect-related Implicational codes provides an important route through which, over the course of development, the form of emotional response can change (or indeed be deliberately modified). Emotional responses will often involve characteristic changes in bodily state. Particularly in situations that elicit an extended emotional response, patterns of Body-state code reflecting the proprioceptive feedback from these effects will be among the features most consistently associated with subsequent emotion production. It follows that elements of Implicational code related to those features will be derived and integrated into the total schematic model for that emotion. In this way, proprioceptive feedback from the bodily changes characteristically associated with a given emotional response, such as facial expression, posture, or bodily arousal, can acquire some ability to elicit the emotion that initially gave rise to those same bodily responses.

In terms of the example of protest-frustration that we have considered, patterns of Body-state code related to proprioceptive feedback from the crying and flailing elicited by the nonarrival of milk may regularly be associated with continued elicitation of the emotional response. The way that the mother reacts to the initial frustration will determine the extent to which this occurs. If she allows the frustrative response to continue unabated, a continuing association will be established, and proprioceptive effects will act to maintain the emotional response. Alternatively, if, by her cuddling or soothing, the initial bodily response is calmed, then more benevolent associations will be established. In this case, Body-state-derived elements will play a lesser role in maintaining and extending the emotional reaction.

We have illustrated how the form of emotional reaction can be modified by adults in the child's environment through effects on bodily emotional response. With development, children eventually reach the point where they themselves can use the same means to regulate their emotional reaction to situations. A child can acquire a powerful method of affect-regulation by voluntarily controlling emotional expressive behaviour that contributes Body-state-derived elements to affect-generating Implicational codes. There is evidence, for example, that "acting brave" and concealing one's emotional reaction in a fearful situation reduces actual emotional response (e.g. Lanzetta, Cartwright-Smith, & Eleck, 1976).

As a result of the developmental changes that we have described, both the situations that elicit emotional responses and the form of those emotional responses can be altered radically from the prepared repertoire with which the neonate arrives in the world. The precise nature of the affect-related Implicational schematic models constructed over the course of development will be influenced considerably by the family and cultural environment within which the child matures. From individual to individual there will be some common features, related to our common "prepared" emotional birthright. However, beyond that there is enormous scope for variation between individuals as a result of differences in experience, and of the interaction of experience with constitutional factors.

To conclude our speculative account of emotional development, we can now offer an answer to the question: Why should the Implicational level, specifically, "inherit" the power to elicit emotion? At birth, certain patterns of sensory information, because they actually elicit prepared emotional responses, will be reliable predictors of the occurrence of those responses. However, as a result of the modifiability of prepared emotional responses over the course of development, there will cease to be such a reliable association between patterns of sensory information and the occurrence of emotion. As our example of the response to a shriek illustrated, patterns of information that reflect an integration of purely sensory-derived information with aspects of the wider informational context (e.g. semantic information indicating that this is a situation of play or make-believe), will be associated more reliably with emotional response than will the sensory information alone. Information reflecting an integration of all aspects of an experience is, of course, precisely what is encoded at the Implicational level. It is because representations at this level are more reliably associated with emotional response that they "inherit" the power to elicit emotion.

Emotion:
"Cognitively Mediated" or "Sensorily Mediated" ?

Affect-related schematic models integrate elements related both to sensory features and to patterns of representational codes reflecting complexes of meanings that have been consistent components of emotion-eliciting situations. So, for example, threat-related schematic models will include elements reflecting characteristic patterns in Acoustic code (e.g. those derived from a shriek) as well as elements reflecting patterns of Propositional meanings indicating imminent bodily danger. The characteristic threat emotional response can be triggered by shriek-derived elements alone (in the absence of meaning-derived elements indicating basic safety), by meaning-derived elements alone, or by integrated patterns including both sensory-derived and meaning-derived elements. *The Implicational code provides a "common currency" in which "sensory" and "cognitive" contributions can be expressed, integrated, and can modulate the production of emotion.* In this way, the ICS approach to emotion offers a resolution to the conflict that at one time raged between those who advocated an exclusively "cognitive" view of emotion and those who maintained the "primacy of affect" (cf. Leventhal & Scherer, 1987).

Body-state-derived Implicational elements related to proprioceptive feedback from the bodily effects of emotional response often provide particularly important sensory contributions to affect-related schematic models. ICS, like Leventhal's (1979; 1984) perceptual-motor theory, Lang's (1985; 1988) bio-informational theory, and Berkowitz's (1993) cognitive-neo-associative approach, recognises that sensory stimuli, such as those related to peripheral bodily effects, can make direct contributions to emotion production and affective evaluation. These contributions are not mediated by propositional-level cognitive appraisals of meaning. For example, snake-phobic subjects may respond with fear to a sinuous stick when they are physiologically aroused through exercise, although they do not at rest (Lang, 1988). Similarly, the evaluation of Walkman headphones is more positive when they are tested while nodding the head in the way usually associated with affirmation, than while shaking the head in the way usually associated with negation (Wells & Petty, 1980, cited by Van den Bergh & Eelen, 1984). ICS suggests that, in such cases, proprioceptive feedback contributes directly to the synthesis of affect-related schematic models, independently of any "cognitive" attributions or appraisals.

"Hot" and "Cold" Representations of Affect-related Material

In Chapter 4 we noted the distinction between "hot" and "cold" representations of emotion-related material as a central difficulty for the associative network theory of mood and memory. Any alternative theoretical approach will have to offer a more satisfactory solution to this problem: How does ICS explain the fact that we can at some times discourse calmly about emotional material that, at another time, will upset us considerably, or that we can remember emotional incidents either with or without re-experiencing the original emotion?

The existence of qualitatively distinct levels of representation and memory stores, each with potentially different functional relationships to affect, makes it relatively easy for ICS to handle the distinction between "hot" and "cold" memories and knowledge. ICS maintains that only representations at the Implicational level can produce an emotional response directly. It is thus quite possible to remember, at the Propositional level, that an upsetting event occurred or, at the Object level, to have a vivid visual image of the event, without necessarily re-experiencing emotion. This latter would depend on accessing affect-related representations of the event at the Implicational level, or re-creating related representations at this level. Similarly, having the inner experience "I have failed" simply as a collection of words (at the Morphonolexical level) or as knowledge of a specific fact (at the Propositional level) would not, by itself, upset me. However, processing an Implicational code pattern prototypical of generalised personal failure and lack of worth, marked by an holistic sense that I might describe to myself as "I have failed", would be an affective "hot" experience. As we shall see, these distinctions will be of crucial importance, not only in unravelling some of the puzzles of mood-congruous cognition, but also in casting light on the treatment of depression and other emotional states.

ICS and the "Prescription" for an Alternative Theoretical Account

At the end of Chapter 4 we laid out a "prescription" for the features that would be desirable in any theoretical account if it was to avoid the problems encountered by Bower's associative network theory. In addition to the need to deal more adequately with the issue of "hot" versus "cold" cognition, we also suggested the need for a framework that recognised several qualitatively distinct levels of representation and memory. As a general psychological theory, it was important that any account meet the need both for representations at levels of abstraction higher than those of the word, concept, or sentence, and for multiple, functionally independent representations in memory of related material. ICS clearly meets the first of these requirements by including the highly abstract schematic model level of Implicational code. ICS meets the second of these requirements by proposing that there are, in all, nine functionally separate memory stores, one for each of the different information codes.

Although, within ICS, representations at one level can be transformed by appropriate processes to related representations at another level, this does not necessarily occur automatically. It follows that, as well as remaining qualitatively distinct, different levels of representation of related material can be "functionally insulated" from each other. Consequently, creation of a higher-level representation does not automatically produce or activate related lower-level representations (and vice versa), and different levels of representation can have functionally distinct relationships with other variables. In this way, ICS avoids the problems of the associative network theory (pp. 41–44) that arise from activation spreading automatically between emotion nodes and the representations of all concepts and events that have been activated concurrently in the past. So, it is quite consistent with the ICS analysis that I can talk about my past failures without getting upset now, and depressed mood may affect my evaluation of my self as a failure without necessarily changing the perceptual threshold for identifying "failure" as a word (p. 39).

In its treatment of emotion, ICS overcomes many of the problems of the network model that we identified in Chapter 4.

ICS and Other Approaches

How does ICS stand in relation to other approaches to understanding information processing in general, and the relationship between cognition and affect in particular?

Few, if any, features of ICS, considered in isolation, are unique to this framework. A distributed modular approach, in which cognitive processing is devolved to specialised, semi-autonomous subsystems, characterises a number of recent developments in cognitive neuropsychology (e.g. Shallice, 1988) and in cognitive science more generally (e.g. Fodor, 1983). Oatley and Johnson-Laird (1987) have presented an analysis of emotion within such a modular cognitive system.

The distinction between a relatively specific and a more model-based level of representation is a commonplace one within psycholinguistics. Leventhal's (1979; 1984) perceptual-motor theory of emotion also recognises different levels of processing and suggests that levels differ in their relationship to emotion. His theory clearly implicates the extraction of prototypical regularities as an important aspect of emotional development, and we acknowledged, earlier, our debt to his theory in the development of our own thinking.

As we have already noted, the sensitivity to total patterns of information, the importance of learning in the development of processing operations, and the approach to analysing the schematic level, are all features that ICS shares with connectionist PDP approaches.

The distinctive contribution of ICS is to combine features that are shared with other approaches in a unique way. The aim to provide a comprehensive, yet potentially detailed, integrative analysis of information-processing and representation, operating under principled constraints, provides the combination of breadth and depth that is particularly necessary in understanding cognitive-affective interactions. The characterisation of the generic, schematic level of representation in the Implicational code of ICS also seems particularly relevant to understanding emotion. Specification of the detailed attributes of this code is still at a relatively early stage. However, as will become clear in our applications of ICS, present conceptualisations of the Implicational level of representation already offer useful insights into understanding cognitive-affective interaction.

Summary

1. ICS proposes that emotion production depends on the Implicational subsystem processing emotion-related schematic models. These models encode the regular co-occurrences in sensory and representational codes that have been prototypical of previous emotion-eliciting situations.

2. In the neonate, emotion consists of prepared "pre-wired" responses to specific configurations of sensory stimuli.

3. With development, patterns of sensory and representational codes that regularly co-occur in situations eliciting prepared emotional reactions are extracted to form affect-related schematic models. These patterns of Implicational code "inherit" from the prepared configurations of sensory stimuli the ability to elicit emotional reactions.

4. Over time, there are changes both in the range of situations that will elicit emotional reactions, and in the form of those reactions. The extraction of communalities of meaning across emotion-eliciting situations allows situations to evoke emotions even when they contain none of the prepared sensory stimuli.

5. The adult emotional reaction is a distributed phenomenon, including subjective, physiological, and action and expressive components. Subjective emotional experience with implicit information content corresponds to activity of the COPY process in the Implicational subsystem. More "physical" subjective emotional experience corresponds to activity of the COPY process in the Body-State subsystem.

6. Affect-related schematic models include important sensory-derived elements, as well as those derived from complexes of lower-level meanings. It follows that ICS, in contrast to more purely "cognitive" models of emotion, recognises a direct contribution to emotion production from sensory stimuli, especially those related to proprioceptive feedback from bodily emotional responses.

7. ICS overcomes the problem of "hot" versus "cold" representations of emotional material by proposing that only affect-related Implicational representations can produce emotion directly. Processing of related representations in other codes, for example, Propositional code patterns encoding specific "affective" meanings, would correspond to "cold" processing of emotional material.

In this and other respects, ICS meets the requirements sketched out at the end of Chapter 4 for a theoretical approach to replace the associative network model.

Recapitulation

We have now completed our initial presentation of the ICS framework. In Part III we begin to apply this approach in more detail to understand specific aspects of cognitive-affective interaction, starting with mood congruous memory. To conclude Part II, it will be useful to re-orient ourselves by briefly recapitulating the story of our attempts to understand depressive thinking so far.

First, we described the clinically derived cognitive model of depression. The inadequacies of this approach prompted exploration of the alternative applied science strategy. Empirical studies firmly established biasing effects of depressed mood on the recall of autobiographical memories in depressed patients and in normal subjects. Bower's associative network theory of mood and memory offered an initially attractive explanatory account of these phenomena. Applied to clinical depression, this model yielded accounts that overcame some of the deficiencies of the Beckian cognitive model, and also generated predictions that empirical studies confirmed. However, closer examination of the network theory and related experimental findings revealed that Bower's model itself had difficulties in important areas. The Interacting Cognitive Subsystems framework was advanced as an alternative approach that overcame these difficulties.

ICS is clearly a complex approach. In Chapter 5, we argued that such complexity was unavoidable in any attempt to provide a comprehensive conceptual framework for understanding cognitive-affective interaction. Given this complexity, it would be as well, before applying ICS to understanding depressive thinking itself, that we evaluate how this approach deals with related findings from controlled laboratory studies. We begin our evaluation in the next chapter by considering mood and memory from the ICS perspective.

PART III

ICS and Mood-congruous
Cognition in the Laboratory

CHAPTER EIGHT

ICS, Mood, and Memory

There are several reasons to begin our more detailed consideration of ICS by looking at the way this framework accounts for mood-congruous memory. From Chapter 2 onwards, we have used a specific focus on the experimentally tractable phenomenon of mood-congruous retrieval to advance our understanding of depressive thinking more generally. Pursuing this strategy, it is obviously important that we satisfy ourselves that the ICS account of mood-congruous retrieval is adequate before adopting ICS as a framework for understanding depressive thinking in general.

The power of experimental paradigms, such as laboratory investigations of mood-congruous memory, is that they provide a wealth of detailed information against which to test and develop the adequacy of theoretical models. The associative network theory of mood and memory initially looked both plausible and attractive. It was only when it was evaluated against the detailed results of experimental investigations that its inadequacies were revealed. In the same way, we can use experimental results from studies of mood-congruous retrieval, and mood-congruous memory more generally, as a "touchstone" with which to assess the adequacy of ICS.

Describing the ICS approach to mood-congruous memory also provides an opportunity to reveal further aspects of this approach that will be directly relevant to our ultimate goal of understanding negative thinking and its role in the maintenance of depression.

Before considering mood-congruous memory itself, it is necessary first to look at what ICS has to say more generally about both mood and memory. We will then summarise the overall findings of experimental studies of mood and memory. Once these essential preliminaries are out of the way, we shall present the ICS accounts of mood-congruous encoding and retrieval and assess them against specific laboratory findings in Chapter 9.

Mood—The ICS Approach

The associative network theory essentially took the view that all moods of a given affective tone were essentially similar; one sad mood, for example, was seen as much the same as another. All sad moods were seen as the result of activity of the sad emotion node and their effects on information processing were expected to be similar.

The ICS view is radically different. It suggests that apparently similar moods may be maintained by quite different underlying mechanisms. In some situations, these differences in underlying mechanism will be reflected in differences in the effects of mood on processing and performance.

Moods are characteristically more pervasive in their effects than the emotional reactions to specific events (e.g. Isen, 1984; Morris, 1989, Chapter 1). Moods also tend to persist for longer periods. What keeps moods going?

In Chapter 7, we saw that the central mechanism in the production of emotion, in general, was the processing by the Implicational subsystem of affect-related schematic models. For an emotional state, such as a mood, to persist the Implicational subsystem has to continue processing patterns of Implicational code characteristic of the schematic models associated with that affect. In other words, the schematic models related to that affect have to be "regenerated" continually over successive processing epochs. There are several ways in which this can occur. Affect-related schematic models may receive contributions from sensory sources (AC and VIS), proprioceptive sources (BS), and semantic sources (PROP). Different mechanisms of mood maintenance reflect different balances in the contributions from these various sources. Some of these different mood maintenance configurations are illustrated in Figs. 8.1-8.5 and discussed in the following paragraphs.

The continuing re-creation of schematic models from elements derived from external sensory input (VIS and AC) depends on the external environment continuing to present the relevant stimuli (Fig. 8.1).

For example, elements derived from visual input (via the VIS→IMPLIC process) reflecting whether it is a bright sunny day, or a dull and cloudy day, will continue to contribute to the generation of, respectively, happy

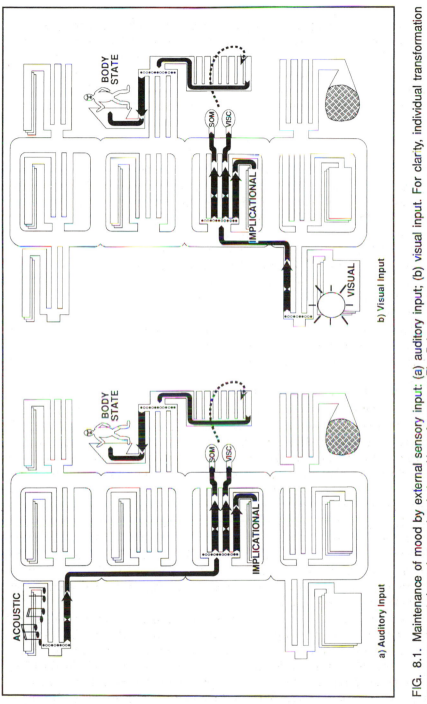

FIG. 8.1. Maintenance of mood by external sensory input: (a) auditory input; (b) visual input. For clarity, individual transformation processes are not shown but can be deduced by reference to Fig. 5.4.

and gloomy moods so long as the weather stays the same. If the weather changes from dull to bright, the VIS-derived contribution to the schematic model maintaining gloomy mood will be removed, and mood may lift. Similarly, elements derived from auditory input (via the AC→IMPLIC process) reflecting, for example, the voice tone in which someone is speaking, or aspects of music being played, will act to maintain a mood state only so long as the related sensory input continues.

On the other hand, the contribution by elements derived from proprioceptive sensory input (via the BS→IMPLIC process) is not so dependent on continuing environmental sensory input. In addition to any effects of "external" taste, smell, or pain stimuli, Implicational elements derived from Body-state sources within the person can contribute to the "internal" regeneration of mood states, as shown in Fig. 8.2.

The feedback loop illustrated in Fig. 8.2 depends on a previous learning history in which a given emotion or mood has been experienced over sustained periods. In this situation, the Implicational subsystem will have continued to process broadly similar affect-related schematic models over consecutive processing epochs. Consequently, Body-state code patterns related to proprioceptive feedback from the emotional reaction produced in one processing epoch will have repeatedly preceded the synthesis, in the next epoch, of an Implicational code pattern similar to the one that led to the emotional reaction that produced them. On this basis, the BS→IMPLIC transformation process will have "learned" to generate, in response to emotion-related proprioceptive feedback, Implicational elements that will facilitate the synthesis of schematic models producing emotional responses similar to those that originally created the proprioceptive feedback. In this way, a self-perpetuating feedback loop (BS→IMPLIC; IMPLIC→VISC/ SOM; VISC/SOM→bodily effects; bodily effects→BS) can act to maintain an affective state.

Elements of Implicational code derived from Propositional sources (via the PROP→IMPLIC process) can contribute to both the "external" and "internal" maintenance of affective states. "External" maintenance occurs when patterns of specific meanings derived from environmental events continue to generate higher-order Implicational meanings with similar thematic content (Fig. 8.3). The affective state elicited in such situations, because it is clearly focused on ongoing events, would normally be described as a continuing emotional reaction rather than a mood state (Morris, 1989, Chapter 1).

Nonetheless, affective reactions to specific events, such as receiving the results of mid-term examinations, have been investigated in studies of mood and memory, sometimes with surprising results (e.g. see the discussion of Parrott & Sabini, 1990, in Chapter 10). As we discuss later, there is reason to expect that the effects of moods maintained by

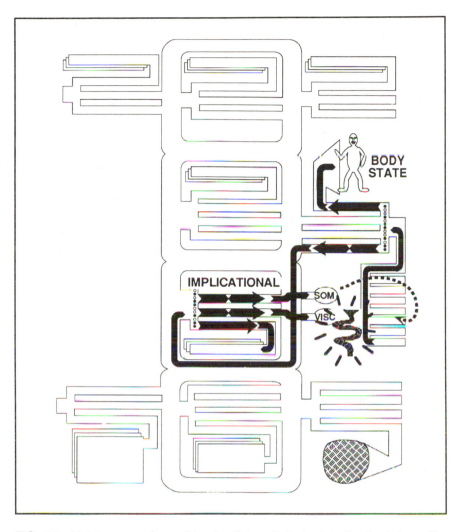

FIG. 8.2. Maintenance of mood by the "internal" Body-state feedback loop. For clarity, individual transformation processes are not shown but can be deduced by reference to Fig. 5.4.

Propositionally derived elements related to continuing external environmental input may not be the same as those where Propositionally derived elements are of more internal origin.

Figure 8.4 illustrates how Propositionally-derived Implicational elements can contribute to the internal regeneration and maintenance of mood states. As we saw in Chapter 6, Implicational schematic models embody much implicit knowledge. This knowledge can be translated into

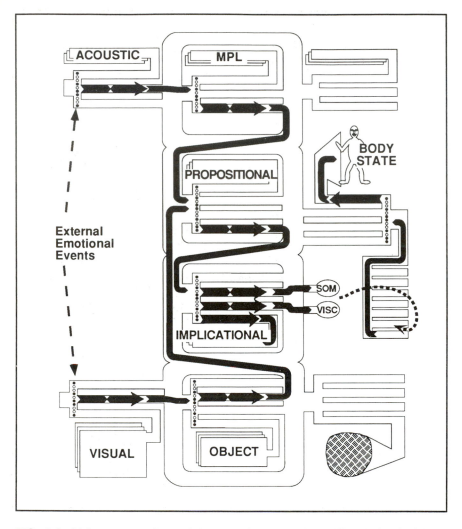

FIG. 8.3. Maintenance of mood by "emotive" meanings. For clarity, individual transformation processes are not shown but can be deduced by reference to Fig. 5.4.

more specific Propositional representations through the IMPLIC→PROP recoding process. For example, the schematic model ["myself as a worthless, useless, culpable person"] will generate specific propositions related to being to blame for something bad that has just happened, or to pessimistic expectations concerning future personal action, or to instructions to access memory records of previous failure-related experiences. These Propositional representations can be processed by the

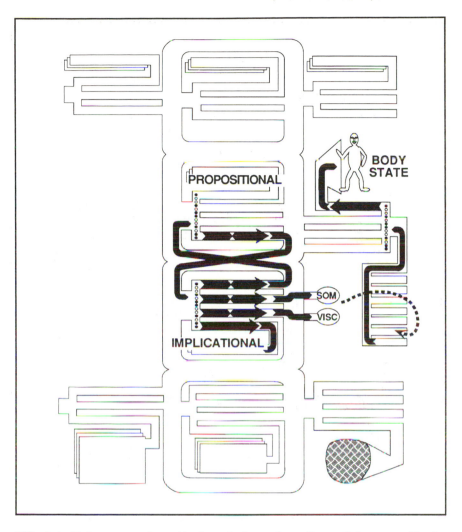

FIG. 8.4. Maintenance of mood by "emotive" meanings, "internally" generated by the [PROP→IMPLIC; IMPLIC→PROP] loop. For clarity, individual transformation processes are not shown but can be deduced by reference to Fig. 5.4.

PROP→IMPLIC process in the Propositional subsystem to produce elements of Implicational code. There is an inherent possibility that the pattern of Implicational code to which these Propositionally derived elements contribute on this processing epoch will recreate a schematic model similar to that from which the Propositional representations were derived in the first place. In this case, the "central engine" of cognition, the Implicational-Propositional loop, can become "locked" onto processing information of a particular theme that re-creates closely related schematic models. In this way, a given mood state will be maintained in the absence of further affect-eliciting environmental input.

The Implicational-Body-state loop (Fig. 8.2) and the Implicational-Propositional loop (Fig. 8.4) can, of course, act to reinforce each others' effects. By each contributing partial fragments of Implicational code that, separately, would not synthesise a schematic model, but, together, form a coherent integrated pattern, affective schematic models may be regenerated from their combined effects (Fig. 8.5).

ICS suggests that the self-regenerating configurations illustrated in Figs. 8.4 and 8.5 are central to the maintenance of certain forms of depressed and other moods. These configurations will also play a prominent role in our analysis of clinical depression later in the book. For now there are two important points to note in relation to these configurations. The first is that the existence of two levels of meaning within ICS, coupled with the possibility of reciprocal transformations between them, makes the development of such "interlocked" processing an inherent possibility. The second point is that the internally regenerating mood maintenance configurations shown in Figs. 8.4 and 8.5 depend for their continued existence on affect-related Implicational models creating Propositional outputs of similar affective or hedonic tone. This is not necessarily true of the more externally maintained mood configurations shown in Figs. 8.1 and 8.3. In these configurations, mood can be maintained by Implicational models synthesised from elements derived from purely external sources without any need for affect-maintaining schematic models to produce congruent Propositional outputs.

The ICS analysis of mood-congruent memory, described in the next chapter, suggests that this phenomenon depends crucially on affect-related Implicational schematic models that produce affectively congruous Propositional outputs. As this is a feature of internally regenerating mood maintenance configurations, but not of externally regenerating configurations, we can anticipate that moods maintained by these two types of configurations will not necessarily show similar effects on mood-congruous memory.

To summarise the important points of this section: (1) moods can be thought of as states dominated by the presence and constant re-creation of affect-related schematic models at the Implicational level; (2) superficially similar moods may be maintained by different underlying processes; and (3) the more "cognitive" consequences of mood states may vary depending on the specific schematic models constructed and the way that they are maintained.

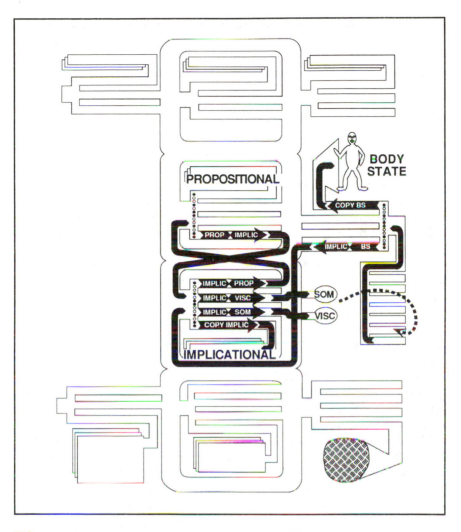

FIG. 8.5. "Internal" maintenance of mood by the combined, "harmonised" effects of the [PROP→IMPLIC; IMPLIC→PROP] loop and the Body-state feedback loop: An "interlocked" configuration.

ICS and Retrieval from Long-term Memory

In ICS, each subsystem has its own memory store. This holds records of all the patterns of information code that enter that subsystem. As each subsystem deals with input in only one information code, the memory store of each subsystem holds records of patterns in only that code. There are as many memory stores as there are subsystems, and parallel representations of a given event, in different codes, can be distributed over several subsystems.

Stored representations are accessed in a manner similar to that suggested by the Descriptions framework of Norman and Bobrow (1979). Retrieval of information depends on the construction of a "description", in the appropriate code, summarising the nature of the required information. Descriptions can be thought of as fragments of the total code pattern that they can access, or as abstract representations of the specific stored representations.

The method by which descriptions access stored information is extremely economical of processing resources, but, for this reason, may appear initially puzzling. There are no special-purpose retrieval resources. Rather, material is "accessed" from memory by being taken as the input to the transformation processes (PROP→IMPLIC; OBJ→PROP, etc.) that normally work on information entering the subsystem from "outside" (from sensory transducers or other subsystems). This "external" input would normally contain sufficient information for a particular process to "fire" to produce an output. However, if the information input is incomplete (as in the case when it is only a description of required information rather than the complete information) then the process will "interrogate" the contents of the memory record to see if patterns that will complete the partial pattern of the description can be discovered. If they can, then the transformation process will operate on the total pattern recovered from the memory record to produce a related output.

Note that, because access to memory records is through the transformation process, stored information is never literally retrieved, as such. Rather, "access" occurs by "processing" to produce an output derived from the stored representation, rather than recovering a faithful record of it. Approximation to the memory records accessed can then be achieved, if necessary, by a reverse transformation in another subsystem: So, a pattern of Morphonolexical code "accessed" via the MPL→PROP transformation process to produce a pattern of Propositional code could be "reconstituted" towards its original form by the inverse PROP→MPL process of the Propositional subsystem.

The information in the memory records of a given subsystem can be "accessed" via descriptions in the code that subsystem takes as input. These descriptions will themselves have been generated, as output, by a different subsystem. We have here the basis of a retrieval mechanism in which a process in one subsystem is used to address information in the memory record of another, so allowing content-addressable access to entries in the latter's memory records. Continuing reciprocal interactions between subsystems may be necessary to construct a detailed representation of an event, drawing on the parallel representations of the event distributed in the memory records of different subsystems.

The fact that continuing reciprocal interactions between subsystems may be required to access information from memory records underlines the general point that normal processing and use of memory records are intimately intertwined. The same processes are involved in using stored information as are involved in generating output directly from fully specified input. Many forms of processing activity across the system as a whole require access to stored representations of recent or past input. Memory access is an integral part of processing operations in general, and cannot be considered in isolation. Rather, memory access, and related overt behavioural phenomena, reflect a continuing dynamic and systemic pattern of mental activity in which memory and processing resources are both utilised.

To summarise, the important points to note in relation to consideration of mood and memory are:

1. the same event may be represented, in patterns of different codes, in the memory records of several subsystems;
2. content-addressable access to memory records of one subsystem depends on the construction of descriptions of the required material by processes in another subsystem;
3. memory access and process functioning are intimately inter-related in evolving cycles of mental activity.

Mood-congruous Memory and its Fickle Ways

Mood-congruous memory refers to superior recall of hedonically valenced material when the tone of the material matches the affective tone of the mood in which it is encoded or retrieved than when there is no match between material and mood. Until now we have focused primarily on mood-congruous retrieval. This is only one of two aspects of mood-congruous memory that can be distinguished:

Mood-congruous Encoding. In this phenomenon material is subsequently better recalled when the mood in which it is encoded is congruous in affective tone with the material, rather than incongruous; for example, better recall of positive material when originally encoded in a happy mood than in an unhappy mood.

Mood-congruous Retrieval. In this phenomenon material is better recalled when retrieval mood is congruous in affective tone with the material rather than incongruous; for example, better recall of negative material in an unhappy retrieval mood than in a happy retrieval mood.

The investigations reported in Chapter 2 provide examples of mood-congruous retrieval of autobiographical memories. Figure 8.6 illustrates an example of mood-congruous retrieval of verbal material presented in the laboratory.

Because of the interpretative difficulties inherent in studies that compare individuals who differ chronically in mood (p. 13) we shall focus on studies that have manipulated mood experimentally. Reviews of experimental studies of mood-congruous memory (Blaney, 1986; Morris, 1989, Chapter 5; Singer & Salovey, 1988) suggest certain broad conclusions. These include the following: (1) Mood-congruous recall of autobiographical memories, and mood-congruous encoding and retrieval of verbal material presented in the laboratory, have been established as empirical phenomena. However, (2) these are not universal phenomena that will always occur with any material that can be categorised as positive or negative in terms of "dictionary defined" meaning. (3) There are strong suggestions that the extent of mood-congruous recall, and, indeed, whether it occurs at all, is a function of the nature of the material used, of the way it is encoded, and of the ways in which differences in mood are created. (4) The variety of experimental outcomes cannot at present be accounted for wholly in terms of any simple empirical generalisation.

Some of the variability in experimental outcomes can be attributed to methodological factors. For example, Bower, Gilligan, and Monteiro's

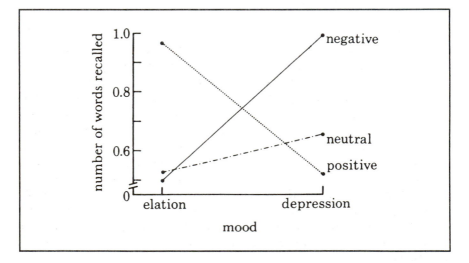

FIG. 8.6. Effects of elated and depressed retrieval mood on recall of positive, negative, and neutral personality trait adjectives, initially presented in neutral mood. Data from Teasdale & Russell (1983). Figure reproduced from Teasdale (1983a) with permission.

(1981) repeated failures to find effects of retrieval mood on recall of happy and sad incidents from continuous narratives have been attributed to the use of connected prose. Within narratives, positive and negative elements are interconnected by the story line. Consequently, at recall, positive and negative elements can cue each other, over-riding effects of mood congruity (Blaney, 1986).

A further methodological factor concerns the type of design used. Studies in which mood is manipulated, and crossed, both at encoding and retrieval can, potentially, demonstrate mood-congruous encoding, mood-congruous retrieval, and mood-state-dependent memory. However, where studies use designs that can, in principle, demonstrate more than one effect of mood on memory, often only one effect emerges as significant: Demonstration of one effect seems to pre-empt the demonstration of other significant effects (Mecklenbraüker & Hager, 1984; Morris, 1989, p. 81; Riskind, 1989).

Methodological factors only account for some of the variability in experimental results; there is evidence for effects of more substantive variables. The kind of material used in experiments appears to influence the results. For example, positive and negative personality trait words generally show mood-congruous retrieval (Carr, 1987 [Experiment 5]; Clark & Martin, in press [self-reference condition]; Clark & Teasdale, 1985 [female subjects]; Isen et al., 1978; Teasdale & Russell, 1983; Willner & Neiva, 1986), but positive and negative abstract nouns do not (Bower et al., 1978; Clark & Teasdale, 1985), nor do unreferred positive and negative mood words (Carr, 1987, Experiment 5.).

There is also evidence that the way material is encoded can be a powerful factor influencing whether mood-congruous effects are observed. Reference of material to the self appears to be an important factor (e.g. Blaney, 1986; Morris, 1989). For example, Clark and Martin (in press) found mood-congruous retrieval when positive and negative trait words were explicitly referred to the self by asking for judgements of their self-descriptiveness. However, when adjectives were referred to another person, mood-congruous retrieval was not observed. Similarly, Brown and Taylor (1986) found evidence of mood-congruous encoding when trait adjectives were rated for their self-descriptiveness ("describes you?"), but not when they were rated for their phonetic features ("rhymes with XXX?"). Nasby (1988), in a study in which subjects rated whether depressed- and non-depressed-content personal adjectives described either themselves or their mothers, found evidence of mood-congruous encoding only for self-referred adjectives.

Evidence such as this suggests that both the nature of the material being remembered and the way that it is encoded have important influences on the extent of mood-congruous memory observed. Although self-reference appears relevant, this factor alone does not seem either necessary or sufficient for the appearance of mood-congruous memory. Blaney (1986, p. 236), in his comprehensive review of the mood and memory literature, concluded that "a prerequisite for mood congruence is not self-referencing set per se but rather some ability of the stimuli (however presented) to contact the subject's customary evaluative construct system. Self-referencing may be one way of enhancing this."

It will be clear from our brief overview that there is considerable variability in the appearance of mood-congruous memory from one study to another. This variability cannot be accounted for adequately in terms of any simple empirical generalisation. ICS has to meet the challenge of explaining both the basic phenomena of mood-congruous encoding and retrieval and also the variability in the appearance of these phenomena from one study to another.

Conclusions

We have covered the preliminary groundwork needed before presenting the ICS analysis of mood-congruous memory.

ICS suggests that moods can be maintained in a variety of ways. A mood maintained by gloomy weather may be rated similarly for despondency to a mood maintained by ruminating over past mistakes. However, the underlying mechanisms maintaining them may be quite different. Further, these differences in mood maintenance processes may be reflected in differences in the effects of the moods on information processing.

ICS suggests that there are nine separate memory systems, each of which can store representations related to a particular event in the information code for which they are specialised. Access to stored representations is by "use" rather than retrieval per se. Material stored in the memory of one subsystem can be accessed by the creation of a "description" of the required material in another subsystem.

Our brief review of the experimental literature suggests that mood-congruous encoding and retrieval are established as empirical phenomena, but there is considerable variability in results from study to study. At present there is no account that adequately explains this variability.

CHAPTER NINE

ICS and Mood-congruous Memory

At the end of Chapter 8 we concluded that the challenge facing ICS was to explain both the basic phenomena of mood-congruous encoding and retrieval and also the variability in the appearance of these phenomena from one study to another. In this chapter we present relevant explanatory accounts, derived within the ICS framework. We shall not at this point discuss the way in which such accounts are derived, nor the relationship between the general-purpose ICS framework and its application to particular topics. These issues are discussed in the concluding chapter of the book. It is, nevertheless, important to note at this stage a crucial aspect of the use of the framework. The ICS architecture does not, in and of itself, provide full explanatory accounts of specific phenomena. It is necessary to supplement the basic concepts by developing additional assumptions concerning the ways in which processes will actually function. These additional assumptions are not simply plucked out of the air: They are constrained by the basic definitions of the cognitive resources, by specific principles governing their operation, and by concerns with consistency and parsimony in the treatment of a wider range of problems.

The ICS analysis of mood-congruous memory takes advantage of the existence of multiple, functionally independent memory stores within the ICS cognitive architecture. The same hedonically valenced event may be represented, in patterns of different information codes, in the memory records of several different subsystems. ICS suggests that mood-congruous encoding and retrieval depend on the creation and storage of affect-related

Implicational representations derived from the to-be-learned material. There is no reason to expect that all hedonically valenced material will necessarily be encoded in this way. For example, the hedonic valence of positive and negative verbal material might be registered in terms of specific Propositional meanings, without any corresponding affect-related Implicational representations being derived. The ICS analysis proposes that representations of material in information codes other than the Implicational will not support mood-congruous memory. By restricting mood congruity to a particular type of encoding in this way, the ICS account is in a position to explain the variable appearance of mood-congruous memory in relation to encoding variables such as the nature of the material, whether it is self-referenced, and so on.

The ICS account suggests a further requirement in the case of mood-congruous retrieval. This is that more "descriptions", or retrieval cues, to access affect-related representations stored in the Implicational memory record should be created in moods congruent with the affective tone of the representations than in moods incongruent with the tone of the representations.

ICS suggests restrictions on the circumstances in which mood-congruous memory will be observed. Variability in results from one study to another is, therefore, not unexpected. Below, we present detailed accounts of mood-congruous encoding and retrieval and illustrate how variability in the appearance of these phenomena is explained.

Mood-congruous Encoding

ICS proposes, very simply, that mood-congruous encoding depends on the creation of more stored representations, with more "routes of access", for material congruent in affective tone with encoding mood than for incongruent material. In other words, more "elaborated" representations, distributed throughout the memory records of several subsystems, and associated with a wider range of other representations, will be created for congruent than incongruent material.

In general, retrieval depends on the generation of descriptions by interactions between subsystems. If many representations related to encoded material are distributed throughout the memory records of these interacting cognitive subsystems, the probability of a description succeeding in accessing a representation will be greater. Consequently, recall of widely represented, congruent material is more likely than that of incongruent material.

Why is congruent material more widely represented? Material will be widely represented if data streams derived from it continue to be selected by transformation processes in the subsystems at which the data streams arrive. Principle 1 of ICS (Barnard, 1985, p. 216) holds that each of these transformation processes can only process one coherent data stream at a time. Consequently, some degree of selection is essential. So, considering, as an example, the IMPLIC→PROP process, many of the streams of Implicational data presented to the Implicational subsystem may remain unselected by this process. Consequently, they will be subject to no further processing. The basis of selection is inherent in the "procedural knowledge" of the IMPLIC→PROP transformation process. Selection reflects both the extent to which elements can be integrated into coherent patterns that the process "recognises" from its previous experience, and the processing priorities assigned to different coherent patterns. The latter reflect the priorities "learned" by the process over the course of its developmental history.

In studies in which encoding mood is experimentally manipulated, the Implicational subsystem will already be processing patterns of Implicational code related to the schematic models maintaining the induced mood. In other words, these affect-related Implicational data streams will already have "won the competition" for selection by the IMPLIC→PROP process, and are likely to retain the processing priority that has been awarded them. The wider representation, on which mood-congruous encoding depends, will be determined by the extent to which elements of Implicational code derived from the to-be-learned material can be integrated with the Implicational data streams maintaining the encoding mood. If such integration can be achieved, a total pattern, incorporating contributions from both sources, can be processed by the IMPLIC→PROP process. The resultant patterns of Propositional code, bearing some relation to the to-be-learned material, can then be the focus of subsequent cognitive operations (PROP→MPL, or PROP→OBJ, or PROP→IMPLIC, etc.). These will leave related representations distributed throughout the memory records of several subsystems.

It will be easier for Implicational elements derived from mood-congruent material to be integrated with the Implicational code patterns maintaining the encoding mood than for Implicational elements derived from mood-incongruent material. This is because congruent material and mood maintaining elements will more often have been encountered together in coherent information streams in the past. Mood-congruent material, by remaining an aspect of the content of a series of information transformations and exchanges between subsystems, will become more widely represented in the memory records of a number of subsystems than mood-incongruent material. For this reason mood-congruent material will subsequently be recalled better, even if recall occurs in neutral mood. Mood- incongruent material, "selected out" from further processing at the Implicational level, will not be widely represented and so will be remembered more poorly.

This account suggests that the critical selection between mood-congruent and mood-incongruent material occurs within the Implicational subsystem, where the schematic models maintaining encoding mood are processed. It follows that mood-congruent biases will only be shown for material if, at encoding, its affect-related features have been extracted and related Implicational representations have been derived. Only in this way can access be achieved to the point in the system where mood-related biases in selection originate.

Mood-congruous Retrieval

The ICS account suggests that mood-congruous retrieval also depends on the creation and storage of Implicational representations encoding the affective or hedonic features of events. Only the Implicational level, directly involved in the production of affective response, captures fully the affect-related dimensions of material. Representations at the Propositional level might well encode whether events or materials are consensually regarded as "good" or "bad". However, this "cold" aspect of hedonic tone does not appear to be the crucial aspect as far as mood-congruent memory is concerned. If it were, then we would expect mood congruence to be shown more universally for all forms of "objectively" positive and negative material. Relatedly, Blaney (1986, p.236), from his extensive review of the mood and memory literature, suggested as a prerequisite for mood congruence that stimuli "contact the subject's customary evaluative system". Within ICS, such contact is much more related to Implicational processing than to Propositional level processing.

In mood-congruent encoding, creation of Implicational representations related to the affective features of material was important because it led to more elaborated and distributed representations of mood-congruent material at encoding. By contrast, in mood-congruent retrieval, the creation of such Implicational representations is important because it allows biased access to mood-congruent Implicational representations at retrieval. This biased access depends, additionally, on retrieval moods that selectively produce more descriptions to access mood-congruent Implicational representations. We now consider in greater detail how this occurs.

Retrieval involves the creation of descriptions to access stored representations. In many situations, production of such descriptions will be the culmination of extensive, interactive processing between subsystems, progressively refining descriptions until they succeed in meeting the requirements of the retrieval task. The "central engine" of cognition [PROP→IMPLIC; IMPLIC→PROP] plays a particularly important part in the elaboration of descriptions. It follows that the descriptions produced can be influenced powerfully by the schematic models controlling activity of the "central engine".

Moods are, necessarily, sustained by the processing of Implicational models related to the affective "themes" of the mood. Consequently, the production of descriptions in the presence of these models may be biased so that production of mood-congruous descriptions is selectively enhanced. As a result, increased access to mood-congruent Implicational representations will occur. These representations, after further elaboration and transformation into "reportable" information codes, will yield a pattern of recall in which memories are retrieved to a greater extent in congruent retrieval moods than in incongruent moods.

The production of descriptions to access mood-congruent representations involves an interchange of mood-congruent information between the Propositional and Implicational subsystems in the operation of the "central engine" of cognition. The production of mood-congruent descriptions in this way will be facilitated by other processing activities that, similarly, include reciprocal PROP→IMPLIC; IMPLIC→PROP transformations focused on mood-congruent material. As we saw in Chapter 8, certain processing configurations supporting the maintenance of mood states also involve continuing reciprocal exchanges of mood-congruent information between the Implicational and Propositional subsystems. We can anticipate that moods maintained in this way will be associated with mood-congruent retrieval, assuming the appropriate Implicational representations were created at encoding.

In Chapter 8 we saw that moods can also be "externally" regenerated without the "central engine" of cognition continually processing mood-congruent information. Such moods would not necessarily be expected to facilitate the production of descriptions to access mood-congruent representations on which mood-congruous retrieval depends. Thus, the ICS approach envisages that moods may vary in their effects depending on the processes maintaining them. This possibility is examined in detail in the next chapter.

Having described the basic accounts of mood-congrous encoding and retrieval, we next consider how the ICS analysis of mood-congruous memory accounts for two generalisations emerging from the experimental literature:

1. self-reference enhances mood-congruous memory;
2. although self-reference is facilitative, self-relatedness is neither necessary nor sufficient for mood-congruous memory.

The Importance of Self-reference

As we have already noted, a number of workers have suggested the importance of self-reference for mood congruence (e.g. Blaney, 1986; Morris, 1989). Findings of mood congruence for personality trait words explicitly referred to the self but not for words referred to another person (e.g. Clark & Martin, in press; Nasby, 1988) fit this view. Why should mood-congruent retrieval occur after subjects have rated the extent to which trait words apply to themselves, but not after they have rated the extent to which the words apply to someone else that they know?

Before answering this question, we should first use this opportunity to note that mood-congruent retrieval can occur in the absence of any obvious emotional reaction at encoding. For example, although trait words often show mood-congruous retrieval it is unlikely that positive and negative trait adjectives, presented in a mixed sequence, will elicit anything approaching an overt emotional reaction. This underlines the ICS position that "causal belongingness" may be a sufficient condition for mood-congruous retrieval, but it is not a necessary condition; establishing the necessary Implicational encodings may not always be accompanied by overt emotional response.

In order to understand the effects of self-reference, it is necessary to consider briefly the representation of self in the cognitive system. Kihlstrom, Cantor, Albright, Chew, Klein, and Niedenthal (1988) point out that, since William James (1890), a distinction has been made between *self as object*, and *self as agent*. The former refers to one's knowledge about and evaluation of oneself, knowledge in principle analogous to our knowledge of other people. The latter refers to an executive structure within the mental system that monitors and controls experience, thought, and action, and is central to the experience of conscious awareness.

Kihlstrom et al. (1988) point out that most experimental work on self-referent encoding has been guided by a focus on *self as object*. For example, a popular view suggests that the self can be represented in an associative network as a node to which are connected representations both of semantic self-related information ("likes Stravinsky", "kind") and episodic self-related information ("helped old man across street") (Kihlstrom et al., 1988). On this view, the representation of the self is not, in principle, different from the representation of others; we have a node representing *self-as-object* in the same way as we have a node representing *other(specified)-as-object*.

However, recent evidence poses difficulty for this view. First, it appears that trait-descriptive and autobiographical event information about the self are not tightly linked, as the network view suggests. For example, they can be addressed independently, without mutual priming (Klein, Loftus, & Burton, 1989). Second, self-related information and other-related information differ in this respect. Klein and Loftus (in press) found that recall of an autobiographical memory related to a trait word did not reduce the time to decide whether a trait word was self-descriptive. However, when the memories and words were related to another (the subject's mother) rather than to the self, overall mutual facilitation between memory recall and decision times was observed.

Such results suggest that decisions on whether a word describes the self are made on a different basis from decisions about whether a word describes another person. In the latter case, decision-making is consistent with the network view of interconnected propositional representations of events and traits attached to a node representing the other as object. In the case of self-referent judgements, we suggest, decisions can also be based on reference to *self as agent*, or *self as subject*, rather than on reference to *self as object*. Reference to *self as subject* would be to one's "sense of self" at any moment rather than to an "objective" description of oneself as an enduring entity.

Within ICS, *self-as-subject* corresponds to the processing of self-related Implicational schematic models, marked by an holistic "sense of self". *Self-as-object* corresponds to stored Propositional representations listing attributes of the self. *Other-as-object* would be represented, Propositionally, in a way analogous to *self-as-object*.

We can now apply these suggestions to account for the observed pattern of results for mood-congruent encoding and retrieval. On this view, judging the self-descriptiveness of positive and negative words would necessarily involve encodings of representations of the words in conjunction with affect-related schematic models of self. Subsequent mood-congruous encoding and retrieval of the trait words would therefore be expected. By contrast, other-referred judgements of words, made using Propositional representations without involvement of affect-related schematic models, would not be expected to yield mood-congruous encoding and retrieval.

The ICS account predicts that, if self-reference mood-congruous effects depend to an important extent on references to *self-as-subject*, then, by using appropriate experimental instructions to lead subjects to base self-referent judgements on *self-as-object* rather than *self-as-subject*, mood-congruous retrieval of self-referred trait words should be reduced or abolished.

A detailed examination of the results of studies investigating self- versus other-reference in mood-congruent encoding supports this ICS analysis of self-reference. Effects of encoding mood on subsequent recall appear to be restricted to yes-rated self-referenced congruent personality trait adjectives (eg. Brown & Taylor, 1986; Nasby, 1988). Such adjectives include positive words that subjects in happy mood endorse as describing themselves, or negative words endorsed as self-descriptive by subjects in unhappy moods. Trait adjectives congruent with encoding mood but rated as not self-descriptive (e.g. positive words rated "no" for self-descriptiveness by subjects in happy moods) do not show effects of mood-congruent encoding.

This pattern of results is wholly consistent with the ICS analysis of self-reference we have presented. Decisions on the self-descriptiveness of personality adjectives involve referring Implicational elements derived from those adjectives to the Implicational schematic models creating the current "sense of self". In mood states, adjectives congruent with the "sense of self" are more likely both to be rated as self-descriptive, and to be incorporated into the mood-dependent schematic self-models being synthesised. Such incorporation means that elements derived from those words are more likely to be included in the further processing that will lead to subsequent enhanced mood-congruent recall. Adjectives that are not congruent with the current "sense of self", even though they may be generally congruent in hedonic tone with the current mood state, will not be incorporated into the schematic models synthesised. Consequently, they will be rated "no" for self-descriptiveness, and will not show enhanced recall.

What of the occurrence of mood-congruous memory for personality trait adjectives when they are not explicitly referred to the self? Mood-congruent retrieval of such words has been observed when subjects, instead of making self-referent judgements, are explicitly instructed to learn the words (e.g. Isen et al., 1978; Teasdale & Russell, 1983 [Fig. 8.6, this volume]) or exposed to them in incidental learning paradigms (e.g. Carr, 1987; Clark & Teasdale, 1985). According to the ICS account, mood-congruent retrieval in these situations depends on incidental incorporation of word-derived representations into self-related Implicational schematic models. In support of this view, Nasby (1988) cites research indicating that, when encoding personality trait adjectives, many subjects report the spontaneous adoption of a self-referent mnemonic (e.g. Rogers, 1977; Turner, 1980; Wells, Hoffman, & Enzle, 1984).

The ease with which words can be self-referred incidentally will obviously vary from one class of words to another, and is likely to be greatest for personality trait adjectives. Other classes of positive and negative words, such as abstract nouns, would be less likely to be self-referred spontaneously. This is probably the reason why, in contrast to personality trait adjectives, positive and negative abstract nouns do not show mood-congruent retrieval in incidental learning paradigms (Clark & Teasdale, 1985).

Self-relatedness is neither Necessary nor Sufficient for Mood-congruous Memory

Self-reference is an important factor affecting the occurrence of mood congruence. Self-relatedness of material per se, however, seems to be neither necessary nor sufficient. By specifying the conditions necessary for mood-congruous encoding and retrieval, the ICS analysis offers a way of understanding when self-relatedness of material is sufficient, and when it is not. This analysis also enables us to understand when material that is not obviously self-related will show mood-congruous memory effects.

Evidence that self-relatedness of material per se is not sufficient for mood congruence comes from a number of sources. For example, Teasdale and Dritschel (submitted) found no mood congruence for material closely related to personal autobiographical events, but mood congruence for material less closely associated with such events. Relatedly, Gilligan and Bower (1983) found no relationship between the extent to which phrases reminded subjects of personal memories and the extent of mood-congruent memory. On the other hand, evidence that self-relatedness is not necessary for the demonstration of mood-congruent memory comes, for example, from Laird et al. (1982, Experiment 1). This study found mood-congruous retrieval for emotionally evocative prose passages—anger-evoking editorials or amusing Woody Allen stories—that, although "personally involving", were not obviously referable to the self. Further, as we have already noted, Blaney (1986, p.236), from his comprehensive review of the mood and memory literature, suggested that "a prerequisite for mood congruence is not self-referencing set per se but rather some ability of the stimuli (however presented) to contact the subject's customary evaluative construct system. Self-referencing may be one way of enhancing this."

The ICS account suggests that mood-congruous retrieval of experimental materials will occur only if encoding involves the production of Implicational schematic models related to the affective content of the material. These conditions are met most obviously where experimental materials themselves elicit emotional reactions. However, as in Laird et al.'s (1982) study in which subjects showed mood-congruous retrieval after reading either anger-evoking editorials or amusing Woody Allen stories, it is not necessary for the materials or the encoding to be obviously referenced to the self. The ICS account predicts that mood-congruent retrieval would be less if such passages were rewritten in a way that retained the same Propositional meaning (including reference to positive and negative features) but that lacked the power to elicit an affective response (cf. prose versus poetry on p. 73).

The present analysis suggests that self-relatedness per se is not sufficient for mood-congruent memory. It suggests that in situations where self-relatedness of material is not also associated with its incorporation into self-related affective Implicational schematic models then mood-congruent memory will not occur. Further, if representations of self-related material can be accessed in ways that bypass the Implicational subsystem then mood-congruent retrieval will not occur. A detailed internal analysis of the previously mentioned study by Teasdale and Dritschel (submitted) supports this view.

It is worth describing these findings in some detail because they were instrumental in convincing one of us (JT) of the difficulty of accounting for the variability of mood-congruous memory in terms of simple empirical generalisations or by Bower's associative network theory. Further, these findings were persuasive that a theoretical approach as complex as ICS was necessary and that ICS, specifically, was able to offer a coherent account of the pattern of results. They may serve the same purpose for the reader.

In Teasdale and Dritschel's (submitted) study, subjects, in normal mood, formed images to written descriptions. Happy and depressed moods were then induced, and incidental recall of the previously presented image descriptions was required. Descriptions that had elicited images closely based on subjects' personal, autobiographical experiences did not show mood-congruent retrieval. In contrast, mood-congruous retrieval was shown for descriptions that had elicited images less related to personal, autobiographical experiences. Creation of these images had depended not so much on recall of autobiographical memories as on the products of creative fabrication. The observed pattern of results was clearly counter to the general trend for mood congruence to be greater for self-relevant material.

ICS offered an account of the overall results of this study that was quite consistent with the detailed pattern of results. This account suggested that directly personally relevant images were based on relatively direct access to visual Object (OBJ) representations of autobiographical events in the memory store of the visual Object subsystem, without the need for much involvement of the Implicational subsystem. Consistent with this suggestion, these images were visually vivid, were formed quickly, and their creation was not accompanied by the experience of emotion. Conversely, less autobiographical, fabricated, images were produced, not by accessing "cold" visual Object stored representations, but by active, extended, elaborative processing, including the synthesis of affect-related themes at the Implicational level. Consistent with this suggestion, these images were rated as less visually vivid, were formed more slowly, and their production was accompanied by the experience of emotion. Although the first type of image was more obviously self-related, it is wholly consistent with the ICS analysis that only the descriptions that produced images of the latter type led to mood-congruous retrieval: It was only in this second case that image production involved the creation of affect-related Implicational representations, the key requisite, according to ICS, for mood-congruent memory.

Conclusions

Accounts of mood-congruous retrieval and encoding can be derived within ICS quite naturally, making few additional or arbitrary assumptions. These accounts provide adequate explanations for the basic phenomena, can explain the variations in the phenomena from study to study, and capture, within a systematic framework, intuitive insights suggested by those reviewing the literature. Testable predictions can also be derived from these accounts.

A major strength of ICS with respect to mood-congruous recall is that it recognises explicitly distinct levels of representation and asserts that these different levels bear different functional relationships to affective phenomena. In explaining mood-congruous recall, central importance has been placed on Implicational level representations. These representations are involved both in the production of mood states and in the encoding of the affective, hedonic, or "hot" qualities of material, so providing a point in the system where these two factors can interact to produce mood-congruous effects. "Good" and "bad" events will be represented in the memory stores of other subsystems. For example, the memory store of the Object subsystem may hold records of the visual objects and their inter-relations involved in events, and the memory store of the Propositional subsystem may store propositions reflecting the content of events including, potentially, the fact that they were evaluated positively or negatively at the time. However, mood-congruous memory for events depends on their hedonic features being encoded at the Implicational level. Unless this occurs, mood congruence would not be expected. Equally, effects of retrieval mood biasing access to congruent memories depends on the retrieval task involving access to "hot" affect-related Implicational records. If the requirements of the memory task can be met without such access (e.g. by direct access to "cold" "scripted" Propositional representations of childhood memories [Salovey & Singer, 1989]; or to "cold" Object level memory records to yield, directly, visually vivid images of events [Teasdale & Dritschel, submitted]), then mood-congruous memory will not be expected. The multiple levels of representation of events, with different functional properties associated with each level, enables ICS to overcome many of the difficulties of the network model of mood and memory.

There is clearly a limit to the extent to which an approach can be strengthened by experimental data that are already available, rather than by generating novel predictions that survive experimental test. Accepting this limitation, the ICS approach seems to have met the challenge of accounting for findings of mood-congruous recall adequately. It also provides insights into an area that has recently become problematic in this field, as we discuss in the next chapter.

CHAPTER TEN

ICS, Mood Maintenance, and Mood-incongruous Memory

The ICS analysis of mood-congruous retrieval has several aspects. In the last chapter we focused primarily on the multiple representation of information in memory and the crucial role played by affective Implicational schematic models. In this chapter we explore further aspects of the ICS analysis of mood states and the production of descriptions to access mood-congruent information.

We begin by extending the analysis of mood previously presented in Chapter 8. We then apply this analysis to recent demonstrations of mood-incongruent memory that pose considerable difficulties for existing theoretical approaches to understanding mood-congruous cognition.

Mood Maintenance and Mood-congruous Memory

The ICS analysis suggests that mood-congruous retrieval depends on retrieval mood facilitating the production of descriptions to access stored congruent Implicational representations. The production of descriptions involves sequences of cognitive operations that have evolved over an individual's cognitive developmental history. There is no necessary reason to expect that these operations will be related similarly to mood states maintained in different ways. The mood-congruent pattern of description production, on which mood-congruent retrieval depends, is not an inherent feature of all mood states. From the ICS perspective, moods that are maintained by different underlying processes may differ in the extent of associated mood-congruous retrieval.

Descriptions to access material in one subsystem have to be created in another subsystem (see p. 108). Descriptions to access congruent Implicational representations will generally be produced by the Propositional subsystem, as the result of an exchange of information related to mood-congruent themes between the Implicational and Propositional subsystems. Such a continuing exchange of mood-congruent information is also a central feature of certain forms of mood maintenance (pp. 103–106). The information flow maintaining these moods is similar to that required for the production of descriptions to access mood-congruent Implicational representations. Consequently, mood-congruent retrieval would be expected in these moods.

ICS suggests that moods can be maintained in a variety of ways (Chapter 8). All of these, necessarily, involve regeneration of affect-related Implicational schematic models. However, not all these schematic models will produce mood-congruent Propositional outputs from which descriptions to access mood-congruent Implicational material can be derived. In situations where mood maintenance does not involve schematic models producing such mood-congruent Propositional representations, mood-congruous retrieval would not be expected.

What characterises moods that produce mood-congruent retrieval descriptions and those that do not? Mood-congruent descriptions are particularly likely to be produced in processing activity that effectively "harmonises" ideation and affect. Within such activity there is coherence and conformity to a continuing affective theme across (1) the Propositional, sensory, and Body-state inputs to the Implicational subsystem; (2) the schematic models synthesised; and (3) the Propositional representational outputs and emotional bodily effects resulting from those models.

Such coherent patterns of processing activity can be thought of as "modes of mind". For example, the mental activity supporting a "sense of self as failure" mode of mind would involve: (1) inputs to the Implicational subsystem consisting of Propositional inputs related to specific failure experiences, and Body-state inputs reflecting sad facial expression and "beaten" posture; (2) synthesis of the ["self as failure"] class of schematic models; and (3) outputs from these schematic models in the form of (a) Propositional representations related to anticipations of future failures, personal attributions for previous failures, or descriptions that will access memories of previous failures; and (b) emotional effector outputs that maintain sad facial expression, "beaten" posture, and general inhibition of action-oriented behaviour.

The idea is that in all of us there exists the potential for a range of such "modes of mind" related to both positive and negative mood states. The mental activity maintaining these modes persists over time by continuing "internal" self-regeneration (Chapter 8). We may slip into such modes, be pushed into them by events, or deliberately, effortfully, work ourselves into them when asked to do so by the mood-induction instructions in an experiment on mood and memory.

Figure 10.1 illustrates an example of a configuration supporting such "harmonised" mental activity.

The figure is, effectively, an annotated version of our previous Fig. 8.5. This illustrated the maintenance of moods by "internal" regeneration of affect-related schematic models as a result of the interlinked, integrated effects of the [PROP→IMPLIC; IMPLIC→PROP] and the [BS→IMPLIC; IMPLIC→VISC/SOM; VISC/SOM→bodily effects; bodily effects→BS] loops.

Particular patterns of "harmonised" processing activity operate as distinctive "modes of mind", which we can recognise in "ruminative" moods with an inherent informational content. Extreme forms of such "harmonised" processing activity underpin the maintenance of neurotic forms of depression (Chapter 12). Laboratory mood inductions, in which subjects actively work at getting themselves into specified moods with the help of verbal or musical cues (Clark, 1983a), can be seen as situations where subjects deliberately enter "harmonised" processing activity corresponding to specific modes of mind.

Although characteristic of certain naturally occurring "modes of mind" and of deliberate efforts at mood induction, the active "harmonisation" of processing activity is not involved in all forms of mood maintenance. This is particularly true of moods maintained by continuing external sensory input. For example, bright sunshine may maintain positive mood through a prepared VIS→IMPLIC transformation, and merely listening to music, without actively trying to "collaborate" with it in an effortful mood induction, may affect mood through the AC→IMPLIC process. In neither case does mood maintenance necessarily involve or require any wider "harmonisation" of ideational content with the directly sensorily derived affective elements. This is because the sensorily derived Implicational elements, by themselves, can create a continuing affective state via the IMPLIC→VISC and IMPLIC→SOM processes.

Sensorily derived elements will only combine with Propositionally derived elements to form an integrated sensori-semantic schematic model of the same affective tone if there has been an appropriate history of co-occurrences. That is, only if good moods induced by sunshine or listening to music have been associated with positively interpreted events. There is no necessary reason why this will be so. Important positive or negative achievement- or relationship-related events probably occur relatively randomly with respect to the weather. Mood-elevating music may have been associated as often with attempts to cheer oneself up after disappointments as with events with positive meanings. In other words,

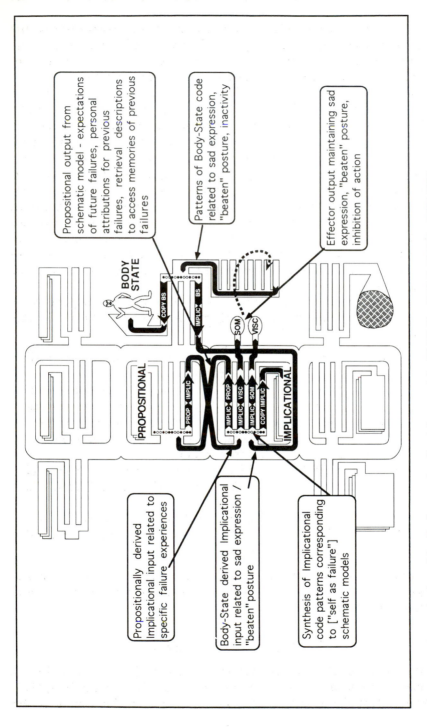

Propositional output from schematic model - expectations of future failures, personal attributions for previous failures, retrieval descriptions of previous failures to access memories of previous failures

Patterns of Body-State code related to sad expression, "beaten" posture, inactivity

Effector output maintaining sad expression, "beaten" posture, inhibition of action

BODY STATE

COPY BS

IMPLIC ▲ BS

PROPOSITIONAL

PROP ▲ IMPLIC

IMPLIC ▲ PROP

IMPLIC ▲ VISC

IMPLIC ▲ SOM

COPY IMPLIC

IMPLICATIONAL

SOM

VISC

Propositionally derived Implicational input related to specific failure experiences

Body-State derived Implicational input related to sad expression / "beaten" posture

Synthesis of Implicational code patterns corresponding to ["self as failure"] schematic models

FIG. 10.1 Harmonisation of the Body-state feedback loop and the [IMPLIC→PROP; PROP→IMPLIC] loop.

there will have been no history of sensori-semantic co-occurrences that would necessarily create the type of schematic model that would yield mood-congruent Propositional outputs, or otherwise support the wider harmonisation of ideational and affective processing activity.

We have discussed the case of Visual and Acoustic sensory inputs. The situation is different with Body-state derived Implicational elements. Reflecting the more "internal" origins of these sensory inputs, there is more likely to have been a history of co-occurrences between specific patterns of Body-state code and affect-related meanings. First, there will have been frequent co-occurences between patterns of Body-state code related to the bodily effects of emotional response and patterns of congruent meanings related to the events that induced the emotional response. Second, pleasant and unpleasant smells and tastes are likely to have been associated with events that, themselves, would have been interpreted positively or negatively. In both cases there is a basis for the development of integrated sensori-semantic schematic models of the type that would support "harmonised" processing activity.

This further discussion of mood-states has made the following key points that are directly relevant to the problems considered in the rest of this chapter:

1. Moods can be maintained in a variety of ways, not all of which will support mood-congruous retrieval.
2. Mood-congruous retrieval depends on the production of mood-congruous descriptions. Production of such descriptions occurs within "harmonised" mental processing activity in which sensory, affective, and meaning components are integrated into thematically coherent "modes of mind".
3. Moods maintained within particular "harmonised modes of mind" necessarily involve related mood-congruent cognitive activity.
4. The extent to which affect-related schematic models generate harmonising mood-congruent Propositional outputs will depend on the previous learning history of co-occurrences.

We now apply our extended perspective on mood maintenance and mood-congruous cognition to understanding the problematic area of mood-incongruous memory.

Mood-incongruent Recall

Recent reports of mood-incongruent encoding (Rinck, Glowalla, & Schneider, 1992) and mood-incongruent retrieval (Parrott & Sabini, 1990) pose a healthy challenge to any theoretical framework that claims to offer a comprehensive account of the effects of mood on memory. How well does ICS meet this challenge?

Mood-incongruent Encoding

Rinck et al. (1992) reported two experiments in which subjects in induced happy or sad moods rated the emotional valence of pleasant and unpleasant words. Half the words had strong affective tone, half had slight affective tone. Subsequently, subjects recalled the words in normal mood. In both experiments, mood-congruent recall was shown for strongly valenced words, but, for slightly pleasant and unpleasant words, significant mood-incongruent recall was observed.

As Rinck et al. (1992) pointed out, their results cannot be accommodated within an unelaborated version of Bower's (1981) associative network theory. They suggested that mood-incongruent recall of slightly toned words arose because decisions on the affective valence of these relatively ambiguous words would be more difficult and take longer in incongruent than in congruent encoding moods. Valence rating times confirmed this suggestion, e.g. slightly pleasant words were rated more quickly in happy mood than in unhappy mood.

Rinck et al. (1992) suggested that the greater difficulty of rating slightly valenced words in incongruent moods is associated with greater elaboration of those words in incongruent than in congruent encoding moods. Consequently, more widespread representations are laid down in incongruent encoding moods. These differences in the extent of encoding elaboration will be reflected in a pattern of recall showing mood-incongruent encoding effects for slightly pleasant and unpleasant words.

The ICS account of mood-congruent encoding (p. 114) suggests that the important factor producing a mood-congruent pattern of recall is the extent to which representations of material are elaborated and distributed throughout the memory records of different subsystems at encoding. In the normal experimental procedure, material congruent with encoding mood will be selected preferentially for further processing, leading to more elaborated, distributed representations. If, as in Rinck et al.'s (1992) study, experimental conditions are arranged so that material incongruent with encoding mood receives more elaborative processing, then the ICS account predicts a pattern of mood-incongruent encoding. In this way, Rinck et al.'s (1992) suggested mechanism for mood-incongruent encoding is quite consistent with the ICS account of mood-congruent encoding: The basic mechanism is the same in both cases.

Rinck et al.'s (1992) findings, that posed problems for the associative network model, are readily explained within the ICS account of mood-congruous encoding. If anything, these findings strengthen that account.

Mood-incongruent Retrieval

Evidence of mood-incongruent retrieval has been reported by Parrott and Sabini (1990). Recall of autobiographical memories was studied in five experiments. Four used "natural" mood inductions (return of graded mid-term examinations, bright versus cloudy weather, and background music). A fifth used a more "artificial" mood induction (a musical mood induction procedure, used in many previous studies, that combined music with instructions to work actively at getting into the mood). Only the last of these inductions produced mood-congruent retrieval. All the more natural inductions yielded significant mood-incongruent retrieval.

Parrott and Sabini took care to dispose of the more obvious artifactual explanations of their results. Let us, pending attempts at replication, assume the validity of their findings and examine their implications.

First, we note that these findings pose enormous difficulties for an unelaborated version of the associative network theory; if mood differences were sufficient to produce any significant memory effects then these effects should be mood-congruent, and should not depend on the "naturalness" or otherwise of the mood induction. Mood-incongruent recall might be explained by suggesting that "mood repair" processes operate to offset the "automatic" effects of mood context, predicted by network theory. However, as well as being a major elaboration of network theory, the notion of mood "repair" is clearly strained when it has to account for mood incongruence involving the greater recall of unpleasant memories in happy mood. This pattern was evident in Parrot and Sabini's results as much, or more, than mood incongruence resulting from greater recall of pleasant memories in unpleasant mood.

How does ICS account for these findings? It should be stressed right away that, in contrast to network theory, it is not inherent in the ICS approach that mood-congruent memory will occur, nor that it will occur for all types of mood, nor that, for a given type of mood, it will occur equally for moods produced in all ways. We discussed this issue at length in the opening section of this chapter. There, we pointed out that, even if Implicational representations of affective events have been encoded in memory, differential access to them in different mood states depends on the differential production of the relevant descriptions.

If the Implicational schematic models maintaining mood do not produce mood-congruent Propositional representations from which mood-congruent retrieval descriptions can be derived, mood-congruent retrieval would not necessarily be expected. In Parrott and Sabini's study, the effects on mood of bright versus cloudy days, or of background music, would operate directly through, respectively, the biologically prepared VIS→IMPLIC, and AC→IMPLIC, transformations. Moods could be maintained through such external sensory input without any need for involvement of [IMPLIC→PROP; PROP→IMPLIC] cycles processing mood-congruent information, and producing the mood-congruent retrieval descriptions on which mood-congruous retrieval depends. Such cycles are more likely to be implicated in the deliberate, controlled efforts to get into a designated mood in the typical laboratory mood induction procedures, whether verbal or musical. It is as if, in these inductions, subjects take a familiar mental mode "off the shelf" and work at maintaining the "harmonisation" of ideation and affect in self-regenerating processing cycles that sustain mood. Mood-congruent retrieval would be expected for moods produced by such inductions to a greater extent than for moods produced by direct, external, sensory input.

Parrott and Sabini (1990) also found mood-incongruent memory when happy and unhappy moods were the result of grades on mid-term examinations that were, respectively, better or worse than students had expected. Here, unlike the case of weather and music, the mood induction has obvious meaning components. Nonetheless, we suggest that in this situation mood was again the direct result of a current external emotion-eliciting event (see p. 102) rather than the result of an "internally regenerating" harmonised configuration focused on personal failure or success.

There are two reasons for this suggestion. First, subjects were allocated to happy and unhappy groups according to whether their examination performance exceeded or fell short of their previously stated expectations. These expectations presumably were based on relatively stable models of self-evaluation and intellectual performance. It seems unlikely that the elation or disappointment that related to a single result that deviated from such stable models would be associated with the creation of either "me as a wonderful success" or "me as a failure" mental modes. The second reason is that a period of distracting activity occurred between receiving the examination grades and memory retrieval. As we discuss more fully later (pp. 177–183), distraction disrupts the processing cycles maintaining "harmonised" affect-related configurations and so, in the present case, would further reduce the possibility of establishing such self-regenerating cycles. For both these reasons, we suggest that moods resulting from feedback on examination performance, like moods created by weather and music, were not maintained by [IMPLIC→PROP; PROP→IMPLIC] cycles processing mood-congruent information. In such moods, there will not be an enhanced production of mood-congruent retrieval descriptions and, hence, no basis for mood-congruent retrieval.

The argument so far explains the absence of mood-congruent memory, but what of the mood-incongruence actually observed by Parrott and Sabini (1990)? ICS necessarily suggests that mood-incongruent retrieval reflects the production of mood-incongruent retrieval descriptions by the Implicational schematic models maintaining moods. Mood-incongruent retrieval of positive memories in unhappy mood can plausibly be related to a "mood repair" processing configuration, based on a learning history of responding to unhappy moods by attending to, remembering, or performing positive activities to restore mood. However, as already noted, mood-incongruent retrieval of negative memories in happy mood appeared to be the more striking pattern in Parrott and Sabini's (1990) study. How is this to be explained ?

Enhanced retrieval of negative memories in certain happy moods depends on schematic models that, themselves, have positive affective content but lead to the production of descriptions to access stored negative material. The abstraction of such models can be understood in terms of the basic processing priority afforded to informational discrepancies within the ICS approach (p. 61, and see also Chapter 14). The importance of informational discrepancies suggests that the system operates with a "default" strategy such as the following: In the absence of more immediately pressing informational discrepancies, the system reconfigures to search its memory records for information related to "unfinished business". Stored representations of such material necessarily encode discrepancies between some state of affairs and the state of affairs that is intended, expected, or desired. Such material is more likely to be rated negatively than positively. Accessing such material in positive mood would yield a pattern of mood-incongruent retrieval.

In positive moods maintained by internally regenerating positive "mental modes", the mood reflects current positive discrepancies between the way things are and some reference state (see Chapter 14). It follows that processing priority will be given to informational discrepancies related to the current topic. Accessing such positive information will preclude the "default" option of accessing more negative information related to previous "unfinished business".

In positive moods maintained by the weather, music, etc., a different situation obtains. Here, mood is maintained by continuing external sensory input rather than by positive discrepancies between current and reference states. Such moods could be described as "everything is basically all right at the moment" modes. Because mood maintenance does not involve informational discrepancies related to the current state of affairs, the system can "indulge" in its default option and search memory for "unfinished business". Further, such moods are already positive and, as we discuss in the next chapter, associated with a general satisfaction with life. Consequently, the system can continue to process negative information related to unfinished business without creating new, current discrepancies related to differences between existing and desired mood states. In normal, less positive mood states, negative information related to unfinished business might be "selected out" from processing in further [IMPLIC→PROP; PROP→IMPLIC] cycles in order to avoid discomfort.

It is not difficult to think of the kind of learning histories that would lead to the development and maintenance of the kind of processing configurations that, according to this analysis, underlie mood-incongruent recall in certain positive moods. For example, the enhanced body tone and equanimity resulting from bright weather or uplifting music might have encouraged a person to tackle unpleasant "chores" that had previously been put off—such as "spring cleaning" or really confronting an ongoing problem previously avoided. As a result of such associations, the schematic models related to these positive states would, subsequently, produce Propositional outputs that would facilitate access to stored representations related to (negatively valenced) "unfinished business".

Although necessarily speculative, the ICS account of mood-incongruent memory is reasonably plausible. It also has important implications for use of the "unnatural" mood induction procedures typically employed in mood and memory experiments. Parrott and Sabini's (1990) findings might lead one to conclude that the bulk of the mood and memory literature is questionable, based as it is on the use of effortful "artificial" mood induction procedures that yield results quite different from those obtained with "natural" mood inductions. We would disagree. Indeed, it was to address the very issue of the ecological validity of early investigations of mood-congruent retrieval using laboratory mood induction procedures that studies were conducted using the same procedures in clinically depressed patients (see Chapter 2). These studies suggested a strong similarity in the results achieved in the two types of study. It seems, perhaps surprisingly, that in this respect, the more "artificially" produced moods are a better analogue of clinically significant depression than more "naturally" occurring states of mild depression. Our interpretation of Parrott and Sabini's (1990) findings is that both clinical depression and typical laboratory mood induction procedures, but not moods produced by sunlight or background music, involve the Propositional-Implicational loop processing mood-congruent information. This processing configuration yields the greater availability of descriptions to access congruent Implicational records on which mood-congruous retrieval depends. As we shall see later (Chapter 12), this same processing configuration is also central to the ICS analysis of the maintenance of clinical depression and negative, depressive thinking.

Conclusions

The analysis of mood-congruous memory developed within ICS has allowed us to develop initially plausible hypotheses in the problematic area of mood-incongruent memory. In the previous chapter we saw how ICS also provides a helpful account of the basic phenomena of mood-congruous encoding and retrieval, and of their variability from one experimental situation to another. We conclude our evaluation of ICS against present evidence of the phenomena of mood-congruous memory with a generally positive verdict. Naturally, this verdict has to remain open pending the results of experiments specifically testing predictions derived from the ICS analysis.

In the next chapter we stay within the realm of experimental studies of mood-congruous cognition, but switch our attention to the biasing effects of mood on evaluative judgements. These effects are clearly highly relevant to our ultimate goal of understanding depressive thinking, where themes of devaluation of "self, the world, and the future" are dominant.

CHAPTER ELEVEN

Mood Effects on Evaluative Judgement

Biasing effects of happy and unhappy moods on evaluative judgements are well-established, robust, phenomena (see reviews by Clark & Isen, 1982; Forgas & Bower, 1988; Morris, 1989, Chapter 5; Schwarz & Clore, 1988). Many of these effects seem of direct relevance to our goal of understanding depressive thinking. For example, compared to happy mood, induced unhappy mood reduces subjects' judgements of their general satisfaction with life (Schwarz & Clore, 1983), of their own social skills (Forgas, Bower, & Krantz, 1984), of their self-evaluation on a number of positive dimensions (Wright & Mischel, 1982), and of their self-efficacy (Kavanagh & Bower, 1985). Unhappy mood increases subjective probabilities of future risk (Johnson & Tversky, 1983) and increases the extent to which subjects attribute failures to their own inadequacies (Forgas, Bower, & Moylan, 1990). Such studies suggest that normal subjects in induced unhappy moods show biases in their judgements parallel to the negative view of "self, world, and future" characteristic of depressed patients (p. 71), although to a lesser extent.

"Natural" mood inductions have often been used in studies of mood and judgement, in contrast to the artificial mood induction procedures typically used in studies of mood and memory. For example, Schwarz and Clore (1983) studied effects of the weather, Isen et al. (1978) studied the effects of free gifts, Forgas and Moylan (1987) compared audiences emerging from happy movies with those who had seen sad or aggressive movies, and Schwarz, Strack, Kommer, and Wagner (1987) compared subjects after their team had won or drawn in a World Cup soccer match. The effects of such natural variations seem generally similar to the effects observed with laboratory mood inductions. This observation is important in two ways. First, it reassures us that the effects observed in laboratory studies are not simply responses to experimental demand. This possibility has to be taken seriously for judgemental tasks where measures often depend entirely on simple ratings, the purpose of which must be quite transparent to experimental subjects. Second, it suggests a contrast with the effects of mood on memory where the findings of Parrott and Sabini (1990), discussed in the last chapter, suggest that some "natural" mood inductions may not produce mood-congruent effects.

How does ICS explain the biasing effects of mood on evaluative judgements? We shall describe the outlines of the ICS account and then contrast this formulation with the alternative proposals offered by Bower's associative network theory and Schwarz and Clore's (1983; 1988) feelings-as-information hypothesis. We shall make these contrasts with respect to a number of specific issues.

The ICS Account of Mood-congruent Evaluative Judgement

In common with other approaches (e.g. Forgas, 1992), the ICS account recognises that judgements can be made in a variety of ways, not all of which would be expected to show effects of mood congruence. So, for example, we may have stored Propositional representations to the effect that "Fred is an excellent chess player", "My income is less than that of my colleagues", or "Socrates was a wise man". If a judgement can be made simply by directly accessing such stored representations, then mood congruence would not be expected.

In many situations the judgemental process will be more active and elaborative, involving information synthesis and production rather than simple information retrieval and reproduction. Within ICS, this more active type of judgemental process depends on the construction of appropriate Implicational schematic models. These schematic models will not be the same as those that would be formed in response to a request to retrieve material from memory. It follows that we should not necessarily expect direct parallels between the effects of mood on recall and the effects of mood on judgements.

Like all Implicational schematic models, those formed to make evaluative judgements can, potentially, receive contributions derived from both semantic (Propositional) and sensory sources. The Propositionally derived elements will, of course, include elements indicating that a judgement is required. If the judgement is performed in a mood state, there may also be contributions to the model from Propositionally derived elements from any [PROP→IMPLIC; IMPLIC→PROP] cycle acting to maintain the mood (pp. 103–106).

Judgement-related schematic models may also receive contributions from mood-related sensory elements. The most important of these will be the Body-state-derived elements resulting from the bodily effects of the mood state, possibly acting to maintain the mood state through the [IMPLIC→VISC/SOM; VISC/SOM→bodily effects; bodily effects→BS; BS→IMPLIC] cycle (p. 102).

The schematic models supporting evaluative judgements made in a mood state may be influenced by pre-existing sensory and informational elements, and the interaction between them. The schematic model "assembled" from the elements available will be processed by the IMPLIC→PROP transformation process to deliver the essential result of the judgement. The influence of mood on this judgement will depend on the extent to which mood-related Implicational elements, of both sensory and semantic origin, have become incorporated into the judgement-related schematic model.

Available Implicational elements will be incorporated into the judgement-related schematic model to the extent that the different sets of elements have co-occurred previously, in the Implicational subsystem's "learning history". Biases in judgement can be expected if, on this basis, mood-related elements can be combined with those related to the judgement task to create a coherent schematic model that, in the past, has delivered mood-congruous judgements via the IMPLIC→PROP process.

Let us consider, as an illustrative example, findings reported by Clark, Milberg, and Ross (1983). Success feedback on a memory task enhanced students' evaluations of various aspects of university life, but only if combined with the high autonomic arousal from stepping up and down on a cinder block for seven minutes. The combination of success feedback and normal arousal did not affect evaluative judgements, nor did high arousal in the absence of success feedback. In this experimental situation, the schematic model assembled for the judgement could draw on elements related to the positive schematic models created following success feedback, together with Body-state-derived elements reflecting either exercise-induced heightened arousal or normal, lower levels of arousal.

Previous experience of successes, and related positive events, will have led to repeated co-occurrences of Propositionally derived Implicational elements related to positive experiences together with Body-state-derived elements related to affect-heightened arousal. These co-occurrences would be encoded in an ["everything in the garden is wonderful"] schematic model. The pattern of Implicational code representing this model would include both semantically and sensorily derived elements.

The experiences leading to the creation of the ["everything in the garden is wonderful"] schematic model would, themselves, have been associated with production of Propositional representations related to positive evaluations of the life experiences fuelling synthesis of this model. The co-occurrences of the model and production of positive evaluations will have been encoded in the procedural knowledge of the IMPLIC→PROP process. As a result, any evaluative judgement based on a schematic model incorporating sufficient elements of the ["everything in the garden is wonderful"] model will deliver positively biased judgements.

In the context of Clark et al.'s (1983) experiment, neither the Implicational elements related to heightened arousal from exercise nor those related to successful task performance were, by themselves, sufficient to create enough of the total pattern of the ["everything in the garden is wonderful"] model to bias judgements of aspects of campus life. However, the combination of elements from the two sources was sufficient to produce a judgement-related schematic model that corresponded closely enough to the total pattern of the ["everything in the garden is wonderful"] model to deliver a positively biased judgement.

By analogous reasoning it is possible to account for the effects of depressed mood, maintained by schematic models such as ["bad self"] or ["bad world"], biasing evaluative judgements negatively. These schematic models will have previously been synthesised in life situations involving personal failure, criticism, loss, or disappointment. Such situations, of course, will also have involved negative evaluations of self or aspects of the world. These co-occurrences will have been encoded in the IMPLIC→PROP process. Presented now with Implicational elements, derived from both Propositional and Body-state sources, that cohere sufficiently to allow synthesis of ["bad self"], ["bad world"], etc. schematic models, the IMPLIC→PROP process will deliver negatively biased evaluative judgements.

We elaborate this basic account as we compare ICS with alternative approaches in relation to a number of specific issues.

The Global Nature of Effects of Mood on Judgement

The effects of mood on evaluative judgements are often wide and global, rather than narrow and specific. For example, Johnson and Tversky (1983) studied the effects of a number of different mood-inducing stories on ratings of subjective risk for a wide range of future disasters. They found that the extent to which judgements of risk were affected by the moods induced by stories was quite unrelated to the extent to which the topic of the story matched the target of the judgement. For example, judgements on the future risk of dying by cancer were increased equally by the negative mood induced by a story describing someone dying of cancer and by a story describing someone dying in a fire. Similarly, a story about someone dying of cancer increased subjective risk of losing one's job just as much as it increased subjective risk of dying of heart disease.

Kavanagh and Bower (1985) reported further data indicating a lack of relationship between the topic of a mood-inducing procedure and the extent to which subjective probabilities for events closely or distantly related to that topic were affected. For example, they found that unhappy mood induced by imaging a romantic failure decreased estimates of successfully coping with handling a snake just as much as it reduced estimates of enjoying eight of one's next ten dates! Both in this and Johnson and Tversky's (1983) study, effects on subjective probabilities appeared to be related solely to the moods induced by the stories and not to the topic of the stories.

Let us now consider these findings in relation to alternative accounts of mood-related biases in judgement.

Accessibility Explanations

Johnson and Tversky (1983) pointed out that the total lack of specificity of mood effects observed in their study poses considerable difficulties for accessibility based explanations for the effects of mood on evaluative judgements, such as those proposed by Bower (1981) and Isen and colleagues (Clark & Isen, 1982; Isen et al., 1978). Accessibility explanations suggest mood-congruent memory as the basis for mood-congruent judgement. These accounts propose that judgements are based on retrieving relevant information from memory. Individuals will rarely retrieve all the information that is potentially relevant to a decision before truncating the search process. Consequently, mood-congruent biases in the accessibility of memories will produce a biased database on which judgements will be based. These judgements, themselves, will therefore show a mood-congruent bias.

Tversky and Kahneman's (1973) availability heuristic proposes that the relative ease with which material can be accessed from memory also affects the weight attached to that information in the judgement process. So, the availability heuristic suggests that, in addition to the effects of the biased database, the readier availability of mood-congruous information will further enhance the mood congruence of judgements.

Johnson and Tversky (1983) argued that the global nature of the effects of mood on judgement that they observed was quite inconsistent with the notion that effects on judgement were mediated through effects on the accessibility of related memories. If they were, they argued, some specificity of effects in relation to the topic of the stories would have been expected. The stories, as well as increasing accessibility of mood-congruent memories generally, should have increased, to a greater extent, the accessibility of material more "locally" related to their specific content. The fact that this pattern of results was not observed poses considerable problems for accessibility accounts of mood-congruous judgement.

The Feelings-as-Information Hypothesis

The global effects of mood-inducing stories on judgements pose no problem for the "feelings-as-information" hypothesis (Schwarz & Clore, 1983; 1988). Indeed, it is wholly consistent with this view.

Schwarz and Clore (1983; 1988) suggested that individuals use their perceived affective reactions as relevant information when making evaluative judgements. They proposed that, particularly where the evaluative judgement may be complex and demanding, we may simplify judgemental tasks by assessing our feelings about the target. Rather than computing a judgement on the basis of recalled features of the target, we may ask ourselves "How do I feel about it?" and in doing so, we may mistake feelings due to a pre-existing state as a reaction to the target stimulus. Mood-congruent evaluative biases can arise in this way; more positive evaluations would be made when pre-existing mood is pleasant rather than unpleasant. From the feelings-as-information perspective, the source of the mood state may often be irrelevant (but see later): The important thing is the informational value of the mood state, however produced.

Mood states are characterised by their diffuse and unfocused quality (Isen, 1984; Morris, 1989, Chapter 1). Emotions, by contrast, are more specific reactions to particular events. So, we are afraid "of" something and happy or angry "about" something, but we tend to be "in" anxious, happy, or sad moods. Schwarz and Clore (1988) suggested that the undifferentiated and unfocused nature of mood states makes them informative for a wide variety of judgements. This is the explanation, on the feelings-as-information view, for the global nature of mood effects on judgement.

The feelings-as-information hypothesis suggests that the informational value of specific emotions is more restricted than that of global moods. Consequently, compared to moods, the more specific information of particular emotions is less likely to be used and misused across a wide range of judgements. Consistent with this view, Gallagher and Clore (1985, cited by Schwarz & Clore, 1988) found that feelings of fear affected judgements of risk, but not of blame, whereas feelings of anger affected judgements of blame, but not of risk.

Clearly, there are some similarities between the feelings-as-information hypothesis and the ICS view that bodily sensations may contribute to the synthesis of Implicational schematic models from which biased evaluative judgements are derived. Further, from the ICS perspective, processing of these models is assumed to be associated with characteristic subjective feeling states (p. 84). However, there are important differences between the ICS and feelings-as-information perspectives in their views on the role of feelings.

Feelings-as-information treats feeling as one of the objects considered by an appraisal process that uses "how do I feel about it?" as an heuristic for making complex evaluation decisions. By contrast, ICS regards subjective feelings as markers of the processing of related Implicational schematic models. On this view, feelings are not a source of information but an indicator that schematic models encoding particular types of information have been synthesised.

The feelings-as-information view, in common with other "cognitive" social psychological approaches to emotion (Berkowitz, 1993), implies an appraisal process in which current sources of information related to an evaluative judgement are weighed and integrated in an apparently "controlled" and "rational" process. By contrast, ICS suggests a much more "implicit" or "automatic" view. In this view, elements contribute to a judgement to an extent largely determined by previous experience of patterns of co-occurrences between representations, encoded in the "procedural knowledge" of recoding processes. Subjects may not be aware of these patterns of covariation, nor of their influence on current evaluative judgements (cf. Lewicki, Czyzewska, & Hoffman, 1987).

The ICS Account

The ICS account suggests that the effects of emotion on evaluative judgements depend on the characteristics of the schematic models synthesised for the judgement task. If the domain of schematic models is extensive, then the state of the model is likely to influence judgements in many areas, creating global effects across a broad range of judgemental tasks. Conversely, if the domain of models is more restricted, the model is likely to influence a narrower range of judgements, and more specific effects on judgemental tasks will be observed.

We can illustrate this contrast by considering ["self-bad"] and ["other-blame-worthiness"] models. Depressed mood often seems to be associated with synthesis of a class of very general ["self-bad"] schematic model. Such a global schematic model would be expected to affect a wide range of judgements. For example, ["self-bad"] implies negative evaluations of general worth, intellectual abilities, social skills, attractiveness, competence to deal with a range of difficulties, etc. Similarly, a ["future-bad"] general schematic model, of the kind also often associated with unhappy mood, not only implies that one is unlikely to succeed on particular tasks, but that losses and disappointments will be more likely, and the risk of future dangers, disasters, and diseases will be higher. Conversely, a narrower anger-related ["other-blameworthiness"] schematic model would affect judgements of culpability in others but would not necessarily affect judgement of one's own worth or capabilities, nor of the risk of future diseases. In an angry mood maintained by an ["other-blameworthiness"] schematic model, anger-related elements are potentially available for incorporation into the schematic models synthesised for judgement tasks. However, the extent to which they actually are incorporated, and bias the judgement made, will depend on the coherence between these elements and those related to the topic of the judgement. If, for example, the judgemental task requires estimates of the risk of flood or cancer, anger-related elements would not be integrated with these judgement-related elements to produce a coherent schematic model. Consequently, these two classes of element will be treated separately, and mood congruence would not occur.

It is important to note that there need be no relationship between the specificity of the event leading to the synthesis of a schematic model, and the extent to which the schematic model synthesised is broad or narrow; a failure in a specific domain may lead to the synthesis of a global ["self-bad"] schematic model. An extreme version of this phenomenon is seen in clinical depression as the "logical distortion" of "overgeneralisation" that we discuss in some detail in Chapter 12 (p. 156).

Why should moods be associated with schematic models with extended rather than restricted domains? The simplest answer seems to be that this is an inherent aspect of what we mean by moods; moods are characterised by their undifferentiated and unfocused nature, as we noted earlier. To be more specific, the key contrast dimension encoded in the schematic models maintaining happy versus unhappy moods appears to be one of general evaluation, perhaps related to the rate of discrepancy reduction between current and goal states (Carver & Scheier, 1990). Some form of general evaluation seems to be a pervasive feature of very many situations. Consequently, there is scope for the extraction of highly generic schematic models. These may be differentiated to some extent in relation to broad classes of topic, such as the self, the world, or the future, but the related models may still be highly generic. These models have global effects on judgements because they can be integrated with elements related to many topics to form coherent schematic models that will deliver biased judgements.

If more specific key contrasts (such as "dangerous-safe") are prominent among the dimensions encoded in schematic models, then the affect associated with those models will take the form of a specific emotion (e.g.

anxiety). As in the example of anger discussed earlier, biasing effects of these more specific emotion-related models will be restricted to judgements in relatively circumscribed domains.

The maintenance of "internally regenerated" moods (pp. 103–107) is dependent to a considerable extent on the global nature of the schematic models maintaining them. As they are global, such models can be regenerated by a wide range of inputs and this is an important feature acting to maintain model-related moods, as we discuss in detail in the next chapter (p. 169).

Dissociation of Mood Effects on Memory and Judgement

The experimental literature contains a number of examples of situations where effects of mood on memory and on judgement appear to be quite unrelated. For example, Bower et al. (1981, Experiment 3) found that retrieval mood affected judgements of the relative number of positive and negative elements in a story, but did not affect measures of the relative recall of positive and negative elements. Conversely, encoding mood affected the memory measure but not the judgement measure. Another example of dissociation is provided by Mathews and MacLeod (cited by Williams et al., 1988, p. 139). In a study of anxious and normal controls, they found no correlation between the judged probability of a number of positive and negative future events and the speed of recalling or imaging specific examples of those events. In a different context, Fiedler, Pampe, and Scherf (1986) studied the effects of elated and neutral mood states on subjects' memory and judgements of a previously described target person. Although the mood manipulation significantly influenced impression judgements in a mood-congruent direction, it did not selectively facilitate recall of mood-congruent material.

Such dissociations, between the effects of mood on judgement and the effects of mood on memory for the material on which judgements are assumed to be based, are embarrassing to accessibility interpretations that suggest mood-congruous memory as the basis for mood-congruous judgement.

Dissociations between effects of mood on memory and judgement cause no problem for the feelings-as-information hypothesis. This view suggests that mood effects on judgement depend on the evidential value of the mood state, rather than any effects of mood biasing retrieval of memories (Schwarz & Clore, 1988).

The ICS account suggests that mood-congruent judgements result from the synthesis of "biased" schematic models, rather than from mood-congruent access to stored information. Consequently, this account has no difficulty with the dissociations between mood effects on judgement and memory, noted earlier. ICS suggests that mood-congruent memory depends on affect-related schematic models generating descriptions to access stored mood-congruent Implicational representations. The biased schematic models that lead to mood-congruent judgements need not necessarily be associated with production of such descriptions. Consequently, they may affect measures of judgement, but not of memory. In practice, many mood-maintaining schematic models will produce both effects. However, in ICS, in contrast to accessibility accounts, judgement effects do not depend on memory effects and so some dissociation can be expected.

The Discounting Effects of Information on Mood Source

Some of the most persuasive evidence for the feelings-as-information hypothesis comes from studies showing that the effects of mood on evaluative judgements can be abolished by providing subjects with information on the source of their moods.

The feelings-as-information view suggests that the impact of affective states on evaluative judgements will be a function of their perceived informational value. Feelings attributed to a source irrelevant to the judgement at hand should be considered uninformative and should therefore be disregarded. The feelings-as-information view suggests that in this situation mood will not affect judgements. A series of studies have tested this prediction, usually in relation to subjects' judgements of how satisfied or happy they were with their "life as a whole".

Schwarz and Clore (1983, Experiment 2) investigated the effects of weather on mood and on judgements of life satisfaction. Subjects were telephoned on sunny and rainy days. When no mention was made of the weather, subjects interviewed on sunny days reported being in a better mood and rated higher general life satisfaction than subjects interviewed on rainy days. In another experimental condition, the subjects' attention was subtly directed to the source of their mood, the weather, by interviewers starting the conversation with the enquiry "By the way, how's the weather down there?". Although this enquiry had no effect on subjects' ratings of their mood, it eliminated the effects of mood on ratings of life satisfaction: These ratings no longer differed on sunny and rainy days. Schwarz and Clore (1983) suggested that subjects discounted their current affective state as a basis for judgement if they could attribute the state to a transient irrelevant source.

In a related study (Schwarz & Clore, 1983, Experiment 1) moods were induced by subjects vividly recalling and describing a positive or a negative life-event. When no external attribution for the resulting mood was made available, subjects who had described a negative life-event reported lower overall life satisfaction than subjects who had described positive events. However, when it was implied that subjects might experience unpleasant feelings as a result of being in an experimental room that had made others tense and depressed, no effects of induced moods on life satisfaction were observed. These findings suggest that subjects based their evaluations of their lives on the informational value of their feeling state, rather than on a review of life-events, even though the mood manipulation itself had rendered a negative event highly salient. Consistent with the feelings-as-information view, measures of subjects' current mood were more strongly correlated with measures of general life satisfaction when their attention was not directed to the experimental room as a possible source of their current feelings than when it was.

Schwarz and Clore (1988) argued that the findings from these studies were incompatible with accessibility accounts of mood-congruent judgement based on selective recall from memory: Inferences based on recalled information about one's life should not be affected by the relative salience of different explanations for one's current mood.

Schwarz and Clore's (1983) findings also pose great difficulties for a variation of the accessibility account that we have not yet considered. In addition to any effects resulting from biased access to stored representations of specific information, mood could affect judgements through its effects on the accessibility of relevant interpretative concepts. Information is encoded in terms of the most accessible applicable constructs (e.g. Higgins, Rholes, & Jones, 1977). If the accessibility of positive and negative interpretative constructs is a function of mood, then positive constructs should be relatively more available in good mood, with negative constructs relatively more available in bad mood. This would be a further factor leading to mood-congruent judgements. From this perspective, the effects of mood on judgements of general life satisfaction could be explained in terms of the greater accessibility of mood-congruent interpretative constructs related to "satisfactoriness-unsatisfactoriness". However, this alternative version of the accessibility account has just as much difficulty in accounting for Schwarz and Clore's (1983) findings as that based on selective recall of stored information: In neither case should effects on judgements be affected by the relative salience of different explanations for one's current mood.

An essential distinction between the view that judgemental biases reflect greater accessibility of mood-congruent interpretative constructs and the ICS view that they result from the construction of biased schematic models concerns the level of abstraction involved. Schematic models reflect the inter-relationships between interpretative constructs, rather than the state of the constructs considered in isolation. Effects at the schematic level, reflecting a wider pattern of information, may well be influenced by the attributions made for the source of mood effects. For this reason, Schwarz and Clore's (1983) findings are understandable from the ICS perspective, as we describe in the next section.

The ICS Explanation of Discounting Effects

The ICS explanation of discounting effects hinges on two aspects of the ICS approach that we have already mentioned. The first is that transformation processes can, effectively, "pattern complete". Presented with partial fragments of an Implicational schematic model previously associated with production of evaluative Propositional output, the IMPLIC→PROP process may deliver judgements comparable to those previously produced by the total model. The second feature is that such pattern completion will not occur if, with the fragments consistent with the pattern of an affect-related schematic model, there are other elements that have been associated discriminatively with the production of other classes of schematic models from those same elements.

We can illustrate the ICS account in relation to the effects of weather-related moods on judgements of general life satisfaction, and their elimination by "incidental" remarks that draw subjects' attention to the weather. The effects of weather are mediated by biologically prepared VIS→IMPLIC; IMPLIC→VISC/SOM transformations. In conditions of low illumination, on dull rainy days, VIS→IMPLIC will produce Implicational elements associated with a basic negative hedonic tone. Processed by IMPLIC→VISC/SOM, these elements will lead to outputs "shutting the body down" by reducing both autonomic arousal and the general disposition to bodily action. The corresponding effects on the body will be picked up by proprioceptive sensory organs to produce patterns of Body-state code corresponding to reduced autonomic arousal, etc. Now, these patterns of Body-state code will be similar to those that have previously been produced by the depressive emotional responses created by ["life as a disappointing, frustrating, depriving experience"] schematic models. It follows that weather-induced Body-state patterns can be processed by BS→IMPLIC to produce elements of Implicational code that, in combination with other compatible elements, and in the absence of incompatible elements, will be treated as fragments of this affect-related schematic model. By "pattern completion" the IMPLIC→PROP process may treat the partial pattern of Implicational elements as the whole schematic model and so deliver negative evaluations of the state of life in general.

However, this will not occur in the presence of elements that have been discriminatively associated with the production, from those same Body-state derived patterns of Implicational code, of other types of schematic model. Propositionally derived elements related to the weather being dull, cloudy, and rainy ("miserable weather") will be an example of these types of elements. There will have been many occasions on dull, rainy days on which, in thought or conversation, such weather-related Propositional representations will have been created. Implicational elements derived from these Propositional representations will regularly have co-occurred with the Body-state derived Implicational elements reflecting the biologically prepared "shut-down" response. Total patterns including both types of element will have been associated discriminatively with specifically weather-related schematic models rather than ["life as a disappointing, frustrating, depriving experience"] models.

In other words, Propositionally derived elements related to the presence of bad weather will be a discriminative marker of when depressive-like Body-state patterns are positively associated with unsatisfactory life situations and when they are not (in general, there will have been no reliable association between bad weather and personal failures, disappointments, and rejections). We know from, for example, the work of Lewicki and colleagues (e.g. Lewicki et al., 1987) that subjects are very sensitive to such markers that show a shift in the relationship between variables. The outcome of all this is that in situations such as Schwarz and Clore's (1983) experiment, introducing Propositionally derived elements related to the weather into the total pattern of Implicational elements will lead to incorporation of Body-state derived fragments into weather-related models. This will prevent "pattern-completion" treating these Body-state derived elements as fragments of the total ["life as a disappointing, frustrating, depriving experience"] model. Consequently, no effect of weather-induced mood on judgement of life satisfaction would be expected. In this way, ICS can provide an understanding of the discounting effects of information observed by Schwarz and Clore (1983) that does not depend on a conscious "rational" appraisal process.

ICS, Feelings-as-information, and Mood Effects on Complex Evaluative Judgements

ICS and the feelings-as-information hypothesis have been able to account equally well for the evidence on the effects of mood on evaluative judgements that we have considered up to now. The superiority of the ICS approach, and the contrast with approaches that view "feelings" as objects to be considered by an appraisal process, rather than as reflections of the state of Implicational schematic processing, becomes apparent when we consider the effects of mood on complex evaluative judgements.

Forgas et al. (1990, Experiment 2), for example, reported a study examining the effects of happy, sad, and control moods, induced by video films, on students' attributions for their successful or unsuccessful performance on end-of-session examinations. Subjects were asked: (a) to attribute their exam performance to four causal categories (effort, ability, luck, and the situation), and (b) to make similar attributions for the performance of an "average" typical student.

In the neutral mood control group, a typical self-serving pattern of attributions was observed: Subjects made more internal attributions for successes than for failures for themselves, but not for others (the "average" student). In positive mood, subjects displayed a similar tendency, attributing their successes internally and failures externally. In this mood, such "benevolent" attributions were also applied to others who also received more internal attributions for success than for failures.

By contrast, subjects in a negative mood made more internal attributions for their own failures than for their successes, in effect "blaming" themselves for failing. This pattern of blaming failure on internal causes only applied to themselves not to others; sad subjects continued to give internal causes for success, and external causes for failure in others. To summarise, happy mood produced a "generous" attributional disposition, with more internal attributions for successes both for the self and for others. In contrast, sad subjects were particularly critical of themselves, taking responsibility for failures but not successes, without being similarly critical of others.

Subjects in good and neutral moods also showed typical self-serving biases in their attributions to stable versus unstable causes. In the negative mood condition, exactly the opposite occurred. Sad subjects attributed their failures to stable causes more than their successes, and did so only for themselves and not for others.

The demonstration that induced sad mood, like clinical depression (Hamilton & Abramson, 1983) increases the extent to which subjects attribute their own failures to internal and stable causes is particularly interesting; this attributional pattern has been implicated as an important factor in the aetiology of depression (Abramson, Seligman, & Teasdale, 1978).

The complex pattern of results observed by Forgas et al. (1990), showing differences in the effects of mood depending on whether the judgements are related to the self or to others, poses problems for the feelings-as-information hypothesis. It is not difficult to accept that judgements about satisfaction with life as a whole, or about personal competence or attractiveness, could be made using the "how-do-I-feel about it?" heuristic: If I feel bad, then my life is probably not satisfactory, and I am not very competent or attractive. It becomes more difficult to see how this heuristic could produce distinctly different patterns of mood effects on complex judgements involving the self, compared to others, of the kind observed by Forgas et al. (1990). There simply does not seem sufficient informational value in undifferentiated happy versus unhappy feelings, regarded as objects of an appraisal process, to allow a subject to conclude, for example, that: 1) happy mood means that success is attributable to internal factors and failure to external factors both for the self and the "average" other student; whereas 2) neutral mood means that success is more attributable than failure to internal factors for the self but not for the "other"; and that 3) sad mood means that failure is more attributable than success to internal factors for the self, but, for the "other", the opposite is true.

The ICS view, by contrast, regards the happy and unhappy feelings induced not simply as crude sources of bipolar information (good versus bad), but as markers of the processing of mood-related schematic models. These models are very rich in "implicit" information. Indeed, the complex set of contrasts between different causal factors for successful versus unsuccessful outcomes, for self versus others, is exactly what would be expected to be encoded in affect-related schematic models. These are just the type of high-order regularities and contrasts, extracted over the experience of many superficially different situations, which are represented in schematic models. The observed pattern of results is wholly consistent with the view that the schematic models supporting, for example, the unhappy mood, embody as an important feature a contrast between the "blameworthiness" for failure of oneself and others.

It is the powerful and distinctive feature of the Implicational level of representation in the ICS framework that it can do justice to complex patterns of inter-relationship between high-order features of experience. This capacity seems particularly important in enabling ICS to handle the complexities of cognitive-affective interactions in judgemental tasks.

Conclusions

In considering the effects of mood on evaluative judgements we have moved closer towards the clinically relevant aspects of depressive thinking that are the practical point of reference of our enterprise. The content of the depressive thought stream with which the book opened was, in effect, an evaluative judgement of "(dis)satisfaction with life as a whole". From the studies we have reviewed, it is clear that parallel, albeit weaker, effects of depressed mood on personally relevant evaluative judgements are well-established phenomena in psychological experiments in normal subjects. Within ICS, these phenomena are understood in terms of the synthesis and use of biased Implicational schematic models.

The account of mood congruence in evaluative judgements developed within the ICS framework handles the existing body of evidence from experimental studies more satisfactorily than other accounts. It also allows us to develop testable predictions. For example, the explanation proposed for the effects of dull rainy weather on judgement of life satisfaction suggests that these are mediated through effects on bodily sensations. This clearly predicts that manipulations that counter reduced physiological arousal, depressive posture, and facial expressions will eliminate weather-induced decrements in judged life-satisfaction. Perhaps this is the origins of the sauna as an antidote to the effects of the long Finnish winter!

As our conclusion of Part III we would argue that ICS has coped satisfactorily with the challenge of explaining effects of mood on evaluative judgements, as it did with explaining mood and memory. We shall assume that ICS has passed the initial test of accounting for the findings reported in the experimental literature in these two areas. From now on, we shall concentrate on developing and evaluating the ICS account of negative thinking and its role in vulnerability to and maintenance of clinical depression. We shall also consider implications for psychological treatments of depression.

PART IV

ICS, Negative Thinking, and the
Maintenance of Depression

CHAPTER TWELVE

Negative Thinking and the Maintenance of Depression: The ICS Account

In this chapter we apply ICS to answer the following questions:

1. Why is the thinking of depressed patients so negative?
2. Why do depressed patients show "logical distortions" such as overgeneralisation of failure?
3. How is the persistence of negative depressive "ruminations" in the absence of any current negative environmental input to be explained?
4. What is the relationship between negative thinking and the maintenance of depression? Do streams of "negative automatic thoughts" play an important part in the maintenance of depression or are they merely epiphenomenal? The answer to this question is of central relevance to psychological treatments for depression: Unless negative thinking plays some role in the maintenance of depression there may be little point targeting our treatments specifically on this aspect of the clinical condition.

The Negative Content of Depressive Thinking

The ICS analyses of mood-congruous memory and judgement provide ways of understanding why thought content is negative in depression. The presence of the depressed state necessarily implies the continuing synthesis of depression-related schematic models in the Implicational subsystem. Our analysis of mood-congruous memory suggested that in "internally regenerated" depressed states (Chapter 10), including certain forms of clinical depression, depression-related schematic models lead to increased production of descriptions to access negative material. It follows that thinking in depressed patients, to the extent that it is influenced by access to stored representations, will be more negative than in subjects in neutral or happy moods. From the ICS perspective, access to memory records and processing are closely interlinked in many forms of cognitive activity. For that reason, biased access to memory records would be expected to have widespread effects in creating negative biases in information processing.

In the preceding chapter we saw how mood-congruent biases in evaluative judgements, in subjective probabilities for future events, and in attributions for success and failure, can arise from incorporation of mood-related elements into the schematic models synthesised to make judgements. The negative evaluations, expectations, and attributions that form such a striking component of the negative thinking of depressed patients are explained in an exactly parallel manner. However, the schematic models synthesised in clinical depression are different from those synthesised by normals in depressed mood. This difference represents a key feature of the ICS analysis of cognitive vulnerability, as we discuss later (Chapter 15). The models synthesised in clinical depression produce more extreme negative evaluations of self and more utterly hopeless pessimistic expectations of the future than the models synthesised in normal depressed moods. In this way, the negative content of the cognitive triad characteristic of the thinking of depressed patients can be explained.

"Logical Distortions" in Depressive Thinking

From clinical observation, Beck (1967; 1976) suggested a number of abnormalities in the form of depressive thinking: He termed these "logical distortions". For illustrative purposes, we shall focus on explaining only one of these "distortions", overgeneralisation. An example of over-generalisation would be drawing the conclusion that one is a total failure as a person following a single experience of failure; e.g. Carver and Ganellen (1983) found that, compared to nondepressed controls, depressed subjects were more likely to endorse items such as "when even one thing goes wrong I begin to feel bad and wonder if I can do well at anything at all".

The essence of the ICS explanation of overgeneralisation is that depressed and nondepressed subjects differ in the pattern of Implicational elements that form the wider context within which specific experiences are interpreted. These differences in pre-existing context themselves reflect differences in the schematic models recently processed by depressed and nondepressed subjects.

We are very familiar with the effects of context at lower levels of representation. For example, at the word level, presenting the letter E has very different consequences if it occurs following the context of the letters WIS rather than DUNC. Similarly, at the sentence level, the word "silence" has very different implications if it occurs in the context: "His joke was followed by total _____" than if it occurs in the context: "The sun was setting, a warm breeze stirred the palm leaves, otherwise there was utter _____". Figure 12.1 illustrates how, at the Implicational level, comparable effects of differences in context can produce "over-generalisation" from a specific failure experience in a depressed patient, but a quite different response in the same person when nondepressed.

The figure uses the convention of representing Implicational schematic models in terms of patterns of variables, each of which represents a high-order dimension into which experience can be "parsed". Each variable can take different values (arbitrarily assigned ○●, ○○, or ●● in the Figure), the pattern of values across variables defining the nature of the schematic model. Figure 12.1 illustrates the response of the same patient to a similar specific failure experience when depressed and when recovered. The difference in prevailing mood state between the depressed and recovered condition is reflected in differences in the values of variables prior to the experience of failure.

In the depressed person, the [○●●●●●●● etc. "(just) adequate self"] pattern already exists at the Implicational level. If this person now experiences a specific failure, the value of the relevant variable will change from ○● to ●●, the schematic model will become [●●●●●●●● etc. "self-as-total-failure"], and the person will have a "sense" of themselves as a total failure as a person.

Beck's clinical cognitive model explains such "overgeneralised" responses to specific experiences by suggesting that those vulnerable to depression have dysfunctional "beliefs" or "attitudes" such as "If I fail at my work, then I am a failure as a person". On this account, both the excessive affective response to failure and the "logical error" of overgeneralisation result from the "faulty premises" underlying depressive thinking. From the ICS perspective, postulating such beliefs can be seen as an attempt to describe effects that are actually mediated by quite different mechanisms, namely, changes in the contexts provided by patterns of Implicational elements.

What of the change to the "functional" response of the recovered depressed person compared to the "dysfunctional response" when

Schematic models and overgeneralisation

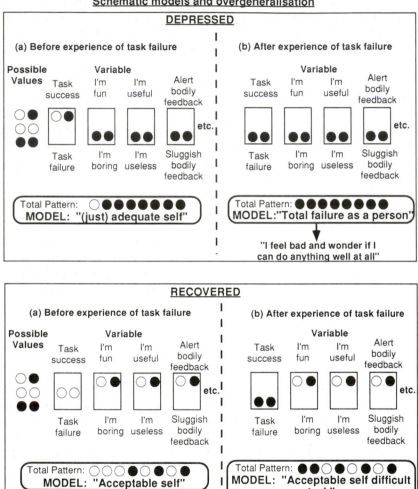

FIG. 12.1. "Overgeneralisation" from a specific failure experience: The different responses in the depressed and nondepressed states reflect differences in the preceding Implicational contexts.

depressed? The ICS account explains this in terms of changes in pre-existing Implicational context. The recovered depressed person's prevailing schematic model is [○○○●●○●○● etc. "Adequate/competent self"]. Given this pre-existing context, a change in value on the single variable related to a specific failure will not disturb the total pattern sufficiently to create a "self-as-total-failure" model. Consequently, in contrast to the situation when depressed, a "functional" response is observed.

Differences between the depressed and nondepressed states reflect differences in the schematic models maintaining these moods. Unlike the situation at the word or sentence level, we are not explicitly aware of the state of the Implicational elements that constitute the pre-existing context at this level of representation. The implicit and highly abstract nature of the contextual elements at the Implicational level may lead us to regard the depressed person's response to failure as some special form of "logical distortion". However, the ICS analysis suggests that this is simply another example of the effects of context.

The ICS analysis of "overgeneralisation" and other "logical distortions" allows us to understand the "dysfunctional" weight depressed patients attach to failure versus success, or to rejection/criticism versus acceptance/liking, in terms of prior learning history. A child's treatment by its family may have led generally to synthesis of ["inadequate/unacceptable self"] schematic models, but successful performance or self-sacrifice by the child may have led, discriminatively, to tolerance or even acceptance by key family figures. In these latter situations ["(just) adequate/acceptable self"] schematic models will have been synthesised, differing from ["inadequate/unacceptable self"] models primarily in the values on variables related to "conformity to self versus other's wishes", or to "success-failure", as in Fig. 12.1. In this situation, the inordinate weight attached to success or failure, or to self-sacrifice versus selfishness, is wholly understandable. In the context of depression-related values on other variables, values on these dimensions represent the only distinguishing feature between schematic models associated with a sense of being "inadequate/unacceptable" as opposed to being "(just) adequate/acceptable".

This analysis suggests that the person prone to depression will attach great importance to success- and criticism-related information to an abnormal extent, but only when other elements of the ["inadequate/unacceptable self"] model are already in place, for example, when the person is already mildly depressed. This explains why those vulnerable to depression can be distinguished from those less vulnerable by measures of dysfunctional attitudes taken in mildly depressed mood, but not by measures taken in normal mood (Chapter 3, and see Chapter 15, p. 219). The increased importance attached to information related to certain goals in depression has direct consequences as far as the motivation to continue processing information related to those goals is concerned. These motivational aspects of negative depressive thinking are considered in detail in Chapter 14.

Stimulus-independent Thought, Negative Thought Streams, and the Maintenance of Depression

Our brief consideration of the content and form of depressive thinking allows us to understand why depressed subjects interpret and respond emotionally to environmental events more negatively than those who are not depressed. We now turn to considering why depressed patients continue to experience streams of negative thoughts, even when there are no immediate environmental events that can be interpreted negatively. As these thoughts generally are quite unrelated to immediate stimulus-input, they can be described as stimulus-independent thoughts (Singer, 1988). We begin by considering the production of stimulus-independent thoughts, in general. We then describe how the ICS analysis explains the continuing domination of such thought streams by negative themes in depression. Finally, we integrate this analysis with an account of the role of negative thinking in the maintenance of depression. For ease of presentation, in this chapter we concentrate on the theoretical analysis of these topics. In the next chapter we describe related empirical research.

Stimulus-independent Thought

Stimulus-independent thoughts (Singer, 1988) are those streams of thoughts or images that we commonly experience when external task demands are low. They are described as stimulus-independent because their content is generally unrelated to current sensory stimulus input. Stimulus-independent thoughts are often experienced as pleasant or useful daydreams (Singer, 1966). However, they can also be troublesome, as in the case of worry or the thoughts that keep us awake at night, or, of course, the streams of negative automatic thoughts experienced in depression.

The core process driving thought production, and responsible for the meaning content of thought streams, is a continuing reciprocal interaction between the Propositional and Implicational subsystems, the familiar "central engine" of cognition (Fig. 6.2). In Chapter 6, we discussed the way in which the reciprocal interaction between the Propositional and Implicational subsystems, handling specific and generic levels of meaning respectively, subserved the comprehension of text. Propositional representations encode the specific meanings of text (e.g. "John knocked the glass off the table. Mary went to the kitchen to fetch a broom"). A more generic Implicational "mental model" of the situation (e.g. related to ["brokenness"]) can be derived from these specific representations. Schematic models, given certain inputs, can generate as outputs predictions, inferences, and recommendations that were not present in the input (e.g. the inference that "something is broken", "someone is to blame").

In text comprehension, Propositional representations of these outputs provide a richer understanding of the specific meanings of the text. These "internally derived" representations can also be integrated with new Propositional representations, derived from further reading of the text, to yield new Implicational schematic models. These, in turn, can generate further specific inferences and predictions. In this way, the process of reading and understanding continues.

Consider now what would happen if, having just read and derived Propositional representations from the sentences "John knocked the glass off the table. Mary went to the kitchen to fetch the broom", we close the book, close our eyes, and let our mind wander. The Implicational schematic model ["brokenness"] will be formed, and will output (via the IMPLIC→PROP process) Propositional representations related to "something is broken", "someone is to blame". With our eyes closed we now have no new input from the text. However, the recently "internally generated" Propositional representations "something is broken", "someone is to blame" may be sufficient to lead to the synthesis (via the PROP→IMPLIC process) of a new Implicational schematic model (e.g. ["guilt-retribution"]). From this model, further, new, specific Propositional meanings, inferences, and predictions can be derived as output (e.g. "there's going to be trouble"), and so the process could continue. In this way, the [PROP→IMPLIC; IMPLIC→PROP] cycle could be maintained on the basis of purely "internally generated" representations. This continuing cycle is the "central engine" for the production of streams of stimulus-independent thoughts.

As the data stream moves to and fro between the Propositional and Implicational subsystems in this cycle, it can also pick up contributions from the memory records of these subsystems. For example, the Propositional output "something is broken" only provides an abstract specification of what is broken. In this respect, this Propositional pattern can act as a "description" (see p. 108), "interrogating" the memory record of the Propositional subsystem to find more extended representations that meet the abstract outline it provides.

In the case of stimulus-independent thought, the memory records accessed could either be ones recently created (e.g. representations of the meanings of recently experienced stimulus-independent thoughts) or records related to the meanings of events or thoughts processed in the distant past. Specific meanings stored in the Propositional memory store and schematic models stored in the Implicational memory store can both be accessed by and incorporated into the data stream as it circulates around the [PROP→IMPLIC; IMPLIC→PROP] cycle. In this way, contributions from the whole of one's life experience are potentially available for inclusion in the stimulus-independent thoughts that comprise the stream of consciousness. Further, the outputs of schematic models will generally be quite different from their inputs, and the schematic models in operation may be constantly varying. Taken together, all this means that the contents of the stream-of-consciousness need not repeatedly run through stereotyped routines (although this can happen—see p. 168), and will often appear fresh and unfamiliar. In this respect, the ICS account differs from purely associationistic accounts of undirected thinking that have been criticised because they do not do justice to the complexity and variety of thought streams (Johnson-Laird, 1988).

Thoughts and Images

The "engine" of the interactive Propositional-Implicational cycle that we have just described can provide the meaning base for a stream of stimulus-independent thought. However, on its own, it would not deliver the subjective experience of streams of images or verbalisable thoughts. So long as the information flow remained confined to the [PROP→IMPLIC; IMPLIC→PROP] loop, our subjective experience would consists of a "sense" or holistic "feel" of knowing what was going on, or of "knowing that" something more specific was the case. To be experienced as a stream of images, or verbalisable thoughts, the information flow would also have to include, respectively, the Object and Morphonolexical subsystems. To understand why this is the case it is necessary to say something more about the ICS perspective on subjective experience.

Subjective Experience and Buffered versus Direct Processing

In Chapter 5 we indicated that, within ICS, activity of the COPY process of each subsystem is the basis for subjective experience. The distinct quality of different forms of subjective experience is related to the activity of the COPY processes in different subsystems, each information code having its own subjective correlates (Table 5.1, p. 52). We now have to consider the nature of subjective experience when whole processing configurations, involving several subsystems, are in operation. What determines the qualities of subjective experience that are most salient, or in the foreground, in these situations? Is our subjective experience some "average" of the qualities corresponding to all the different subsystems involved, or is it particularly affected by some subsystems more than others? If it is, what determines the "weights" attached to the contributions from different subsystems?

We can be either diffusely or focally aware of subjective experience within a particular modality. In diffuse awareness we may be no more than dimly conscious of processing related to that modality. In focal awareness we will be much more highly conscious of definite "focused" experiences, of high clarity, related to one particular form of information.

Whether we are diffusely or focally aware of a particular facet of experience depends on the extent to which related, extended patterns of information derived from that aspect of experience are COPIED throughout the subsystems that make up a processing configuration. This, in turn, is influenced to a great extent by the internal configuration of processing resources within the subsystem dealing with the information code corresponding to that facet of experience. Figure 12.2 illustrates two configurations in which the transformation processes within subsystems can operate; direct and buffered processing.

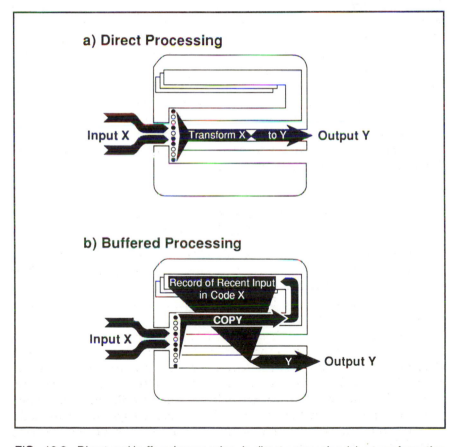

FIG. 12.2. Direct and buffered processing: In direct processing (a) a transformation process takes input on-line: in buffered processing (b) a transformation process takes input from the memory record of its subsystem.

In direct processing, transformation processes take their input "on-line" directly from the streams of information arriving from other subsystems (Fig. 12.2a). In buffered processing, a transformation process within a subsystem takes as input extended patterns of information from the recent sections of the subsystem's memory records (Fig. 12.2b). These patterns of information correspond to those that have just arrived in the subsystem over the data network and have been "copied" into the subsystem's memory store by the COPY process (p. 56).

Within ICS, focal awareness of a particular form of information is associated with buffered processing in the corresponding subsystem. By taking its information from the recent contents of the memory record, a transformation process uses an extended representation rather than moment-to-moment dynamic transitions in the incoming data. This wider representation will usually be associated with more extensive subsequent processing of related information through other subsystems. The repeated COPYING of related patterns of information across subsystems provides the basis for the quality of "focal" awareness associated with buffered processing. Where information processing is highly integrated in this way, many COPY processes are handling variants of the same basic information that can be "overlaid" and "resonate" to produce a vivid, multidimensional, entity in "phenomenal space". ICS maintains that, within any given processing configuration, there will be only one process operating in buffered mode. It will be that process that determines the "foreground" quality of subjective experience, the specific nature of the phenomenal experience depending on the information code being processed in buffered mode.

From the ICS perspective, differences in subjective experience are markers of different underlying configurations of information processing. On this view, subjective experience, which is accessible to us and reflects the products of information processing, allows us to monitor, modify, and make inferences about the information processing operations to which we have no direct access. Armed with this further elaboration of the ICS analysis of subjective experience, let us now return to the topic of thoughts and images.

Streams of Thoughts and Streams of Images

Figure 12.3 illustrates the way that the central engine of reciprocally linked Propositional and Implicational processing can be extended by further processing "loops" that incorporate, respectively, the Morphonolexical subsystem (Fig. 12.3a) and the Object subsystem (Fig. 12.3b). In each case, the additional subsystem incorporated into the configuration is in buffered mode. The first of these configurations supports the production of streams of verbalisable thoughts, the second the production of streams of images. In each case, subjective experience is determined largely by the subsystem in the total configuration that is in buffered mode.

The data stream's trip out to the Morphonolexical subsystem (Fig. 12.3a) gives the "mind's ear" potential access to the verbalisable content of information circulating round the [PROP→IMPLIC; IMPLIC→PROP] loop that would not otherwise be available. Similarly, involvement of the Object subsystem (Fig. 12.3b) in the wider configuration gives the "mind's eye" potential access to imageable aspects of that information content.

The additional involvement of the Morphonolexical and Object subsystems in these configurations can also substantially alter the form and content of the circulating information. First, their inclusion allows the configuration to draw on the more specialised "information processing skills" that these subsystems have acquired, over the course of development, as a result of handling information more directly derived from external sources. For example, the OBJ→PROP transformation process will be highly "skilled" at extracting specific meanings from complex patterns of spatial information. In certain tasks it will be easier for the "central engine" to draw on these skills than to perform the information processing required all by itself. For example, in a game of noughts and crosses (tic-tac-toe), the system can simulate the consequences of a potential move by transforming the relevant Propositional information into patterns of Object code, adding these to the image-level representations of the existing state of play in the "working memory" section of the Object subsystem's memory records, and, via the OBJ→PROP process (in buffered mode), directly "read off" the meaning of the resultant pattern. Similarly, involvement of the Morphonolexical subsystem in a total processing configuration allows use of "transformation skills" developed on speech-level input, e.g. those related to verbalised self-instructions.

A second way in which the involvement of extra subsystems may alter the form and content of the circulating information is by allowing access to additional memory records. The memory records of the Morphonolexical and Object subsystems are likely to contain representations of material for which corresponding representations simply do not exist in the records of the Propositional and Implicational subsystems, or exist in much less detail.

Finally, involvement of either the Morphonolexical or Object subsystems in buffered mode will have effects on the form and content of the information circulating by shifting the effective "centre of gravity" of processing configurations. Within a total configuration, any subsystem

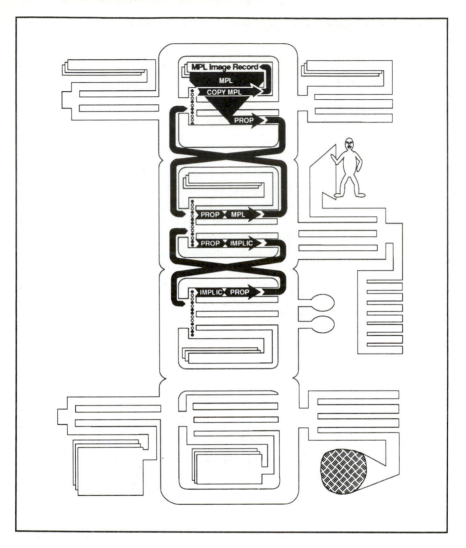

FIG. 12.3a. The extended loop supporting verbalised thoughts. Here MPL to Propositional recoding is buffered corresponding to heightened awareness of verbalised thoughts.

operating in buffered mode will have an enhanced influence over the total pattern of processing, as a result of the "higher quality" information with which it is dealing. It follows that the subsystem within a configuration that is in buffered mode can exert a "rate-limiting effect" on the processing and form of information dealt with by the system as a whole. For example, in the configuration subserving the production of streams of verbalisable

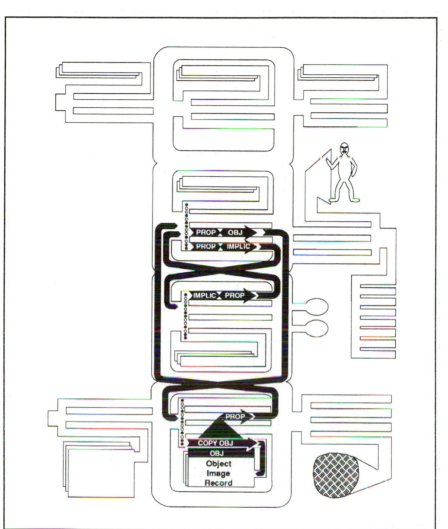

FIG. 12.3b The extended loop supporting visual imagery. Buffered processing of the Object to Propositional transformation corresponds to heightened awareness of visual object-based imagery.

thoughts (Fig. 12.3a), buffered processing in the Morphonolexical subsystem will have the effect of slowing the rate of information processing of the configuration as a whole to that which is consistent with dealing with speech-level information. Similarly, the domination by speech-level forms implies data streams narrowly focused on a single topic at a time, rather than the simultaneous focus on a wide range of topics available in image-level information, and captured in the dictum: "A picture is worth a thousand words".

These considerations suggest that the configurations illustrated in, respectively, Figs. 12.3a and 12.3b may be switched in and out according to the particular processing needs of different situations. Consistent with this view, Borkovec and Inz (1990) found that in patients with generalised anxiety disorders, for whom thought content is often dominated by themes of threat, streams of stimulus-independent thought were more likely to be in verbal rather than image mode. For normal controls the converse was true. However, when the normal control subjects were instructed to worry, the form of their thought streams changed so that it became more like that of the patients; verbal form increasing, image form decreasing.

ICS and the Production of Streams of Negative Thoughts

In applying our general account of the production of stimulus-independent thought to the streams of negative stimulus-independent thoughts in depressed patients, we have to explain why thought content is negative and why it remains so. The persistence of a narrow range of negative themes in depressive thinking stands in contrast to the continuing evolution and variety of thematic content of most normal daydreaming.

The "engine" driving the production of stimulus-independent thought is the [IMPLIC→PROP; PROP→IMPLIC] cycle. The negative content of depressive thinking reflects the domination of this cycle by a general class of depression-related Implicational schematic models. These models themselves have negative thematic content and they also produce negative Propositional output. This output takes the form of negative evaluations, pessimistic expectations, self-blaming attributions, descriptions to access failure-related information, etc. In other words, these schematic models produce outputs that, after further processing, produce inputs to the Implicational subsystem that regenerate the same, or a closely similar, schematic model. In this situation, the "engine" of stimulus-independent thought production becomes "locked" onto processing material on a narrow range of negative themes. When this material is also the subject of buffered processing in the Morphonolexical subsystem, these themes will be reflected in the experience of continuing streams of "negative automatic thoughts".

Such "thematic interlock" does not usually occur with most forms of stimulus-independent thought. Its emergence depends on schematic models with certain characteristics. On the sensory side, the emotional response resulting from synthesis of the model must lead to bodily effects that create patterns of Body-state code with particular features. These

Body-state code patterns, after processing by the BS→IMPLIC process, yield Implicational elements corresponding to fragments of the schematic model that originally produced the emotion (cf. p. 102). This situation will be the result of learning histories involving extended periods of depression that allow the co-occurrences between the Body-state patterns, elicited by depressive symptoms, and the continuing subsequent synthesis of depression-related schematic models to be encoded in the procedural knowledge of the BS→IMPLIC process. Such associations would be involved, for example, in extended periods of loss, separation, or rejection as a child, or, indeed, in previous episodes of depression itself.

On the semantic side, the likelihood of depressive interlock is crucially dependent on the Propositional inputs to Implicational schematic models and the Propositional outputs from those models. Schematic models that engender depressive interlock can be synthesised from Propositionally derived elements related to a wide range of patterns of specific meanings. As a result, the informational content of the circulating data stream can be returned constantly to the same recurring themes. These schematic models will be related to highly generic "global" domains, so that the models can be synthesised and re-synthesised from a very wide range of patterns of lower-level codes. Global ["negative-self"] models meet these requirements, as do other highly generic schematic models that are not focused primarily on the self.

Depressive interlock requires that the negative schematic models involved produce thematically congruent Propositional output. This can take the form of descriptions to access mood-congruous representations in memory, or mood-congruous evaluations, expectations, attributions, etc. Without this characteristic feature on the output (IMPLIC→PROP) side, schematic models encoding themes of loss, disappointment, and the like will be unlikely to create self-regenerating depressive interlock. As we discuss further in Chapters 13 and 14, the tendency to create thematically congruous semantic outputs from depressive schematic models seems to be an important feature of differences between individuals. Differences between people in this respect are related to their tendency to becomes depressed and for their depression to persist.

Figure 12.4, adapted from typical depressive responses to an item in Fennell and Campbell's (1984) Cognitions Questionnaire, illustrates the way a highly generic, negative-self, schematic model ["myself as a useless, worthless, culpable, and responsible total failure as a person"] can generate and be regenerated by congruous Propositional output.

A total configuration of processing resources will "settle" into depressive interlock as a result of the combined effect of a number of influences. Interlock is most likely when the sensory and semantic feedback loops both contribute to the regeneration of the same class of schematic models (cf. p.

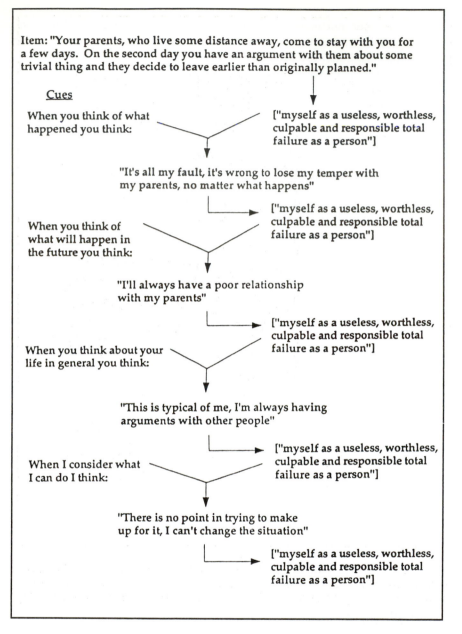

Item: "Your parents, who live some distance away, come to stay with you for a few days. On the second day you have an argument with them about some trivial thing and they decide to leave earlier than originally planned."

Cues

When you think of what happened you think: → ["myself as a useless, worthless, culpable and responsible total failure as a person"]

"It's all my fault, it's wrong to lose my temper with my parents, no matter what happens"

→ ["myself as a useless, worthless, culpable and responsible total failure as a person"]

When you think of what will happen in the future you think:

"I'll always have a poor relationship with my parents"

→ ["myself as a useless, worthless, culpable and responsible total failure as a person"]

When you think about your life in general you think:

"This is typical of me, I'm always having arguments with other people"

→ ["myself as a useless, worthless, culpable and responsible total failure as a person"]

When I consider what I can do I think:

"There is no point in trying to make up for it, I can't change the situation"

→ ["myself as a useless, worthless, culpable and responsible total failure as a person"]

FIG. 12.4. Re-generation of a highly generic schematic model ["myself as a useless, worthless, culpable, and responsible total failure as a person"], illustrated by depressive responses to Item E of the Cognitions Questionnaire, Fennell and Campbell, (1984).

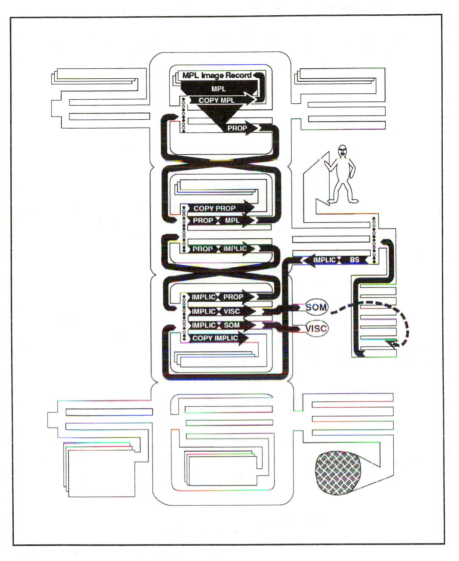

FIG. 12.5. Depressive interlock: The Body-state feedback loop and the linked Implicational-Propositional and Propositional-MPL loops reinforce each other to create a self-regenerating configuration circulating depression-maintaining information.

106). In this situation, the contributions from the sensory and semantic streams can be integrated and so mutually reinforce each other's effects. This is the situation illustrated in Fig. 12.5, which is likely to characterise most persistent depressions.

Negative Thought Production and
the Maintenance of Depression

Our account suggests that, in the absence of immediate negative environmental input, the maintenance of streams of negative automatic thoughts depends on the establishment of depressive interlock. The central feature of this processing configuration is the continuing regeneration of depression-related Implicational schematic models. From the ICS perspective this, of course, is the necessary condition for the continuing production of the depressed state. It follows that the depressive interlock configuration, illustrated in Fig. 12.5, also represents the ICS analysis of the maintenance of depression in the absence of external depressing stimuli.

Figure 12.5 also illustrates the ICS perspective on the relationship between negative thought production and the maintenance of depression. The ICS account suggests that it is most appropriate to think of the maintenance of depression as depending on the total self-regenerating processing configuration, illustrated in Fig. 12.5. It suggests that it may be less helpful to isolate specific components of the total configuration as *the* antecedent to depression. To the extent that any single part of the total configuration plays a pivotal role, it is, according to ICS, the synthesis of depression-related schematic models in the Implicational subsystem. In attaching primary importance to high-order meaning in this way, the ICS analysis contrasts with the suggestion from the Beckian clinical cognitive model that consciously accessible negative thoughts and images are the antecedents to depression. The contrast between the two positions is illustrated in Fig. 12.6.

From the ICS perspective, the content of consciously accessible thoughts and images may provide potentially useful, but necessarily partial, markers of the information circulating round the total processing configuration maintaining depression. However, unlike the Beckian clinical cognitive model, the ICS analysis suggests high-level meanings, rather than consciously accessible negative thoughts or low-level meanings, as the immediate antecedents to the emotional response. The contrast between these two positions has important implications for psychological treatment of depression; these are discussed in Chapter 16.

Both the Beckian and ICS analyses suggest that interfering with the processing configurations that maintain negative thought production should also break into the processes actively maintaining depression. Thus, both predict that procedures that reduce the frequency of negative depressive thoughts should alleviate depression. Testing this prediction is the first topic we consider in the next chapter, which discusses empirical evidence in relation to the theoretical accounts we have just outlined. First,

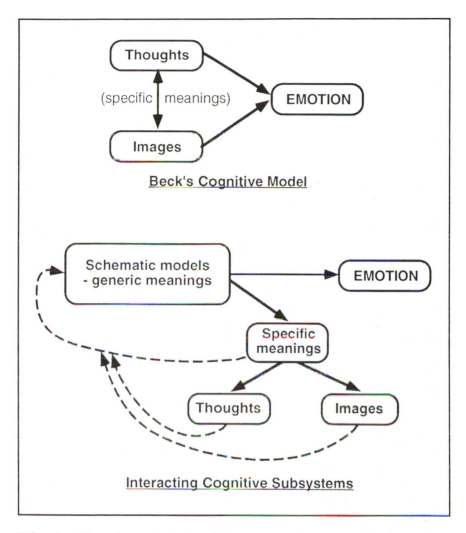

FIG. 12.6. The role of thoughts and images in emotion production: Contrasting positions from Beck's cognitive model (upper panel) and Interacting Cognitive Subsystems (lower panel)

however, we conclude our theoretical discussion by noting a further important aspect of the ICS analysis.

The depressive interlock configuration, once established, will show a degree of resistance to disruption. The information flow maintaining depressive interlock can be interrupted by tasks that require the same transformation processes and have, temporarily, a higher processing priority (e.g. experimental distraction tasks—see p. 178). However, once the competing, disruptive processing is completed, there is an inherent possibility that processing will revert to the previous depressive interlock configuration. This is because, as a result of the preceding interlock processing, the recent sections of the memory records of the subsystems involved will largely be "populated" with stored representations with depressive thematic content. In particular, the recent contents of the Implicational subsystem's memory store will be dominated by representations of depressogenic schematic models.

Access to memory records, particularly of recently encoded material, is an aspect of much processing in ICS. It follows that there is an inherent possibility that the memory access involved in the processing that follows a disruption may allow representations of global depressogenic models, from the recent sections of Implicational memory, to be re-introduced into the circulating data stream. These models could then lead to the re-establishment of depressive interlock.

The "tenacity" of the depressive interlock configuration will be greater the longer this configuration has already been in operation—the proportion of recent memory records "populated" by depressive material will be directly related to the proportion of time the system has recently spent in the depressive interlock configuration. It is for this reason that brief distractions, which may be highly effective in dispelling brief depressed moods in normal people, may produce only temporary alleviation in patients who have been depressed for some time.

Summary

The ICS analysis suggests that the negative content of depressive thinking reflects the output of the schematic models maintaining clinical depression. These operate to produce negatively biased descriptions for memory retrieval and negatively biased evaluative judgements, much as we described in Chapters 10 and 11.

The form of depressive thinking also reflects aspects of the schematic models specifically associated with the maintenance of depressed states of clinical severity. The suggestion that logical distortions are the result of contextual effects at the level of generic, implicit, Implicational information provides a simple parsimonious account of these effects. It also explains the observation that logical distortions are mood-state-dependent.

The persistence of streams of negative automatic thoughts in the absence of depressing external stimuli reflects self-regenerating cycles of activity in the "central engine" of cognition, extended by a loop that includes the Morphonolexical subsystem, and reinforced by the action of the Body-state loop. This configuration of "depressive interlock" also supports the maintenance of clinical depression in the absence of depressing environmental events. ICS suggests that the immediate antecedent to depression is the processing of depression-related schematic models, rather than the experience of consciously accessible negative automatic thoughts related to specific meanings, as suggested by Beck's clinical cognitive theory.

CHAPTER THIRTEEN

Negative Thought Production and the Maintenance of Depression: Empirical Evidence

In this chapter we review empirical evidence that is directly relevant to assessing the theoretical account described in the previous chapter. As the ICS account has been developed only recently, much of the evidence we review was not collected specifically with a view to evaluating these ideas.

We begin by considering the central question: Is there evidence that negative thought production is actually involved in the maintenance of depression, rather than being merely an epiphenomenal aspect of the disorder?

Experimental Investigation of Negative Thought Production and the Maintenance of Depression

The ICS analysis of depression maintenance suggests that reports by depressed patients of streams of negative stimulus-independent thoughts can be used as markers that the processing configuration illustrated in Fig. 12.5 (p. 171) has been established. On this view, interventions that interrupt the flow of negative stimulus-independent thoughts do so by disrupting this processing configuration. As a result, the "internal regeneration" of the depressed state would be interrupted, and alleviation of depression would be expected. This analysis predicts that interventions that reduce the frequency of negative stimulus-independent thoughts experienced by depressed patients should alleviate their depression.

Teasdale and his colleagues obtained evidence relevant to this prediction in a number of studies examining the immediate effects of brief distraction procedures on patients with major depression (Fennell & Teasdale, 1984; Fennell, Teasdale, Jones, & Damlé, 1987; Teasdale & Rezin, 1978). Fennell et al. (1987) reported findings typical of the earlier reports. This study compared the effects of a distraction procedure, in which patients described to themselves the contents of a series of slides projected onto a wall, with a control condition in which patients simply sat looking at a patch of light projected on the wall. Frequency of depressing thoughts was measured by a probe-and-report thought sampling technique, and state of depression by a self-report measure of depressed mood and measures of psychomotor speed.

We focus primarily on the results for patients with neurotic depression (defined by a score of three or less on the Newcastle Diagnosis Scale [Carney, Roth, & Garside, 1965]). In the control condition, thoughts with depressing content were reported on no less than 56% of occasions. Most of these depressing thoughts were "stimulus-independent", related to concerns quite outside the experimental situation. The distraction procedure was effective in reducing the frequency of depressing thoughts from 56% to less than 10%. This reduction in depressing thoughts was associated with significant reductions in state depression, measured both by self-reported mood and psychomotor performance. The extent of thought reduction and mood improvement were substantially and significantly correlated.

The results of this simple experiment suggest that negative thoughts, or the processes underlying their production, do seem to be actively involved in the maintenance of the depressed state, rather than being merely epiphenomenal. The ICS analysis, of course, suggests that it is the total configuration producing negative stimulus-independent thoughts, rather than the thoughts per se, that is the important factor maintaining depression.

In neurotic depression, negative thought production does seem to be linked to the processes actually producing the depressed state, rather than being only an epiphenomenal consequence of that depression. A different relationship between negative thoughts and the depressed state may exist in more endogenous forms of depression. Fennell et al. (1987) found that in these patients negative thoughts appeared more epiphenomenal and less directly involved in the maintenance of depression, replicating a pattern observed in earlier studies.

A further conclusion suggested by Fennell et al.'s (1987) results is that the state of neurotic depression has to be constantly recreated, from moment to moment, in order to be sustained. This conclusion, wholly consistent with the ICS analysis presented in the last chapter, follows from the observation that interruption of the negative thought production process leads to an immediate improvement in mood.

The interference with thought production by distraction observed by Fennell et al. (1987) suggests that the processes underlying performance on these two tasks share at least some cognitive resources in common. Assuming these resources are limited, diversion of resources to the distraction task would be expected to reduce those available for thought production and depression maintenance. Consequently, engagement in the distraction task would be expected to reduce both negative thinking and the state of depression.

The ICS analysis indicates quite clearly the cognitive resources assumed to underlie production of negative stimulus-independent thoughts and the maintenance of depression. Fennell et al.'s (1987) findings can provide only limited support to the ICS proposals concerning the more precise nature of the cognitive resources involved. This is because the distraction task used in their study, describing in detail pictures projected on a wall, is complex, involving many different types of cognitive resource. For this reason, we can draw few conclusions about the specific cognitive resources that the distraction task shares in common with negative thought production. We could draw more specific conclusions by observing the extent to which "purer" forms of distraction task, targeted on specific types of cognitive resource, interfere with thought production. For this purpose we will turn, in due course, to consideration of experimental investigations of the production of stimulus-independent thoughts in normal subjects. However, we will first consider a further line of evidence that is directly relevant to the ICS analysis of the maintenance of depression.

Responses to Depressed Mood— Distraction versus Rumination

The analysis presented in the preceding chapter suggests that maintenance of depression depends on establishing a processing configuration, characterised by persistent "ruminative" activity on depressive themes, that we described as "depressive interlock". Amongst the many influences that may determine whether the system "settles" into depressive interlock or "escapes" into processing other material, the [IMPLIC→PROP] process is at a particularly pivotal point. If, presented with an Implicational schematic model that produces a depressive emotional response, this process yields Propositional output that maintains the continuity of negative ruminative information flow, then depression will be maintained. On the other hand if, presented with depression-related Implicational input, the [IMPLIC→PROP] process outputs patterns of Propositional code related to instructions to process other types of information or to engage in externally directed behaviours, then "escape" from depressive interlock is likely.

Consistent with this analysis, Nolen-Hoeksema (1987; 1991) has suggested that the ways people respond to their depression will be related to the subsequent duration of the depression (Nolen-Hoeksema, 1991, p. 569): "People who engage in ruminative responses to depression, focusing on their symptoms and the possible causes and consequences of their symptoms, will show longer depressions than people who take action to distract themselves from their symptoms." Nolen-Hoeksema (1991) reviews a number of empirical studies supporting her proposal. As much of this evidence is directly relevant to our evaluation of the ICS account of depressive maintenance, we summarise it here.

Morrow and Nolen-Hoeksema (1990) studied the effects of four activities on induced depressed mood. In the ruminative-passive condition, subjects read neutral sentences designed to encourage self-focusing, emotion-focusing, or self-questioning (e.g. "I wonder why things turn out the way they do" and "I want to understand things"). In the distracting-passive condition subjects read sentences that simply stated facts such as "Canada's biggest industry is lumber". In the ruminative-active condition, subjects sorted cards printed with positive and negative adjectives according to how well each adjective described them. The markers for the piles covered the length of an 8-foot table. Consequently, subjects had to walk around to sort and were more physically active than subjects in the passive conditions. In the distracting-active condition, subjects sorted cards printed with the names of countries of the world in terms of their level of industrialisation, again walking around a table as they sorted.

Results showed that the greatest remediation of induced depressive affect was shown in the distracting-active condition, followed in order by the distracting-passive condition, the ruminative-active condition, and the ruminative-passive condition. These results are particularly interesting from the ICS perspective. They suggest that maintenance of depression was influenced not only by manipulations directed at influencing the semantic content of the information circulating around the [PROP→IMPLIC; IMPLIC→PROP] loop (i.e. the distracting versus ruminative conditions), but also by manipulations that would affect the Body-state representations circulating around the [IMPLIC→VISC/SOM; VISC/SOM→bodily responses; bodily response→BS; BS→IMPLIC] loop (i.e. the active versus passive conditions).

In a similar study Nolen-Hoeksema and Morrow (submitted) found that subjects with naturally occurring depressed mood who engaged in a ruminative-passive task were significantly more depressed following the task than subjects who engaged in a distracting-passive task. In nondepressed control subjects, neither the ruminative nor distracting tasks led to significant changes in mood, suggesting that ruminative focusing is not inherently depressing, but can act to prolong an existing depressed mood.

Nolen-Hoeksema, Morrow and Fredrickson (submitted) studied daily fluctuations in mood, and responses to these moods, in a group of subjects over 30 consecutive days. Subjects were consistent in the way they responded to depressed mood, either ruminating or distracting. Subjects with more ruminative styles of responding had significantly longer episodes of depressed mood. Importantly, a significant relationship between ruminative responses and duration of depressed mood remained after initial severity of depression was taken into account. This suggests that the effects of ruminative response style were not simply a reflection of more intense depressed moods in subjects showing that style.

Nolen-Hoeksema and Morrow (1991) found that measures of the way students responded to depression predicted the duration of their depression following a natural disaster, the 1989 Loma Prieta Earthquake. Students who, on measures taken before the earthquake, had a more ruminative style of responding to depressed mood, were significantly more likely to be depressed ten days and seven weeks following the earthquake than were students with a less ruminative style. Again, this relationship held when the effect of initial levels of depression were taken into account.

Nolen-Hoeksema, Parker, and Larson (submitted) studied the correlates of more severe levels of depression in a group of close relatives of the terminally ill. Regression analyses showed that more ruminative, less distracting styles of responding to mood were associated with more severe levels of depression. This relationship held after history of previous depressions, sex, age, and relationship to the terminally ill patient were taken into account. Further, people with a more ruminative, less distracting response style were significantly more likely to have a history of previous clinical depressions.

In summary, experimental and correlational studies conducted by Nolen-Hoeksema and her colleagues have consistently suggested that ruminative responses to depressed moods tend to maintain them, whereas distracting responses tend to alleviate them. This conclusion is wholly consistent with the ICS analysis. This suggests that the maintenance of depression in the absence of depressive external input depends on the establishment of a configuration of "depressive interlock" characterised by "ruminative" processing focused on depression-related material.

ICS suggests that the tendency to establish a configuration of "depressive interlock" is an important aspect of cognitive vulnerability to depression. Individuals will differ in the ways that processing configurations evolve dynamically when they experience depressing events. In vulnerable individuals processing will "settle" into self-maintaining "interlock" configurations so that initial depressive reactions persist and become more intense states of depression. Less vulnerable individuals will "escape" the progression into interlock, and their depressive reactions will remain mild or transient. The work of Nolen-Hoeksema and her colleagues supports the idea that individuals differ in their habitual response to states of mild depression, and that these differences are related to the future course of those depressions. Most importantly, there is evidence that the greatest single risk factor for depression, being female, is itself associated with an increased tendency to respond "ruminatively" to depressed states (Nolen-Hoeksema, 1991).

It seems clear that the way people respond to depression is an important factor influencing the future course of the depression. The ICS analysis provides an additional, complementary perspective on this issue that goes beyond that offered by Nolen-Hoeksema (1991) herself. Her view, quoted earlier (p. 180), seems to be very much along the lines: All of us get depressed; some of us respond ruminatively, some of us respond with distraction; if we respond ruminatively our depressions will be more intense and last longer. The response to depression, whether ruminative or distractive, is regarded essentially as a coping response that has been learned to deal with an unpleasant affective state that is much the same from one person to another. In ICS terms, this view would correspond to the [IMPLIC→PROP] process, presented with the same depression-related schematic model, producing rumination-enhancing Propositional output in one individual, but distraction-related Propositional output in another individual.

The ICS analysis raises an alternative possibility. This is that ruminative versus distractive responses reflect, not simply different outputs from [IMPLIC→PROP] to the input of the same depression-related schematic model, but differences in the kind of depression-related schematic models the [IMPLIC→PROP] process takes as input. In other words, differences in the response to depression may reflect differences in the "view" or "model" of depression implicit in depression-related schematic models. For example, my model of depression may be that it is a common, normative, unpleasant affective state that affects us all from time to time, but that, with appropriate coping action, this state need only be a temporary nuisance. If I hold this model of depression then I will be quite likely to engage in distractive coping responses. However, if my model of depression is that it is much more a reflection of "me", my inadequacies and weaknesses, then I may be less likely to engage in active-distractive coping and more likely to puzzle ruminatively over what is wrong with me and what, in the long term, I can do about it.

This alternative possibility is consistent with the general view of cognitive vulnerability to depression that we describe in the next chapter.

This alternative view also has clear implications for the treatment of depression. We discuss these in Chapter 16. For now, let us return to consideration of distraction in relation to stimulus-independent thought.

The work of Nolen-Hoeksema, like the study of Fennell at al. (1987) described earlier, points clearly to the effectiveness of distraction tasks in reducing depressive ruminations, and, thereby, alleviating depression. However, this type of work does not provide a very precise indication of the type of cognitive resources that distraction tasks must occupy in order to interfere with depressive stimulus-independent thought. Consequently, it provides us with only limited guidance as to the nature of the critical cognitive resources that are required for the maintenance of streams of stimulus-independent thoughts. As we indicated earlier, for this purpose we need to examine the effects of more precisely focused interfering tasks. To this end, we turn to consideration of studies of the production of stimulus-independent thought in normal subjects.

Experimental Investigations of the Production of Stimulus-independent Thoughts in Normal Subjects

According to the analysis of stimulus-independent thought production presented in Chapter 12, the central "engine" driving the production of thought streams is a continuing, reciprocally influencing, exchange of information between the Propositional and Implicational subsystems. As we noted earlier, in Chapter 6, the control and co-ordination functions normally attributed to a central executive in other cognitive architectures are also realised, within ICS, by this same configuration of processing resources. According to Principle One of the ICS approach (Barnard, 1985, p. 216), the transformation processes supporting this pattern of information flow can themselves only handle one coherent data stream at a time. It follows that mutual interference would be expected between the production of stimulus-independent thought and tasks in which performance makes continuing demands on the resources required for control and co-ordination. In other words, on this analysis, "distraction" tasks would be expected to interfere with the production of stimulus-independent thoughts to the extent that they make demands on such resources. Does existing experimental evidence fit this view?

Early Studies

Pioneering experimental investigations of stimulus-independent thought were conducted by Antrobus and Singer (reviewed in Singer, 1988). These studies were based on a model in which a common, limited-capacity central cognitive operator dealt with information from both external (sensory-perceptual) and internal (memory) sources (Antrobus, 1968). Stimulus-independent thought was seen as the product of operations on information from internal sources. It was assumed that the essential limitation on this system was the overall rate at which the common operator could process information (calculated in the classic sense of number of bits per second). It followed that tasks would suppress stimulus-independent thoughts to an extent directly related to the rate at which they presented external information. Consistent with this suggestion, Antrobus (1968) found a substantial negative linear relationship between the rate of information presentation in a tone detection task and the frequency with which stimulus-independent thoughts were reported.

Antrobus and Singer's approach to stimulus-independent thought was based on a view that limitations of human performance can be accounted for in terms of a limited supply of general-purpose processing capacity. More recently, such views have been severely criticised (e.g. Allport, 1980) and there has been a move towards models, such as ICS, in which processing capacity and memory is distributed throughout the cognitive system in the form of relatively autonomous, special-purpose subsystems.

From the ICS perspective, Antrobus' (1968) results would be accounted for by suggesting that, in the particular experimental situation studied, external information load and the demand for "central executive" control and co-ordination resources were highly correlated. From this perspective, the results observed by Antrobus are wholly consistent with the ICS proposal that tasks interfere with production of stimulus-independent thoughts to the extent that they make demands on "central executive" control resources (the inverted commas remind us that, from the ICS perspective, there is no separate "central executive" structure, as such).

Recent Studies

The distinction between the Antrobus and ICS perspectives becomes clearer, and different predictions from the two approaches emerge, when the effects of practice are considered. In the Antrobus limited-capacity information channel model, the limit on capacity is explicitly the rate of information processing, calculated in bits per second from the rates and uncertainties of stimulus presentation and response production. By contrast, ICS suggests that the limit on capacity is in terms of the resources available for the control and co-ordination of the sub-processes involved in task performance. From the Antrobus view, the processing of the same rate of external information in a task when it is novel and when, following extended practise, it has become automated and proceduralised, should be equally disruptive of thought production. By contrast, the demands on control and co-ordinating resources will be much greater for tasks when they are novel than when they are well-practised and when relatively automated routines have been developed. According to the ICS analysis, even though the rate of information processing (calculated in bits per second) may be the same when a task is novel and when it is practised, the effects of the task in suppressing stimulus-independent thoughts should be greater when the task is novel.

Teasdale, Dritschel, et al. (submitted) reported findings consistent with the predictions from ICS. As shown in Fig. 13.1, prior practice on a pursuit rotor or simple memory task reduced the extent to which such tasks interfered with concurrent production of stimulus-independent thoughts. More stimulus-independent thoughts were experienced during practised tasks, even though level of performance on the pursuit rotor was actually superior following practice on this task than following no practice.

Teasdale, Dritschel, et al. (submitted), in a study of random number generation, reported further evidence consistent with the ICS proposal that production of stimulus-independent thoughts and "central executive" function compete for the same limited processing resources. Random number generation has been proposed as a paradigmatic "central executive" task (Baddeley, 1986, Chapter 10). In this task, subjects have to overcome habitual tendencies to count in the normal forward sequence, or to count backwards, or in series of odd or even numbers, or other

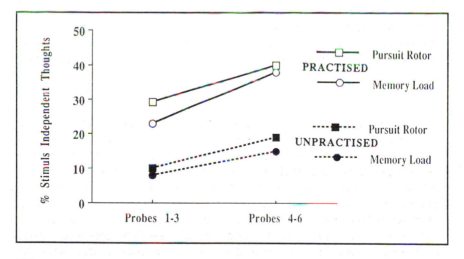

FIG. 13.1. Effects of prior practice on pursuit rotor and memory tasks on frequency of stimulus-independent thoughts experienced during task performance. Data from Teasdale, Dritschel, et al. (submitted).

stereotyped sequences, in order to produce strings of numbers that are truly random. The randomness of the numbers generated can be used as an indication of the extent to which "central executive" resources have been deployed to the generation task and away from tasks competing for the same resources. If random number generation and production of stimulus-independent thoughts both compete for limited "central executive" control resources, then mutual interference between these two tasks would be expected. Teasdale, Dritschel, et al. (submitted) obtained evidence supporting this prediction. Subjects generated random numbers continuously once every second. At intervals they were stopped and asked to report what was going "through their mind" at the time they were stopped. Thought reports were categorised by independent judges into those which showed evidence of stimulus-independent thought and those where thought content was exclusively related to task stimuli or absent. Consistent with the predictions from the ICS analysis, randomness was significantly less in the intervals that preceded occasions on which stimulus-independent thoughts were reported than in the intervals preceding occasions on which thought content was exclusively task-related or absent.

The two experiments we have described formed part of a longer series of experiments conducted by Teasdale and colleagues (Teasdale, 1989; Teasdale, Dritschel, et al., submitted; Teasdale, Proctor, & Baddeley, submitted; Teasdale, Proctor, Lloyd, & Baddeley, submitted) investigating the production of stimulus-independent thoughts in normal subjects. The overall conclusion emerging from the total sequence of investigations was that tasks interfered with thought production to the extent that they made continuous demands on "central executive" resources of control and co-ordination. This is, of course, exactly what the ICS account predicts.

Effective Distraction

These findings also provide guidelines for the development of effective "distraction" procedures that can be used as short-term coping strategies to reduce the frequency of unwanted stimulus-independent thoughts. Sheer "busyness" in a task would be expected to be ineffective in reducing thoughts if the task can be performed on "automatic pilot" without making demands on control resources. For example, a relatively simple articulatory suppression task, such as continuously repeating "the, the, the", would be expected to have only limited effectiveness, which would decline with practice. To make this a more effective distraction task, it would be necessary to incorporate a greater demand on control and co-ordination resources. Interestingly, this is exactly what Levey, Aldaz,

Watts, and Coyle (1991) found in a clinical study of methods for dealing with unwanted thoughts; in this particular case, the intrusive thoughts that keep insomniacs awake at night. Simple repetition of "the, the, the" had only limited effects. However, when subjects were asked to generate "the" at constantly varying random intervals, the effectiveness of the procedure improved considerably. Clearly, the latter variation of the task would make many more, and continuing, demands on central executive resources, much as in the task of generating random numbers.

To summarise, the evidence available from studies that have examined the effects of tasks interfering with stimulus-independent thought production, both in normal subjects and in depressed patients, is wholly consistent with the analysis presented in the previous chapter.

Cognitive Deficits in Depression

The interfering effects of distraction on depression represent a situation in which the competition for access to the transformation processes of the [PROP→IMPLIC; IMPLIC→PROP] "central engine" of cognition is won by information related to the distraction task. Where the competition is won by depression-related stimuli, deficits on concurrently performed cognitive tasks would be expected. Interestingly, and consistent with the ICS analysis we have presented, such depressive deficits appear greatest on tasks that depend to a considerable extent on "controlled process" resources (Ellis & Ashbrook, 1988; Hartlage et al., 1993; Watts, 1993). Deficits are much less evident on tasks that can be performed more "automatically".

An attractive strength of the ICS approach is its ability to offer, within the same explanatory framework, integrated accounts of "central executive" function, of the production of streams of stimulus-independent thoughts, of their negative content and form in depression, of the maintenance of depression, of the alleviation of depression by distraction, and of the nature of cognitive deficits in depression. As we indicated when we described ICS initially (p. 62), the necessary complexity of a comprehensive framework is more than compensated for by its ability to offer unifying accounts of diverse phenomena. The alternative is a number of isolated "custom-built" analyses of specific phenomena, which then have to be "cobbled" together if one wants a satisfying account of a wide problem area.

In the final section of this chapter, we consider a study specifically designed to test the account, offered by ICS to explain mood-related negative biases in the thinking of depressed patients, against the alternative account, offered by the associative network model.

Mood-dependent Depressive Thinking—
Effects of Increased Accessibility of Negative
Constructs or of Shifts in Schematic Models?

In Chapter 3, we outlined the associative network theory's explanation for mood-dependent negative thinking in depression. Essentially, this view suggested that negative thinking was the result of depressed mood selectively increasing the activation or accessibility of specific negative interpretative constructs, representations of specific meanings, and representations of events.

By contrast, the ICS account suggests that negative depressive thinking depends on the regeneration of depression-related schematic models that output biased lower-level meanings in the form of evaluations, attributions, predictions, retrieval descriptions, etc. These biased lower-level meanings, after translation into speech-level or visual-object-level codes, lead to streams of negative thoughts and images.

Much depressive thinking is mood-dependent; most measures of negative thinking return to normal levels as depressed mood remits. ICS and the associative network model offer contrasting accounts of the levels of representation at which these mood-related changes occur. The associative network model suggests that thinking becomes less negative as a result of changes in the accessibility or activation of representations at the level of specific constructs or clusters of constructs. The ICS analysis, on the other hand, suggests that thinking becomes less negative as a result of changes in wider configurations of processing patterns. It is not really meaningful to isolate particular aspects of such total processing configurations as *the* critical focus of change. To the extent that one can do so, ICS suggests that thinking becomes less negative as depressed mood remits as a result of shifts in the prevailing schematic mental models dominating information processing. The focus of such schematic models is the inter-relationship between constellations of constructs (and sensory elements), rather than simply the level of activation of individual constructs. On the ICS account, change in mood is accompanied by a shift in schematic models, the implicit knowledge of what leads to what.

Often changes at the schematic model level will be reflected in congruous changes at the level of specific constructs. However, because schematic models and specific constructs are at different levels of abstraction, it is possible to arrange situations in which effects at these two levels operate in opposite directions. By exploiting such a situation, Teasdale, Taylor, Cooper, Hayhurst, and Paykel (in preparation) were able to pit predictions from Bower's associative network model and from ICS against each other.

Teasdale et al.'s (in preparation) investigation focused on changes in measures of dysfunctional attitudes as depressed patients recover. As we saw in Chapter 1, the mood-dependency of such dysfunctional attitudes is well established. As we noted earlier (p. 9), the return of depressed patients' scores to normal values on recovery has been an important source of embarrassment to the Beckian cognitive model. Dysfunctional attitudes are typically measured with Weissman and Beck's (1978) Dysfunctional Attitude Scale (DAS). The following is an illustrative item from the DAS: "If a person I love does not love me it means I am unlovable". The extent to which patients endorse agreement with such attitudes typically declines as their depression remits. How are such changes to be explained? Considering the illustrative item, the Bower network model suggests that endorsement of this attitude when depressed is primarily a reflection of a general increase in activation and accessibility of depressogenic constructs, such as "unlovable self", associatively linked to the depression emotion node. As mood recovers, activation from the depression node is reduced and so endorsement of the dysfunctional attitude is less likely. ICS, by contrast, suggests that the changes in endorsement of such attitudes as mood improves reflect shifts in schematic models, the implicit knowledge of what particular patterns of lower-level meanings (and sensory elements) signify.

By appropriate rewriting of selected DAS items, Teasdale et al. (in preparation) created an experimental situation in which predictions from the Bower and ICS accounts were pitted against each other. Attitude statements were rewritten so that dysfunctional depression-related schematic models would be expressed by statements requiring completion by positive constructs. Conversely, functional schematic models were expressed by statements requiring completion by negative constructs. For example, dysfunctional completions of the stem "Always to put others' interests before your own is a recipe for _____" would involve positive constructs such as "happiness", whereas more functional completions would involve negative constructs such as "disaster".

In this way, a situation was arranged in which the ICS approach, which concentrates on the inter-relationships between patterns of specific meanings encoded in schematic models, makes the counter-intuitive prediction that depressed patients, operating with dysfunctional schematic models, should make more positive completions than the nondepressed. With recovery, there should be a reduction in the number of positive completions. By contrast, the associative network approach, focusing on the activation of specific constructs, predicts that depressed patients will be less likely to make positive completions, but positive completions should increase with recovery.

Teasdale et al. (in preparation) tested these contrasting predictions in a study in which patients with major depression were tested initially while depressed and, again, three months later, when a majority were considerably less depressed. Patients were divided into those whose mood had improved over the three months and those whose mood had stayed the same or deteriorated. Consistent with the predictions from the ICS account: (1) at initial testing, the group of depressed patients as a whole gave significantly more positive completions than nondepressed controls; and (2) patients who were less depressed at retest showed a reduction in positive completions, whereas those who were unimproved showed an increase in positive completions. Table 13.1 shows a particularly striking illustration of the changes in the case of one patient whose mood improved considerably. It does, indeed, seem that as mood shifts so do our schematic models of self and world—in different moods we inhabit, mentally, different "alternative realities".

These results support the ICS proposal that affect-related biases in information processing are better understood in terms of effects at the generic schematic level rather than at the level of the activation of specific constructs. We can use this experiment as a further example to illustrate in more detail the ICS account of the effects of depression on the form and content of thinking. Figure 13.2 illustrates fragments of the total pattern of Implicational code assumed to be present in a depressed person immediately before and after presentation of the sentence blank "Always to put others' interests before your own is a recipe for _____".

The figure uses the same convention for representing Implicational schematic models as we used previously in Fig. 12.1 (p. 158). Figure 13.2 also illustrates the response of the same patient to the same sentence stem when recovered. The difference in prevailing mood state between the depressed and recovered condition is reflected in the change in the values of variables prior to item presentation. As in our earlier discussion of

TABLE 13.1

Changes in Sentence Completions produced by an individual Patient with recovery from Depressed to Normal mood-state. As depression reduces, completions change from Positive (Dysfunctional) to Negative (Functional).

Example—Patient number 33	Depressed	Recovered
Always to put others' interests before your own is a recipe for _____	success	disaster
If I could always be right then others would _____ me	like	hate
For everyone to look to me for guidance and advice would make me _____	important	frightened
Always seeking the approval of other people is the road to _____	happiness	disaster

Schematic models and mood dependent thinking

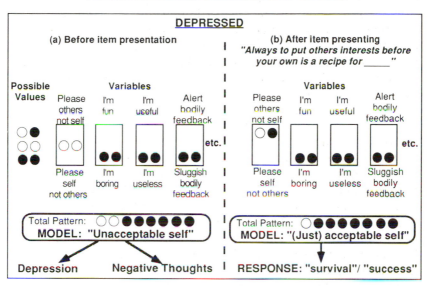

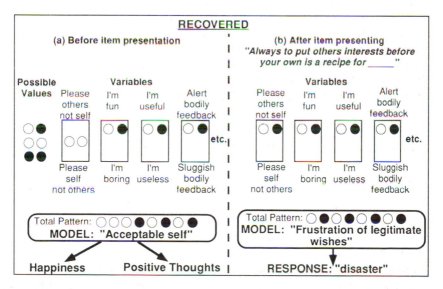

FIG. 13.2. Effects of mood-related Implicational context on the anticipated consequencs of events: The response to the sentence blank "Always to put others' interests before your own is a recipe for _____"in a patient when depressed and when recovered.

overgeneralisation (p. 156–159), the "dysfunctional" response of the depressed person is explicable in terms of the "implicit informational context" at the Implicational level associated with the schematic models maintaining the depressed state. With recovery, there will be changes in the pre-existing Implicational context related to changes in the schematic models maintaining mood. Given the recovered depressed person's prevailing schematic model ([○○○●○●○● etc.] "acceptable self"), a change in value on the single variable related to pleasing others versus pleasing self will not disturb the total pattern sufficiently to create an "unacceptable self" model. Consequently, in contrast to the situation when depressed, a "functional" response is observed.

The ICS analysis handles the change in response with recovery with ease. This contrasts with the formidable difficulties that the apparent mood-state dependency of "dysfunctional beliefs" causes for the view that those vulnerable to depression possess such attitudes as relatively enduring cognitive structures. This problem disappears as soon as one regards "dysfunctional attitudes" as approximate and inadequate descriptions of the operation of schematic models, rather than as the mechanisms underlying the production of negative thoughts.

Conclusions

Our evaluation of the ICS analysis must inevitably be limited by the fact that little work has, as yet, been conducted specifically to test out this approach to negative thought production and depression maintenance. Nonetheless, we conclude that ICS has provided a very helpful integrative account of existing empirical evidence closely related to the target clinical problem that is our continuing point of reference. Evidence from studies of the effects of distraction on negative thought production and the maintenance of depression, of the effects of ruminative versus distractive responses to depression, of the production of stimulus-independent thought, of depressive cognitive deficits, and of the changes in negative thinking with recovery from depression, are all quite consistent with the ICS analysis of negative thought production and the maintenance of depression. Perhaps the most important contribution from the ICS analysis at this stage is that, as in the immediately preceding section, ICS provides a perspective for approaching well-established clinical phenomena in a way that provides useful new insights and generates novel testable predictions.

In the next chapter, we add a motivational dimension to our analysis by considering self-regulatory and intention-based approaches to depression from the ICS perspective.

CHAPTER FOURTEEN

ICS and Self-regulatory, Motivational Models of Depression

It is time to address a number of inter-related issues concerning motivational aspects of patterns of processing activity. We have suggested that mood-congruous retrieval depends on the production of descriptions to access mood-congruous material, but we have not indicated why the system should have "learned" to do this in the first place. We have suggested that certain "normal" moods and states of clinical depression both depend on "interlocked" configurations in which reciprocal Propositional and Implicational processing regenerates mood-related schematic models. However, again, we have said little about the motivational basis of such activity. Finally, the question arises: If certain normal moods and clinical depression both depend on self-regenerating interlocked configurations, why are the former normally transient, whereas the latter are more persistent? We touched on this issue in the previous chapter but it deserves further consideration.

In addressing these issues, we introduce a motivational perspective into ICS analyses of cognitive-affective phenomena. First, we will discuss the importance of informational discrepancies as a guiding influence within the ICS framework. We will then describe two self-regulatory approaches to understanding depression; the self-awareness theory of Pyszcynski and Greenberg (1987) and Kuhl and Helle's (1986) degenerated-intention hypothesis. Discussion of these approaches will provide an opportunity to extend our present ICS analysis of mood-congruous cognition and depression by including a motivational perspective that incorporates and extends their insights, and will offer answers to the three issues raised in the opening paragraph.

Informational Discrepancy and
Motivated Processing

We have already indicated (p. 61) that ICS, in common with other cognitive science approaches, attaches a central operating priority to the reduction of informational discrepancies. Important sources of informational discrepancies include situations where representations of the current, past, or anticipated states of the world are discrepant from internally generated representations of how the world is expected to be, intended to be, desired to be, or should be. There are two broad strategies that the system can use to reduce such discrepancies. The first is to operate on the external world to create changes in the sensory input entering the system. These can then lead to changes in related representations of the external world within the system. The second strategy is for the system to engage in "internal" work to create new representations, or to modify existing representations, so that discrepancies between related internal representations are reduced, and representations related to a given topic throughout the system are "concordant". In both strategies, the system achieves its long-term goal of discrepancy reduction by assigning a priority to processing discrepancy-related information.

Informational discrepancies are of central relevance to affect in general, and to depression in particular. It is a commonplace that happiness results from concordance between the way things are and the way we want, or intend, them to be, whereas unhappiness results from discrepancies between the real and desired states of affairs. Higgins' (1987) self-discrepancy theory provides a recent, more formal statement of this general position.

Carver and Scheier (1990) have recently proposed an interesting variant on the generally accepted view of the relation between discrepancy and affect. They suggest that affect is related, not to the absolute magnitude of the discrepancy between current and desired states, but to the rate at which that discrepancy is being reduced, compared to a reference rate of discrepancy reduction. Positive affect occurs when the rate at which the discrepancy between current and goal states is being reduced exceeds a reference rate of discrepancy reduction. Conversely, negative affect occurs when the rate at which the discrepancy between current and goal states is being reduced falls short of the reference rate of discrepancy reduction. The important point for our present discussion is that Carver and Scheier's (1990) analysis suggests that both positive and negative affect mark a discrepancy from a reference rate for disparity reduction. On this view, at least some of the consequences that derive from assigning processing priority to discrepancy-related information, and its reduction, may be shown similarly for both negative affect and positive affect.

Our own analysis, presented in detail in the next chapter, suggests that among the dimensions encoded in depressogenic schematic models, those related to discrepancies between present state and some desired, expected state are particularly important. Such goal-related discrepancies are central features of the two self-regulatory, motivational approaches to depression that we now describe.

Self-awareness Models of Depression

At the empirical level, there are many similarities between depression and states of self-focused attention (Musson & Alloy, 1988). Such findings have led a number of workers to propose self-attentional models of depression. For example, Pyszczynski and Greenberg (1987) recently described a self-awareness theory of reactive depression, rooted in Carver and Scheier's (1981) cybernetic model of self-regulation.

Carver and Scheier (1981) conceptualised self-awareness, or self-focus, as part of a self-regulatory negative feedback cycle that keeps a person "on track" in pursuit of important goals. Self-focus is seen as the "test" segment of a test-operate-test-exit sequence in which a comparison is made between current state and a standard. If the person meets or exceeds the standard, then he or she exits the cycle and self-focus is terminated. On the other hand, if the person falls short of the standard then he or she enters the "operate" phase, in which attempts are made to bring current state into line with the standard. Subsequent "tests" will detect whether or not the "operate" phase has been successful in eliminating the discrepancy. If the discrepancy is eliminated, the person exits the cycle. Otherwise, test-operate-test phases continue.

If matching-to-standard is impeded or disrupted, then, according to Carver and Scheier, the likelihood of reducing the discrepancy between present state and standard is assessed. If the subjective probability of successful discrepancy reduction is high, the matching-to-standard process continues until the discrepancy is eliminated. However, when the subjective probability of discrepancy reduction is very low, the test-operate-test sequence is abandoned, further self-focus is terminated, and efforts at discrepancy reduction cease. It is suggested that disengagement from the self-regulatory cycle is adaptive in such situations because it avoids negative affect generated by awareness of the negative discrepancy and prevents fruitless persistence in pursuit of an unattainable goal.

On this view, the course of life involves many irreducible discrepancies. Normally, attempts to reduce such discrepancies are abandoned without great difficulty. In such situations, exit from the self-regulatory cycle is often facilitated by switching to the pursuit of substitute goals, or derogating the unattainable goal.

The essence of Pyszczynski and Greenberg's (1987) self-awareness theory is that depression occurs where the person is unable or unwilling to give up the desired or unattainable goal. This is particularly likely when the goal concerns a lost or unattainable object of central importance to the person. In this situation, the person does not exit the self-regulatory cycle, but, instead, becomes stuck in a cycle aimed at achieving a goal that he or she can neither attain nor relinquish. This cycle, it is suggested, will be associated with a virtually constant state of self-focus centred on awareness of the irreducible negative discrepancy.

Pyszczynski and Greenberg point out that, in contrast to theories that conceptualise depression as a phenomenon in which a person gives up on unattainable goals, their own theory suggests that depression occurs as the result of an inability to give up when it would be adaptive to do so.

Kuhl's Degenerated-intention Hypothesis of Depression

Kuhl's degenerated-intention hypothesis of depression springs from a wide and detailed analysis of intentional and motivational phenomena from a volitional perspective (Kuhl & Kazen-Saad, 1988). Within this framework, a distinction is made between two influences determining whether a behaviour will be performed: one is the history of reinforcement for that behaviour in the past; the other is a cognitive analysis of the anticipated future consequences of that behaviour. This latter is a central aspect of intentional behaviour.

Kuhl suggests that "intentions" correspond to semantic representations of action schemas, selected for execution as a result of an analysis of the long-term consequences of action alternatives. Kuhl proposes a specific mechanism, the volitional system, through the operation of which behaviour can be brought under the control of intentions. In this way, we are able to perform actions with a view to their anticipated long-term consequences, rather than their past history of reinforcement. So, for example, we can decide to give up smoking as a result of knowledge of its health consequences and (sometimes!) use this cognitively derived intention to over-ride the motivation to smoke based on a long history of positive reinforcement for smoking behaviour. The operation of intentions in this way depends, Kuhl suggests, on the activation of intentions in contexts where they are relevant, and their de-activation in irrelevant contexts.

Kuhl suggests that individuals differ in their ability to deactivate context-inadequate intentions, and has devised a questionnaire (The Action Control Measure Scale, Kuhl, 1981) for this aspect of individual difference. The questionnaire presents hypothetical situations with two response alternatives, one characteristic of the ability to deactivate context-inadequate intentions (Action-orientation), the other characteristic of the inability to deactivate such intentions (State-orientation). For example, to the item "When a new appliance falls on the floor by accident ..." the Action-oriented response is "I concentrate fully on what should be done" (reparative action being a context-adequate intention) whereas the State-oriented response is "I can't stop thinking about how this could happen" (trying to understand the origins of what has happened is an inadequate intention in the context of the need for immediate reparative action). Clearly, there are parallels between Action-versus State-orientation and Nolen-Hoeksema's (1991) proposal that individuals have characteristic response styles to depression; distractive versus ruminative. However, Action- versus State-orientation is assumed to be a much more general characteristic applying to a wide range of intentional phenomena, not only those related to depression.

The importance of Action- versus State-orientation originally appeared in studies conducted within the learned helplessness paradigm (Kuhl, 1981; Kuhl & Weiss, 1985, cited by Kuhl & Kazen-Saad, 1988). It was found that, following experience of uncontrollable failure, deficits on subsequent task performance could be attributed to an inability to de-activate concepts related to the intention to solve the original task. This inability, it was suggested, caused a perseveration of failure-related cognitions and emotions when the subject attempted to concentrate on the subsequent (solvable) task. Generalised performance deficits following helplessness pretreatment were observed only in State-oriented subjects. Thought-sampling procedures showed that these subjects were highly motivated to perform well on the second task, but were not able to keep failure-related thoughts from intruding into consciousness. The perseveration of failure-related thoughts in State-oriented subjects in these studies is clearly closely related to Pyszczynski and Greenberg's (1987) concept of negative self-focus involving continuing self-regulatory cycles aimed at reducing the discrepancy between current and goal states.

From the degenerated-intention perspective, depression is seen as an extreme form of State-orientation. It involves excessive perseveration of intentional states related to unfulfilled goals arising from events such as separation, object loss, or loss of control. As in the Pyszczynski and Greenberg (1987) self-awareness theory, it is assumed that, normally, unattainable goals are renounced after a certain number of futile attempts to attain them (Kuhl & Helle, 1986, p. 247): "The antecedent event is expected to lead to a depressive disorder only if the individual is unable to eliminate the intention." Processing related to such perseverating intentional states is assumed to preclude the performance of actions motivated by inherently positive reinforcing outcomes. In this way a negative affective state is maintained. Such processing is also assumed to take up working memory resources, and so to create cognitive performance deficits. Kuhl and Helle (1986) report evidence consistent with this latter suggestion.

As with the self-awareness theory, Kuhl's approach to depression points out the important motivational aspects of the processing configurations underlying the disorder. Kuhl's theory is particularly attractive because it specifies the nature of intentions in precise terms and places their operation in an overall motivational-volitional framework.

ICS, Self-regulation, and Intention-related Behaviour

The insights of Pyszczynski and Greenberg's (1987) self-awareness theory, and of Kuhl's intentional perspective (Kuhl & Helle, 1986; Kuhl & Kazen-Saad, 1988) can be mapped very directly into the ICS conceptual framework. In this section we focus on "normal" action control. In subsequent sections we extend this basic account to consider how "negative self-focus", "the perseveration of intentional states", and "interlock configurations" differ from such "normal function". We will then consider the difficulties of disengagement from such processing configurations in clinical depression. In discussing these topics we will suggest a motivational basis for production of mood-congruous retrieval descriptions. Finally, we will consider the "added value" that the ICS perspective contributes to existing accounts.

As we noted in our discussion of the ICS perspective on controlled processing (p. 80), there are two ways in which motivation, or goal orientation, can affect the direction in which information processing develops. The first of these is through the effects of previous experience (or innately prepared responses), as embodied in the procedural knowledge of transformation processes. Previous experience will, of course, reflect the input-output relations that have "paid off" in the past. These relations, encoded in the procedural knowledge of a transformation process, will determine, for example, selection between alternative data streams competing for access to the process, and the kind of output that will be produced from a given input. The "motivations" or "goals" that drive the direction of processing, and of action, in this way need not be "conscious" (cf. Brewin, 1989).

The second way in which goals can affect the evolution of processing sequences is by the creation of Propositional representations reflecting, on the one hand, intended or desired states of affairs and, on the other hand, the current state of affairs. Creation of Implicational code patterns that reflect the discrepancy between these representations can then effectively monitor progress towards goal attainment. The resulting Implicational patterns will then contribute to the synthesis of schematic models that will either facilitate further progress towards the goal, or, if appropriate, disengagement from the goal.

As in other aspects of "controlled processing" (p. 80), reciprocal interactions between the Propositional and Implicational subsystems play a central role in the evolution of such intention-related processing sequences. The self-regulatory cycle of self-awareness theory, and the perseveration of intention-related processing in Kuhl's approach, correspond to activity of the Propositional-Implicational cycles of the "central engine of cognition" as it controls intentional behaviour. The "semantic representations of action schemas selected for execution" that comprise intentions in Kuhl's framework correspond to related patterns of Propositional code, stored in the memory record of the Propositional subsystem. Intentional behaviour depends on an interaction between specific Propositional representations of the intended outcome, of the current state, and of the effects of recent effector actions, with the generic knowledge of problem-solving and goal attainment incorporated in Implicational schematic models. The resultant Propositional outputs indicate the next actions to be attempted, further information to be accessed from memory, and so on. The consequences of these actions are fed back into continuing cycles of test-operate-test, at the heart of which lies the "engine" of the [PROP→IMPLIC→PROP] cycle.

The Propositional representations that comprise an intention are themselves created by the Implicational subsystem (via IMPLIC→PROP) and reflect the schematic models being processed. Normal disengagement from unattainable goals after repeated unsuccessful attempts at goal attainment is seen in terms of the dynamic evolution of the schematic models synthesised. With continuing failure to achieve the intended goal, Propositional information accumulates indicating repeated non-attainment of goals on all earlier processing cycles. There will also be increasing Body-state information related to the fatigue resulting from repeated, unsuccessful attempts at goal attainment. The combined effect of the Implicational elements derived from these two sources eventually, over successive cycles, transforms the schematic models synthesised by the Implicational subsystem from ones that could be characterised as ["go for it"] models to patterns of Implicational code more characteristic of ["give up"] schematic models. As the schematic models change, their Propositional outputs change, effectively "removing the commitment marker" (Kuhl & Kazen-Saad, 1988) from intention-related representations in the Propositional memory record.

From the ICS perspective, Pyszczynski and Greenberg's (1987) "negative self-focus" and Kuhl's "State-orientation" correspond directly to "interlocked" processing configurations. What does a motivational analysis contribute to understanding the difference between these states and the more "normal" controlled processing involved in goal-oriented behaviour that we have just described?

Negative Self-focus, State-orientation, and Interlocked Processing Configurations

Kuhl's concept of Action- versus State-orientation (Kuhl & Kazen-Saad, 1988) implies relatively general differences between individuals in their ability to "deactivate" intentions irrelevant to the present context. Pyszczynski and Greenberg (1987) provide a somewhat different perspective by suggesting that "negative self-focus" persists because of the difficulty of disengaging from certain goals. We can incorporate this view into our ICS analysis to suggest that the perseveration of certain intentional states in "interlocked" configurations reflects, not so much a general deficiency in "screening out" all forms of context-irrelevant intentions but, rather, differences in the goals that the intentions concern. These differences in goals, in turn, reflect differences in the schematic models from which they were derived.

We can illustrate this analysis using the findings of a series of studies on the effects of failure on children, conducted by Dweck and her colleagues (reviewed by Dweck & Leggett, 1988). Some children show a "mastery-oriented" response to the experience of failure, characterised by enhancement of performance, test-focused cognitions, and positive affect. Other equally able children show a "helpless" response to failure, associated with deterioration of performance, negative self-cognitions, and negative affect. The state of these children after failure appears to correspond very closely to "State-orientation" and "negative self-focus".

Dweck and her colleagues showed that differences in response to failure were related to differences in the goals that children were pursuing. Helpless children, when they perceived their present ability as low, had the goal of avoiding negative judgements of their competence. When they perceived their present ability as high, the goal of these children was to gain positive judgements of their competence. By contrast, the goal orientation of children who responded positively to failure was to learn more and to increase their own competence. These differences in goal orientation, in turn, were related to differences in children's implicit theories, or schematic models, of the nature of intelligence. Helpless children held a view of intelligence as a fixed, limited entity. By contrast, mastery children held a view of intelligence as malleable and extensible by their own effort.

Consistent with their analysis, Dweck and her colleagues showed that they could create either helpless or mastery patterns of response to failure by manipulating children's goal orientation experimentally. When children were oriented towards skill acquisition they showed the mastery-oriented pattern, whereas when they were oriented towards evaluation of their performance they showed the helpless pattern.

Dweck's findings and analysis supports the view that, in ICS terms, individuals differ in the implicit views of themselves and their worlds encoded in Implicational schematic models. In performance related situations these differences in implicit generic models will be reflected in differences in the goals and intentions encoded in the Propositional representations derived from those models.

The Motivational Origins of Interlock Configurations

Attempts to achieve particular goals or intentions will be implemented using information-processing strategies and routines that have been extracted from previous situations in which the system has been working towards related goals. Production of representations that can act as retrieval descriptions will have been an important aspect of these strategies. These representations may be produced specifically as a means to access stored information relevant to goal attainment. Alternatively, fragments of representations may act "incidentally" as retrieval descriptions, e.g. self-derogatory representations, produced as part of a strategy for pre-empting adult criticism (e.g. Forrest & Hokanson, 1975), may act as descriptions to access negative self-related information. In both cases, the interacting cognitive subsystems of the developing child will "learn" strategies for goal attainment that involve access to stored representations and the creation of retrieval descriptions.

The nature of the information that will be accessed will vary from one goal to another. If the goal is to learn more about the task and so to extend one's capacity, then the important information to access is that related to the current task, the outcomes of immediately preceding actions, and possibilities of future action. By contrast, if one's goal is to avoid or minimise negative judgements of oneself, then the information accessed will be different and is likely to include negative self-related information. Production of mood-congruous retrieval descriptions by the Implicational models extracted from these situations can be seen as an aspect of the information-processing strategy that a child has used in those situations.

It follows from this analysis that differences in goals will create tendencies for some (State-oriented) individuals to ruminate over previous failures and for other (Action-oriented) individuals to process information related to current task performance. There are obvious parallels with our earlier discussion of Nolen-Hoeksema's (1991) contrast between ruminative and distractive responses to depression. The ICS analysis regards Dweck's helpless children, Kuhl's State-oriented individuals, and Nolen-Hoeksema's ruminative responders as all being liable to enter interlocked processing configurations as a result of the particular kinds of intentions generated by the schematic models dominating processing cycles.

We have some evidence indicating the type of developmental histories that lead to the goal-orientation characteristic of State-orientation and other forms of interlock. Nolen-Hoeksema, Wolfson, Mumme, and Guskin (1990, cited by Nolen-Hoeksema, 1991), in a study of mothers' styles of responding to their children when they were frustrated, found that the mothers of children who tended to become helpless and passive when upset were (a) intrusive and did not allow their children to solve many of their own problems, (b) did not teach their children to respond to negative affect by trying new approaches to a problem, and (c) were unsupportive and critical when their children failed. This kind of parental reaction is, of course, likely to lead to the development of intentions related more to protecting self-evaluation rather than to task solution, and, also, to the development of information-processing strategies involving access to negative self-related information.

This analysis of interlocked configurations can be extended to depression. The essential point is that such configurations arise from information-processing strategies extracted from previous situations involving attempts to attain certain types of goals. In common with the goal-orientation of Dweck's helpless children, the goals in the situations from which depression-related processing strategies are extracted will be primarily to reduce negative outcomes, rather than to attain positive outcomes. As we indicate in Chapter 15, depression arises in response to situations where negative outcomes are experienced that can be neither escaped nor avoided, and that are likely to persist. The response to such situations is likely to involve intentional behaviour attempting to minimise the effects of those negative outcomes. The information-processing strategies that are extracted into related Implicational schematic models from these situations are likely to include the production of Propositional outputs that can act, directly or indirectly, as descriptions that will access negative information. Such access will have been an inherent part of the goal-related information processing occurring in those situations. Further, the important information to access in such situations is inherently likely to be self-related.

The Implicational models extracted from recurring experiences of depressing situations "learn" to produce representations that can act as retrieval descriptions to access negative self-related information. These same models are responsible for the production of the depressed affect characteristic of these episodes of unsuccessful goal attainment. This provides an explanation for the origins of the production by depression-related schematic models of retrieval descriptions to access congruous self-related information. Such production, we have proposed, is the basis for mood-congruous retrieval in depressed mood, and of the maintenance of "normal" and clinical states of depression. This developmental account helps us understand why mood-congruous retrieval is, in general, more likely to be shown for self-related material than for other-related material (Chapter 9).

It is important to remember the demonstration, by Dweck and her colleagues, which showed that even mastery-oriented children manifested signs of ruminative, interlocked, processing when conditions were arranged so that they worked to the goal of avoiding negative evaluations of their performance. This suggests that, although some individuals may be characteristically more vulnerable to enter interlocked configurations than others, this possibility is open to most of us in certain circumstances. We have, of course, previously suggested (Chapter 10) that many positive demonstrations of mood-congruous retrieval depend on experimental subjects being able to enter mood-related interlock configurations "at will" in the course of deliberate mood induction procedures. In other words, it seems that the ability to establish interlock configurations, related to performance evaluation and other self-related themes, is an inherent part of the processing "repertoire" in most of us. What, then, distinguishes between interlock configurations that support relatively transient, easily disrupted states such as normal depressed mood, and the more persistent states of clinical depression?

Failure of Disengagement:
Transient versus Persistent Interlock

In normal, intention-related, controlled processing, persistent failure to achieve a goal will eventually lead to disengagement from attempts to attain the goal. The persistence of intention-related processing seen in state orientation, in certain normal depressed moods and in clinical depression, reflects the greater "cost" of abandoning the intention-directing goal-oriented behaviour. For example, where an intention to avoid negative performance-related evaluations was initially created by a schematic model related to personal worth, abandoning the intention implies that the system will accept the risk, or reality, of reduced evaluations of worth in the eyes of others or the self. The "costs" of accepting this outcome are likely to be greater than the "costs" of accepting the abandonment of intentions unrelated to worth. Consequently, in the face of Propositionally derived elements indicating repeated and continuing failure to realise the intended outcome, the Implicational subsystem will be more likely to create outputs that act to maintain, or re-instate, the intention rather than to abandon it.

In milder, "normal" states of depression, or state orientation, it is likely that the "costs" of a mild "dent" to evaluations of one's worth (or of other comparably important outcomes) are not so great that the system will persist indefinitely in the attempt to implement intentions related to attaining that outcome. Eventually, processing resources are likely to be taken over by competing demands with higher processing priorities.

By contrast, depressive interlock in clinical depression appears to be much more persistent. We can understand the greater persistence of the depressive interlock of clinical depression in terms of greater "costs" of accepting the consequences of nonattainment of the goal. Our earlier discussion of the type of schematic models that engender lock-up provides a way of understanding why disengagement from certain types of goal is so difficult for those prone to clinical depression. Consideration of dysfunctional attitudes (pp. 190–192), overgeneralisation (pp. 156–159), and cognitive vulnerability (pp. 219–221) suggests that the schematic models synthesised by vulnerable individuals are related to global, persistent, negative themes such as ["global negative self"] or ["future totally hopeless"]. Further, changes in the values on a limited number of Implicational variables in such models can alter the total pattern of values to create a shift from one schematic model to another with radically different implications. For example, shifts on the variables ["pleasing others rather than self" versus "pleasing self rather than others"] (p. 191) or ["succeeding at tasks" versus "failing at tasks"] (p. 158) can transform ["unacceptable self"] models into ["(just) acceptable self"] models. It follows that differences in the state of the values on such variables can have enormous implications for individuals.

In a situation where the rest of the Implicational context conforms to a pattern of values on variables that approximates a ["global negative self"] or ["future totally hopeless"] model, the incentive to achieve a value on any variable that will prevent the pattern "completing" into such models will be extremely high. From this perspective, clinically depressed patients fail to disengage from their attempts to win others' approval, or to succeed, or to regain lost relationships, because the implications of doing so for their total view of themselves and the future are so grave.

In Chapter 12 (p. 159) we speculated briefly on the type of family backgrounds that might lead to development of schematic models that would support depressive interlock in the way we have just discussed.

Gains from the ICS Perspective

The basic ICS account of the maintenance of depression can be expanded very usefully by incorporating the motivational, goal-oriented, self-regulatory perspective of the self-awareness theory of depression, and Kuhl's intentional approach. In return, the ICS perspective can offer benefits to these theories.

For example, Pyszczynski, Hamilton, Herring, and Greenberg (1989) observed negatively biased recall in mildly depressed students on an autobiographical memory task under conditions of self-focused attention. The bias was eliminated under conditions of external attention focus. In discussing their findings, Pyszczynski et al. (1989) contrast as *alternative* explanations: (1) the possibility that external focus decreased negative memory bias because it deactivated depressed subjects' self-schemata; and (2) the possibility that it did so through its effects in reducing negative affect. From the ICS perspective there is, of course, no real conflict between these views: Any procedure that, by creating an "external focus" of attention, disrupts an interlocked configuration maintaining depressed mood by regeneration of self-related depressive schematic models, will have a number of effects. Such a procedure will: (1) "deactivate" negative self-schemata; (2) reduce depressed mood; (3) reduce the production of negative retrieval descriptions, and so reduce negative memory bias; and (4) reduce the production of pessimistic future expectations, a finding which Pyszczynski, Holt, and Greenberg (1987) reported in an earlier study. In this way, the ICS view—of depressed mood states as self-regenerating processing configurations dominated by depression-related schematic models—allows us to view otherwise opposed perspectives simply as two sides of the same coin.

ICS allows us to broaden our view of motivated depression-related processing. As we noted earlier, from the ICS perspective "externally oriented" intention-related processing is only one of the possible routes to discrepancy reduction. The other is "internal" discrepancy reduction via directly mediated changes in stored representations or transformation processes. Adding this perspective to that offered by the more intention-related theories is important, because "ruminative" processing in emotional disorders (such as depression) often seems as much motivated by attempts to "make sense" or "understand" situations as by attempts to generate constructive action. As in the external, intention-related strategy, such internally oriented activity is likely to involve access to depression-related material via the production of mood-congruous retrieval descriptions. Similarly, there will be difficulty in disengagement from such "internal" activity as a result of the importance attached to the problem to be understood.

The ICS framework, in specifying two levels of semantic representation, allows us to get a wider perspective on intention-related behaviour by including in our view the schematic models from which intentions are derived. The Propositional representations that comprise an intention are themselves created by the Implicational subsystem (via IMPLIC→PROP) and reflect the schematic models being processed. As we noted earlier, changes in these schematic models following repeated unsuccessful attempts to achieve an intended goal state form the basis for disengagement from intentions.

Changes in schematic models as a result of "internal" discrepancy reducing processes can also produce effects on intention-related Propositional outputs. For example, behaviours related to intentions to change one's partner's behaviour to be more like oneself are a common cause of marital distress. These intentions, in turn, are derived from schematic models encoding a dependence of one's own well-being on others being similar to oneself. A shift to an alternative model, in which one's well-being depends on complimentarity rather than similarity of personal style, will lead to consequent changes in the type of intention-related Propositional output generated. This example illustrates how informational discrepancies can be reduced by internal changes related to "insight and understanding" as well as by intention-based action directed at the world. These possibilities are explored further in Part V, when we consider psychological treatments from the ICS perspective.

Conclusions

Consideration of Pyszczynski and Greenberg's (1987) self-awareness and Kuhl's (Kuhl & Helle, 1986) degenerated-intention theories of depression has allowed us to add a motivational and intentional perspective to the ICS account of depression. In order to understand fully the processing activity within depressive interlock, it is necessary to consider how goals and intentions originally led to the long-term development of this pattern of activity, and how they act to maintain it in current states of depression. Awareness that depressive interlock is oriented towards the attainment of goals, determined and maintained by the implicit theories represented in Implicational schematic models, is of particular importance if we wish to bring about change. Lack of awareness that, from its own "point of view", the system has good motivational reasons to maintain patterns of processing that, from the outside, appear self-destructive, may lead us to attempt to make changes that the system will itself counteract. Such issues are of obvious relevance to the psychological treatment of depression.

In the next two chapters we look more closely at the contrasting perspectives on depression and its treatment offered by the ICS analysis and the clinical cognitive model. Before doing so, it is appropriate to summarise the ICS perspective in a core model comprised of three conjectures.

Three Conjectures:
A Core Model of Cognitive-affective Interaction
Applied to Depression

We can express our core model of cognitive-affective interaction, and its dysfunction in depression, in terms of three inter-related conjectures. Illustrative supporting hypotheses are also listed.

Conjecture 1:
Affect-related schematic models, synthesised at the Implicational level, play a central role in cognitive-affective phenomena.

Working Hypothesis: Mood-congruous effects in studies of memory are directly related to circumstances in which cycles of processing activity result in the construction, storage, and use of affect-related Implicational schematic models. These models incorporate hedonic elements together with wider cognitions linked to a generic sense of *self-as-subject*, or to core evaluative constructs of personal significance.

Conjecture 2:
Potential discrepancies among stored representations have priority in the control of cycles of processing activity.

Working Hypothesis: Other things being equal, priority "value" will be related to the size and personal importance of the discrepancy.

Conjecture 3:
Processing cycles can become "interlocked". In these circumstances, depressogenic schematic models synthesised at the Implicational level can continually be regenerated by feedback from the Propositional and Body-state levels.

Working Hypotheses: Learning histories that lead to the abstraction of global, negative, self-related schematic models predispose individuals to dynamic, depressive interlock; Implicational input from direct sensory and/or proprioceptive routes, when integrated with other inputs at the Implicational level, can reinforce the interlock.

These three conjectures do a reasonable job of synthesising what we know about the empirical phenomena associated with cognition and affect. With appropriate additional assumptions it is also possible to derive working hypotheses from these conjectures. Testable predictions can then be generated from those hypotheses.

In Part V we look more closely at the clinical implications of the core model that has been developed.

PART V

ICS, Depression, and
Psychological Treatment

CHAPTER FIFTEEN

ICS and Beck's Cognitive Theory of Depression

The ICS account suggests that the maintenance of depression depends on the regeneration of depression-related schematic models. Continuing synthesis of such models will maintain a continuing depressive response. We now elaborate this basic account and compare it with the highly influential clinical cognitive theory of Beck and his colleagues (Beck et al., 1979).

A difficulty in making the comparison with Beck's theory is that his is a clinical, rather than scientific, theory. As a clinical theory, it has served very effectively its function of providing a framework to guide therapists in their treatment of patients. In meeting this need, it has not been necessary to specify the theory in the kind of detail that might be expected of a more scientific theory. Nor, as the theory has developed and evolved, has it been necessary formally to acknowledge deficiencies of earlier statements and to replace them with explicit reformulations. Instead, at different times and in different places, Beck and his colleagues have highlighted many of the clinical phenomena that seem central to an understanding of the relations between cognition and affect and have incorporated them into the corpus that might be called the clinical cognitive theory.

These features of clinical cognitive theory create difficulties for the task of comparing this theory with others, such as the ICS approach to depression that we have described. On the one hand, without some reasonably stable, formalised statement of the clinical theory it is not possible to draw the kind of contrasts with, and distinctions from, alternative approaches on which scientific advance depends: You make no sparks by striking earth on a flint, as the saying goes. On the other hand, it would not be fair to the clinical cognitive theory to fail to acknowledge that developments have occurred, somewhat organically, in response to the recognition of difficulties with earlier versions of this approach.

Our solution to this problem is to compare the ICS approach to understanding depression, and its treatment, with the "modal" version of the clinical cognitive theory that is described in Beck et al. (1979) and earlier publications. This version is still widely adopted, and, because Beck et al. (1979) is the definitive treatment manual employed in trials evaluating the clinical effectiveness of cognitive therapy for depression, it is directly relevant to our discussion of cognitive therapy in the next chapter. It is, nonetheless, important to acknowledge that further developments of clinical cognitive theory have occurred since its publication. Indeed, some of these more recent developments in the clinical cognitive approach are very much in line with the ICS analysis we present. ICS can provide a useful framework for the more formal statement of some of these ideas.

One further caveat is that we assume that the aetiology of clinically significant depression is heterogeneous. The ICS analysis is not equally applicable to all forms of depression. The analysis is specifically directed towards unipolar neurotic depression of the kind that Fennel et al. (1987) found responsive to the effects of distraction (p. 178).

We begin our further elaboration of the ICS approach to depression by considering in greater detail the dimensions encoded in depression-related schematic models.

Depression-related Schematic Models

Depression-related Implicational models encode the high-order recurring features, or dimensions, extracted from previous situations that have produced depression. We must now offer some working conclusions on the nature of these dimensions.

Elsewhere, Teasdale (1985; 1991) has suggested setting conditions for depression such as the following (1991, p. 43):

> ... depression is a response to the experience of highly aversive outcomes perceived as uncontrollable and likely to continue. In humans, the aversive outcomes will often not be events that are inherently noxious, such as electric shocks or other sources of physical pain. Rather, they will involve the non-arrival of expected or desired positive outcomes (that is, losses, disappointments, chronic frustration of goals). Experimental studies in

animals by workers such as Jeffrey Gray have shown such situations of frustrative non-reward to be functionally equivalent to the delivery of more obviously noxious aversive outcomes. The essence of these setting conditions is that I become depressed when I am experiencing now something extremely unpleasant that I cannot escape or avoid and that seems likely to continue, or when I am not getting something that I very much want (that may recently have been taken away from me) and see no way in which I can get it by my own actions or expect that it will happen otherwise.

These setting conditions emphasise the importance of three dimensions of experience as critical for depression: aversiveness, perceived controllability, and expected persistence.

Setting conditions such as these are suggested by studies of the effects of uncontrollable aversive outcomes, such as those conducted within the learned helplessness and related paradigms (Seligman, 1975; Abramson, Seligman, & Teasdale, 1978; Abramson, Metalsky, & Alloy, 1989). These setting conditions are also consistent with the findings of epidemiological studies examining the relationship between life-events and depression (e.g. Brown & Harris, 1978).

What are the origins of the dimensions encoded in depression-related schematic models? In many species, experience of repeated failure to terminate aversive or painful stimuli, or of repeated failure to obtain highly desired outcomes, elicits a biologically prepared "depression-like" response. This response is mediated, biologically, by neuroendocrine depletion (Anisman & Zacharko, 1982). There also appears to be a prepared "depression-like" response when infant primates are separated from their mothers and unable to become reunited (McKinney & Bunney, 1969).

From the ICS perspective, these biologically prepared reactions form the basic substrate underpinning the development of depression-related Implicational schematic models. From repeated experiences of situations eliciting the prepared responses the higher-order semantic dimensions will be extracted and will become incorporated into schematic models. Reflecting the nature of the situations in which the eliciting stimuli have occurred, these generic semantic dimensions will encode the conjunction of aversiveness, uncontrollability, and persistence. The schematic models will also include Implicational elements related to the recurring sensory features of depression-eliciting situations.

The generic semantic dimensions extracted will often be encoded into models that "package" the features of broad classes of experience. For example, the ["global negative self"] family of models will encode (1) aversiveness, related to childhood experiences of repeated failure to be loved or approved, or to criticism, rejection, or abuse, by close family members; (2) uncontrollability, related to the child's helplessness and inadequacy at preventing or alleviating such aversive experiences; and (3) persistence, related to the chronicity of the ill-treatment by other family members and the child's inability to escape or avoid. These dimensions are particularly likely to be extracted if the child accepts that the cause of their suffering is their own characterological inadequacy.

Our chacterisation of the dimensions encoded in depression-related schematic models is, necessarily, speculative. Establishing the nature of these dimensions more definitively will depend on further investigations. For the moment, we adopt the dimensions we have outlined as useful working hypotheses.

Having elaborated this aspect of the ICS analysis, we now examine ICS and the Beckian cognitive account in relation to a number of key issues.

The Role of Environmental Factors

Early versions of Beck's cognitive theory were criticised for their neglect of environmental factors. For example, Brown and Harris (1978, p. 267) criticised Beck's view that depressions are set off by incidents "triggering" latent cognitive structures ("like an explosive charge ready to be detonated by an appropriate set of conditions" in Beck's [1967, p. 277] phrase), the incidents themselves being quite minor. Brown and Harris' (1978) own epidemiological studies have shown that the environmental events provoking onsets of depression are associated with marked or moderate long-term threat, and have much more than a simple "triggering" effect. The same workers found that it was only a minority of women exposed to such events who became depressed. Vulnerability was associated with factors such as a marital relationship rated low on intimacy. Brown and Harris suggested that these factors increased vulnerability by reducing self-esteem and increasing the generalisation of hopelessness following a threatening loss event. Subsequent prospective studies (e.g. Brown, Andrews, Harris, Adler, & Bridge, 1986) have confirmed the importance of low self-esteem as a factor that increases the risk of becoming depressed in the face of a threatening loss event.

Both environmental events and the settings in which they occur are accorded importance in the ICS analysis. On this view, the core process producing depression is the synthesis of depression-related schematic models. The tendency to synthesise such models in response to environmental events will be a joint function of the nature of the input from the environment and the state of the internal "Implicational context" already existing as a result of recent processing.

Some experiences, by their nature, are inherently likely to lead to synthesis of schematic models related to aversiveness, uncontrollability, and persistence—for example, the loss of a loved one through death.

Equally, wider aspects of experience, such as the extent of available social support, will affect the Implicational models synthesised from specific experiences—even if I cannot control an aversive situation myself but I know I can rely on the support of someone who can, then I will not "interpret" the situation Implicationally as uncontrollable and likely to persist.

The "Implicational interpretation" of a situation is also, very importantly, a function of the state of the pre-existing Implicational context, that is, the pattern of values across Implicational elements that already exists before the situation or event is encountered. In Chapter 11, we saw how pre-existing mood-related Implicational elements can become incorporated into the schematic models synthesised for judgement tasks, and so bias the evaluations, attributions, and expectations generated. In the same way, Implicational models encoding dimensions of aversiveness, uncontrollability, and persistence are more likely to be synthesised in a person who is already in a depressed state than in one who is not. Most importantly, ICS suggests that other pre-existing Implicational contexts, not necessarily associated with marked depressed mood, can also operate in a similar way. For example, in vulnerable individuals, ongoing difficulties in family relationships may produce patterns of values on Implicational elements equivalent to models associated with a "sense of low personal worth". Although such models may not themselves produce marked depression, they may provide an Implicational context that, with the addition of loss-event-related elements, completes the pattern of a depression-related schematic model.

The role of reduced self-esteem increasing vulnerability to depression, observed by Brown and colleagues, would be wholly consistent with this analysis. The ICS approach also captures the "dynamic" character of self-esteem suggested by Brown's group (Brown, Bifulco, Veiel, & Andrews, 1990). Rather than seeing negative self-evaluation as a fixed trait, or as simply a direct reflection of mood state, these workers suggest that self-esteem reflects an ongoing integration of the state of key aspects of a person's life, particularly the state of close interpersonal relationships. The notion of "Implicational context" provides a way of incorporating this view into an integrated information-processing framework.

What Level of Representation Generates Affect?

Beck's theory suggests that negative thoughts and images produce depression because they reflect related negative meanings. Although clinical cognitive theory refers to a schematic level (usually expressed in the form of basic assumptions and attitudes), this theory, unlike ICS, does not appear to recognise qualitatively distinct levels of meaning. This becomes clear in the way Beckian theory handles the contrast between "intellectual" and "emotional" belief, or "knowing with the head" versus "knowing with the heart". For example, depressed patients may say "I know, intellectually, that I am not worthless, but I don't believe it emotionally". The clinical cognitive theory suggests that such distinctions merely reflect quantitative variations within a single type of meaning (Beck et al., 1979, p. 302): "Patients often confuse the terms 'thinking' and 'feeling' ... The therapist can tell the patient that a person cannot believe anything 'emotionally' ... when the patient says he believes or does not believe anything emotionally, he is talking about *degree of belief*" (original italics).

Such quotations suggest that Beck and his colleagues have in mind only a single level of meaning. Further, it seems that this single level of meaning corresponds to the lower, specific, Propositional level of meaning within the ICS analysis. Meaning at this level corresponds to thoughts and beliefs that assert specific propositions with a truth value that can be assessed. Consistent with a focus on lower-level meaning, the treatment approach derived from Beck's cognitive theory, cognitive therapy (Beck et al., 1979), includes procedures and strategies designed primarily to evaluate and challenge the truth value of specific propositions. For example, cognitive therapy involves the collection of evidence for and against beliefs, hypothesis testing, analogies with the investigative procedures of scientists, and the use of Socratic dialogue. These, like the use of syllogistic reasoning as a model of the derivation of negative cognitions from dysfunctional attitudes (p. 8), all suggest a concern with meaning at a specific rather than generic level.

ICS, by contrast, recognises two distinct levels of meaning and suggests that only the more generic of these is directly linked to emotion. On this analysis, the immediate antecedent to depressed emotion is the processing of the higher-level meanings encoded in depression-related Implicational schematic models. From this perspective, verbalisable negative automatic thoughts, negative visual images, and negative specific meanings are not the immediate antecedents to depression and have no direct effect on depression. The contrast between the two positions was illustrated in Fig. 12.6.

Depression-related Implicational schematic models that produce depression may also produce, "downline", thematically related specific meanings and negative verbalisable thoughts or images. This may give the impression that such thoughts and images are antecedents to depression. However, from the ICS perspective, any apparent direct causal relationship is illusory. ICS suggests that specific meanings (and related thoughts and images) have no direct effects on emotion production. Nonetheless, they may effect depression production indirectly through their contribution to the synthesis of depression-related schematic models.

In the ICS analysis, in contrast to the clinical cognitive view, a negative low-level meaning is only one of a large number of elements contributing to the total pattern making up an Implicational generic meaning. Consequently, the contribution of one specific meaning can be offset by other elements of the total pattern. These might include elements related to other specific meanings, filling out a wider semantic context, or elements related to sensory-derived elements, for example, elements related to a smiling facial expression.

Negative thoughts and images may be useful markers of the state of the "parent" schematic model from which they were derived. Consequently, in certain situations, interventions that change "marker" thoughts may also change depressogenic schematic models and so reduce depression. However, the higher-level meanings that produce emotion will not always be reflected in the content of consciously accessible thoughts and images: We can be upset without knowing, consciously, why.

ICS and the clinical cognitive model clearly differ in their view of the role of specific meanings, thoughts, and images as antecedents to depression. Consequently the two approaches make different prescriptions for therapy. We consider these in detail in Chapter 16.

ICS suggests depression-related schematic models as the immediate antecedents to depressive emotional responses. However, from the ICS perspective it is not really meaningful to isolate one aspect of the configuration maintaining depression as *the* critical component. It is more realistic to think in terms of a total processing configuration maintaining depressive "interlock". This view enables ICS to resolve an issue that has sometimes appeared problematic for the clinical cognitive model.

Negative Thinking— Antecedent to or Consequence of Depression?

Beck's cognitive model of depression initially attracted a great deal of attention and interest because it asserted boldly that depression was primarily a cognitive disorder, the other signs and symptoms being secondary consequences of distorted negative thinking. So, as we have already noted (p. 7), Beck et al. (1979, p. 11) maintained: "The cognitive model views the other signs and symptoms of the depressive syndrome as consequences of the activation of the negative cognitive patterns. For example, if the patient incorrectly *thinks* he is being rejected, he will react with the same negative affect (for example, sadness, anger) that occurs with *actual* rejection." Similarly (Kovacs & Beck, 1978, p. 525): "The cognitive view of behaviour assigns primary importance to the self-evident fact that people think. It assumes that the nature and characteristics of thinking and resultant conclusions determine what people feel and do and how they act and react."

As we noted in Chapter 1 (p. 8), evidence suggesting that negative thinking may be a consequence rather than antecedent of depression posed problems for this original form of the cognitive model. In the face of such evidence, more recent statements have placed less emphasis on the primacy of cognition, e.g. (Beck et al., 1983, p. 2): "Distorted cognitive phenomena are not necessarily the causes of affective, vegetative, motivational, and behavioural symptoms (e.g. biological factors can play a causal role), but they constitute a major component of the depressive state that can be a target for treatment and a means of reducing the other symptoms."

On the face of it, this appears to represent a move away from the original "cognitive primacy" view. The ICS analysis of depression maintenance allows us to retain the essential insights of both earlier and later versions of the clinical cognitive model. ICS suggests that the "internal" maintenance of depression depends on the total processing configuration that we have labelled "depressive interlock". To the extent that any one component of this total configuration can be isolated as "causal" it would be the synthesis of depression-related Implicational schematic models. These, it is proposed, are the immediate antecedents to the depressive response. However, the synthesis of such models will be powerfully affected by the biological state of the person, reflected in the Body-state-derived elements contributing to the patterns of Implicational code. It follows that the nature of such schematic models can equally well be seen as consequences of emotional state. For such reasons, the notion that depression-related schematic models are antecedents of the depressed state and the notion that they are also consequences of the depressed state are not mutually incompatible.

Beck's cognitive model, of course, suggested consciously accessible negative thoughts, rather than implicit schematic models, as the antecedents to depression. In this respect, the two approaches obviously differ. However, the ICS view that maintenance of depression depends on the continuity of a total processing configuration implies that such maintenance may be interrupted by changes to any of the components of the total configuration. Further, changes in one component are likely to be reflected in changes in other components. It follows that, in situations where depression is being maintained by the typical "depressive interlock" configuration, interventions that are successful in changing "negative automatic thoughts" may also successfully reduce depression. This could occur either because the interventions targeted on the thoughts were also actually effective in changing the "parent" schematic model, or because regeneration of depression-related schematic models depended critically on elements derived from further processing of "thought-level" MPL information.

Cognitive Vulnerability to Depression

The Beckian cognitive model suggests that individuals become clinically depressed because they possess relatively enduring dysfunctional attitudes. When such individuals encounter negative events that mesh with the content of their attitudes, negative thoughts are produced and depression follows. For example, it is proposed that when a person with the attitude "My worth depends on what others think of me" is criticised, the dysfunctional attitude leads to the conclusion "I am worthless" and, as a result, they feel depressed.

At least some statements of the clinical cognitive model regard the dysfunctional attitudes that underly cognitive vulnerability as stable characteristics of those prone to depression, e.g. (Kovacs & Beck, 1978, p. 530) "certain cognitive processes seem chronically atypical among depressed patients and may represent a stable characteristic of their personality". As we saw in Chapter 1, there have been repeated failures to find evidence of dysfunctional attitudes that persist once depressed individuals have recovered. Such failures have been an empirical embarrassment to the clinical cognitive theory's account of cognitive vulnerability.

In Chapter 3 we described evidence suggesting that, in contrast to the lack of difference found in normal mood, those vulnerable to depression could be differentiated from controls on measures of dysfunctional attitudes and globally negative self-view taken in mildly depressed mood. How does ICS explain both these findings and cognitive vulnerability to depression more generally?

ICS suggests that the tendency to establish a configuration of depressive interlock is an important aspect of cognitive vulnerability to depression. Individuals will differ in the way that processing configurations evolve dynamically when depressing events or biologically driven fluctuations in affective state are experienced. In vulnerable individuals processing is more likely to "settle" into self-maintaining interlock configurations. Consequently, initial depressive reactions will persist and become more intense states of depression. Less vulnerable individuals will "escape" the progression into interlock, and their depressive reactions will remain mild or transient.

In Chapter 12 (pp. 168–169) we suggested that differences in the schematic models producing depression were an important factor affecting the likelihood of settling into interlock. In particular, we suggested that highly global schematic models, such as those related to a globally negative self-view, were likely to facilitate interlock. In Chapter 13, we proposed that differences in the implicit view of depression encoded in the schematic models creating depression were responsible for differences in the tendency to respond to depressed affect with rumination, itself a factor associated with the persistence of the depressed state. Thus, the ICS account of cognitive vulnerability attaches central importance to differences between individuals in the nature of the schematic models synthesised in depressed mood, vulnerable individuals being more likely to synthesise globally negative models. How does this proposal explain the available evidence?

As a result of the differences in the schematic models that they synthesise, vulnerable and nonvulnerable subjects will differ in the Implicational contexts prevailing in mildly depressed moods. These differences in Implicational context, in turn, are responsible for the differences between vulnerable and nonvulnerable individuals that are observed on measures of dysfunctional attitudes and measures of global negative self-view administered in mildly depressed, but not in normal mood (Chapter 3). The way in which Implicational context produces elevated scores on measures of dysfunctional attitudes in depression, and the way these were reduced with recovery, was described in Chapter 13 (p. 192). Similarly, in Chapter 12 (p. 158), we saw how the effects of Implicational context can explain the "logical distortions", such as overgeneralisation of failure, shown by patients when depressed. Changes in prevailing Implicational context also account for the disappearance of such "distortions" with recovery. In each case, it is the Implicational contexts provided by the globally negative schematic models prevailing in vulnerable individuals in depressed mood that lead to dysfunctional responses. When the mood of these individuals returns to normal, the Implicational context prevailing is no longer sufficient to produce elevated scores on measures of dysfunctional attitudes, or of global negative self-view. Consequently, in normal mood, these vulnerable individuals are no longer different from controls on such measures.

The Differential Activation hypothesis (p. 31), derived from associative network theory, suggested that vulnerable and nonvulnerable individuals differ in the type of memories and interpretative constructs that become accessible in mildly depressed mood. On this view, the depressed mood produced by environmental events and mood induction procedures is much the same in the two groups. By contrast, the ICS view suggests that vulnerable and nonvulnerable individuals differ in the mildly depressed moods produced in these situations. This view suggests that moods are actually maintained by different types of schematic models in the two groups. The ICS analysis predicts that these differences in mood will be reflected in scores on appropriate mood descriptors. Although the depressed moods of the more vulnerable may be rated similarly to those of the less vulnerable on adjectives such as "gloomy", "despondent", or "fed up", the ICS analysis predicts differences if more discriminating adjectives such as "worthless" or "hopeless" are used to rate the quality of subjective mood, or "sense".

Studies examining the persistence of depression lend further support to the ICS contention that differences between individuals in the schematic models synthesised in depressed mood, and maintaining the depressed state, are a central aspect of cognitive vulnerability to intense or persistent depression. Dent and Teasdale (1988) administered measures of depression and the same measure of global negative self-view as that used by Teasdale and Dent (1987) (see p. 33, this volume) to a community sample of depressed women. The women were followed for five months, when measures of depression were then re-administered. Multiple regression analysis showed that the initial measure of global negative self-view predicted follow-up scores of depression, independently of initial levels of depression: For women who were equally depressed initially, those with more negative self-views were more likely to remain depressed than those with less negative self-views. This is wholly consistent with the ICS proposal that schematic models related to a globally negative self-view are particularly likely to engender self-perpetuating depressive interlock. Lewinsohn, Steinmetz, Larson, and Franklin (1981) have reported similar evidence of cognitive measures taken in the depressed state predicting subsequent persistence of depression.

The ICS suggestion, that cognitive vulnerability to depression depends on the likelihood of "settling" into depressive interlock, retains positive features of the Differential Activation hypothesis. The ICS account has the advantage that it does not depend on the associative network metaphor, which, as we saw in Chapter 4, has encountered considerable problems. ICS also offers a broader, novel perspective. In particular, in suggesting that the schematic models that engender interlock encode implicit views of depression and what to do about it (p. 182), the ICS approach to vulnerability has direct implications for treatment. We discuss these in the next chapter. First, we consider briefly more enduring cognitive characteristics associated with vulnerability to depression.

Neuroticism and Vulnerability

It has been difficult to demonstrate enduring, trait-like differences related to vulnerability using measures of dysfunctional attitudes and related constructs. There is, nonetheless, evidence for persistent psychological differences in vulnerable individuals. For example, high scores on the personality dimension of neuroticism (N) have repeatedly been shown to be associated with elevated risk for depression, and for depression, once established, to persist (e.g. see Martin, 1985). This is particularly interesting in relation to the current discussion in view of the relationship between neuroticism and retrieval of positive and negative autobiographical memories. A number of studies (reviewed by Martin,

1985) have examined the relationship between scores on questionnaire measures of neuroticism and retrieval of autobiographical memories, using paradigms very similar to those described in Chapter 2 to study the effects of mood on autobiographical recall. These studies have consistently found that high neuroticism, like depressed mood, increases the relative recall of negative memories. Most interestingly, the effects of neuroticism in these studies could not be accounted for by effects of depressed mood, suggesting two independent influences on the hedonic tone of the memories retrieved. The Neuroticism as Cognitive Predisposition to Depression hypothesis (Martin, 1985) suggests that the elevated risk of clinical depression in high-N individuals exposed to depressing events results from the conjunction of stable (neuroticism) and transient (mood) factors that both act to increase accessibility of negative self-related material. The combined effect of both factors is held to increase the chance that mood-perpetuating cognitive cycles will become established.

From the ICS perspective, the effects of neuroticism on both autobiographical recall and risk of depression would be interpreted in terms of long-term biases in the "Implicational context" of high-N individuals. As a result of current or recent processing, the Implicational subsystems of such individuals frequently contain sub-patterns of elements related to ["negative-self"] models. These elements will usually be insufficient, alone, to maintain a depressed state of any intensity. However, the contribution of such elements can be revealed in the presence of additional coherent Implicational elements associated with certain induced or naturally occurring moods. Equally, the presence of such elements can be revealed, in normal mood, through the biased retrieval descriptions they help create when autobiographical recall is required.

Conclusions

In Chapter 3 we saw how attempts to understand the phenomena of clinical depression from the perspective of the associative network theory of mood and memory overcame a number of the difficulties inherent in Beck's cognitive model. Subsequently, we documented the problems of the associative network theory with respect to the detailed findings of laboratory experiments, and argued that, overall, ICS gave a more satisfactory account. In the present chapter, we have described an extended ICS account of depression that retains the gains offered by the insights from associative network theory but, at the same time, extends the scope of our applied science analysis of clinical depression. In contrast to both Beck's clinical model and Bower's associative network theory, the ICS analysis suggests that the immediate antecedent to depression is the processing of generic depression-related meanings, rather than the specific meanings emphasised by the two earlier approaches. This radical difference in emphasis has important consequences for the way we understand and design psychological treatments. In the next, penultimate chapter of this book we describe cognitive therapy, the psychological treatment derived from Beck's clinical cognitive model of depression, and discuss ways in which the understanding and effectiveness of this treatment might be improved through application of the ICS perspective.

CHAPTER SIXTEEN

Psychological Treatment for Depression—The ICS Perspective

Our attempts to understand negative depressive thinking and its relation to the production and maintenance of depression have been substantially motivated by a practical goal. This is to improve the effectiveness and efficiency of methods for relieving and preventing disabling depression. There is already excellent evidence for the efficacy of a range of psychological treatments for depression (Williams, 1992). However, there is considerable scope for further improvements in the effectiveness and efficiency of psychological interventions. In particular, it is most unlikely that existing treatments, based on the traditional format of an extended series of face-to-face contacts between a depressed client and a highly trained professional, will ever make a substantial impact on overall levels of disabling depression. Given the high prevalence of this problem, there are simply not the resources, either professional or financial, to support the extent of psychotherapeutic contact that would be required. It follows that creation of further variations on the basic theme of one-to-one psychological treatments for depression is unlikely to be the most productive strategy for the future development of interventions. An alternative strategy is to identify the essential psychological processes on which alleviation and prevention of depression depends, and then to incorporate these core ingredients into interventions that deliver them most effectively and efficiently. Such interventions might not look very much like existing approaches to individual psychotherapy administered by highly trained professionals.

This alternative strategy depends on establishing clearly the central effective psychological processes and procedures that have to be incorporated into interventions. We believe that an applied science approach to better understanding of the production and maintenance of depression, of the kind that we have described in this book, provides a foundation from which future improvements in psychological treatment can rationally be developed.

ICS and the Future Development of Psychological Treatments for Depression

Experience with the treatment of phobias (e.g. Mathews, Gelder, & Johnston, 1981) suggests a useful strategy to achieve further improvements in the effectiveness and efficiency of psychological treatments for depression. This strategy suggests that a very effective approach is to combine: (1) the insights and inventions of skilled clinicians; (2) the systematic empirical evaluation of well-described treatment procedures; and (3) accounts of clinical conditions and central effective therapeutic mechanisms expressed in terms of explicit, research-driven, psychological paradigms.

This combined interactive approach enables us to build systematically on those techniques, developed by creative clinicians, that are actually effective. Research and theoretical analysis can then identify and isolate the essential psychological processes through which these techniques work, and allow us to understand their action in relation to an explicit formulation of the disorder being treated. This information can be used to guide creative clinicians in the development of new treatment procedures that incorporate the identified essential change process mechanisms more effectively and efficiently. By using such a strategy, the efficiency of psychological treatments for agoraphobia was increased almost twenty-fold over a short time-period, with the additional bonus of an increase in effectiveness as well as efficiency (Mathews et al., 1981).

In order to apply this general strategy to improve psychological treatments for depression further, it is necessary to have an initial explanatory framework that accounts reasonably adequately for what we already know about the nature of depression and the effectiveness of existing treatment approaches. We suggest that ICS provides such a framework.

In this chapter we look first, in general terms, at the implications for psychological treatment of the ICS analysis of depression and depressive thinking that we have developed. We then apply this perspective to cognitive therapy, the psychological treatment derived from Beck's clinical cognitive model of depression (Beck et al., 1979). The ICS perspective, which retains many of the strengths of the clinical cognitive model, also overcomes a number of its difficulties. The ICS analysis of cognitive therapy expresses, in an explicit theory, views that many skilled cognitive therapists have developed, implicitly, as a result of their own clinical experience. Further, ICS provides a way of understanding the effectiveness of a range of other, "noncognitive" psychological treatments for depression. ICS offers a novel view of the central effective mechanisms in treatments that have already been shown to be effective. In doing so, it opens the possibility of retaining what is of value in those approaches while incorporating those features, along with others, into the development of treatments of even greater effectiveness and efficiency.

The ICS Prescription for the Psychological Treatment of Depression

The ICS analysis suggests that certain forms of persistent, disabling depression are maintained by the regeneration of depressogenic Implicational schematic models. It follows that the central goal of therapy should be to replace the synthesis of such models by the synthesis of more adaptive models. How this is achieved in any particular case will depend on the actual mechanism maintaining the regeneration of depressogenic models in that person (cf. Chapter 10). For example, where synthesis of such models is largely maintained on the basis of input from persistent, uncontrollable, highly aversive environmental events, then some form of problem-solving activity directed at reducing the persistence and aversiveness of those events, and increasing their controllability, would be appropriate. Consistent with this view, where depression is associated with chronic relationship difficulties in a marriage, marital therapy is effective at reducing depression (e.g. Jacobson et al., 1991). Similarly, there is encouraging evidence that treatment approaches teaching general problem-solving skills are effective at reducing depression (e.g. Nezu & Perri, 1989).

There are many situations in which depression does not seem to be maintained by a continuing barrage of environmental events that are inherently highly aversive, uncontrollable, and persistent. In these situations, we have suggested, the regeneration of depressogenic schematic models depends on the establishment of configurations of depressive interlock. It is likely that such configurations also play some role in the maintenance of depression even where there is a contribution from ongoing environmental events. How should psychological treatments intervene to break up, or resolve, depressive interlock?

The central aim of such interventions should be to redeploy the resources maintaining the depressive interlock configuration to the processing of other data streams. It will be recalled that the first operating principle of ICS asserts that any given transformation process can only handle one coherent data stream at a time. It follows that the establishment of an alternative processing configuration, competing for the same resources as those of the interlock configuration, will, inevitably, disrupt interlock. Establishing an alternative configuration necessarily involves synthesis of schematic models other than the depressogenic models maintaining interlock. Consequently, the regeneration of the depressed state that depended on the continuing synthesis of depressogenic models will cease, and depression will be reduced.

Although depressogenic Implicational schematic models are the immediate antecedents to depression, the maintenance of depression depends on the integrity of the total processing configuration of depressive interlock. The maintenance of this configuration depends on a number of interlinked feedback loops so the total configuration is vulnerable to attack at a number of points. Consequently, in addition to therapeutic change occurring from techniques specifically directed at the schematic level, benefits may also result from techniques directed at changing specific meanings, negative thoughts, or sensory inputs (especially those related to depression-produced changes in Body-state) (Fig. 16.1). It should come as no surprise, therefore, that a number of different psychological treatments, with quite different explicit targets, have been shown to be effective in reducing depression (Williams, 1992). At least some of the effectiveness of these treatments may depend on their specific effects on their designated targets. For example, the effectiveness of programmes of physical exercise (Simons et al., 1985) could be interpreted in terms of disruption of the depressive interlock configuration by changes in Body-state feedback. In the same way, at least some of the beneficial effects of cognitive therapy may, indeed, be mediated through changes in specific meanings and negative thoughts.

In Chapter 13 we described the effects of brief distraction tasks that alleviated depression by taking over the resources supporting maintenance of the interlock configuration (p. 178). However, we also noted (p. 173) the "tenacity" of depressive interlock in situations where that configuration had already been in operation for some time. This "tenacity" refers to the tendency to revert to the interlock configuration after brief interruptions such as distracting tasks. This tendency is the result of the "population" of recent sections of Implicational memory by representations related to the depressogenic schematic models that have been maintaining interlock. Whenever subsequent processing involves access to these recent "working memory" sections of the Implicational memory record, there is the possibility that these stored representations may become re-integrated into the circulating data stream and so re-establish depressive interlock.

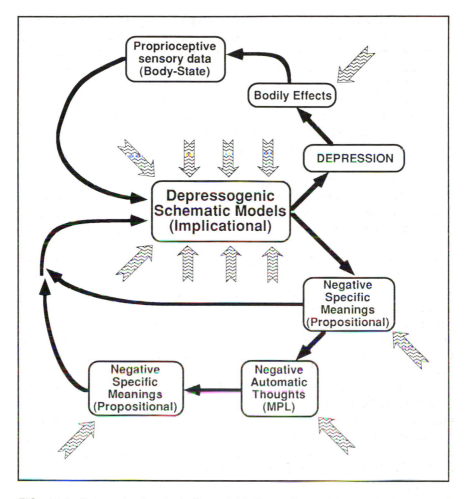

FIG. 16.1. Depressive interlock: Potential indirect effects of interventions targeted on negative automatic thoughts, and on specific meanings and depressive bodily state. Interventions targeted at any of the points marked with broad arrow-heads could indirectly change depressogenic schematic models. The primary targets are the depressogenic models themselves, marked by a ring of arrow-heads.

As a result, the effects on established depression of brief distraction, or other purely disruptive procedures, are likely to be relatively short-lived.

More enduring alleviation of depression requires that the recent sections of Implicational memory be "re-populated" by nondepressogenic schematic models. This might be achieved, for example, as a result of extended processing on topics completely unrelated to depression. Repeated synthesis, and storage, of schematic models irrelevant to depression would be associated with such processing. However, given the processing priority normally afforded to discrepancy-related information (such as that encoded in recently stored depressogenic schematic models), extended processing of nondepressive information in this situation is likely to require a lot of "effortful" "controlled" processing. Such processing may be difficult to sustain.

A more effective strategy is to replace the schematic models maintaining depression with more adaptive schematic models related to the same topics. In the next section we illustrate how this could be achieved by considering the effects of psychological treatments on problem-related schematic models, especially those related to depression itself. The essential suggestion is that a range of psychological treatments for depression have the effect of creating new, nondepressogenic, schematic models related to depression. These new models supplant the depressogenic models maintaining depressive interlock, disrupt the interlock configuration, and so reduce depression.

Depression About Depression

The ICS analysis of depression (p. 213) suggested that the schematic models that maintain depression encode a combination of the dimensions of aversiveness, uncontrollability, and anticipated persistence. Events are depressing to the extent that they support production of schematic models involving this combination of features. We suggest that, in addition to any ongoing life problems, the events that are important in regenerating depressogenic schematic models often include the symptoms and effects of depression itself. In other words, it is the patient's higher-order "view" of depression, and related problems, that sustains the self-regenerating cycles of depressive interlock that maintain depression.

The symptoms and effects of depression are themselves inherently aversive, may be difficult to control, and are likely to persist. The tendency for depression-maintaining schematic models to be synthesised on the basis of these "natural" characteristics of depression can be enhanced by a combination of lack of information about depression and mood-related information-processing biases. Rather than viewing themselves as the unfortunate sufferers of a well-recognised negative affective state, depressed individuals often tend to view their depression as an aspect of characterological deficiency that is relatively irremediable.

From schematic models related to such views, self-blaming attributions for depression and hopeless expectations about the outcome of possible coping or problem-solving actions will be derived. These serve to regenerate the parent schematic model and also to reduce the probability of effective action directed at relieving symptoms of depression or at changing problematic life situations. The effects of this inaction further "confirm" the hopelessness of the situation. Often such "depression about depression" seems to be an important feature maintaining depression (Teasdale, 1985).

At least some of the effectiveness of cognitive therapy, and of a range of other psychological treatments for depression, can be understood in terms of the impact of these interventions in breaking up self-perpetuating vicious cycles of "depression about depression". A number of workers (e.g. Teasdale, 1985; Zeiss, Lewinsohn, & Munoz, 1979) have suggested that key features shared by effective psychological treatments for depression include high structure, an explanation for depression linked to a credible treatment rationale, training in coping responses linked to that rationale, action plans, and active, collaborative involvement of the client. From the ICS perspective, the total "package" of such features can be seen as an effective way of changing the key dimensions of aversiveness, uncontrollability, and anticipated persistence that are embodied in the schematic models maintaining "depression about depression". The effect is to replace these models by alternatives that embody an "implicit" view of depression as a normative, understandable response that is modifiable. (Compare this with our discussion of the schematic models leading to ruminative versus distractive responses to depression on p. 182).

These alternative schematic models lead to the execution of active coping responses directed at changing depression and the situations producing it. Both the performance of these coping actions and the resultant effects on the internal and external worlds would tend to reinforce "coping" schematic models, and further undermine the state of "depression about depression".

It is suggested that change in the schematic models maintaining "depression about depression" is a central process in many effective psychological treatments for depression. It is important to stress that the models created in these treatments encode much more than an alternative "conceptual level" explanation of depression. They also encode an active-coping-problem-solving "set", derived from repeated experiences, within therapy, of applying the coping techniques taught by the particular treatment approach. Further, repeated experiences of the transience of depressed states, within therapy, will lead to modification of the variables in depression-related models that encode parameters related to persistence and duration of depression.

In this analysis, the specifics of the explanations offered and the coping responses "prescribed" by different treatment approaches may matter relatively little, so long as they are credible, coherent, and produce some changes in the internal or external worlds. Implicational schematic models are at a high level of abstraction. Consequently, psychological treatments that are quite different at a superficial level may produce closely similar effects at a more generic level, and be effective in reducing depression for similar reasons. Thus, on this view, much of the effectiveness of cognitive therapy may be through a generic mechanism that it shares with a number of other treatments, rather than through specifically "cognitive" mechanisms.

Consistent with this analysis, Fennell and Teasdale (1987) found that patients who improved most from cognitive therapy for depression were those who, very early in therapy, indicated close identification with the "view" of depression outlined in a handout describing that treatment approach. Such patients would clearly be those in whom more functional schematic models of their depression could easily be established by the particular treatment approach that they were receiving. Consistent with the view that synthesis of such models requires an "enactive" component, rather than simply the provision of information, these patients only began to show their superior rate of improvement after the alternative "view" described in the handout was reinforced by related homework assignments.

Similar evidence that psychological treatments are effective through reinforcing or reinstating alternative functional, schematic models of depression and depression-related problems was reported by Addis, Truax, and Jacobson (1991). They found that the extent to which patients benefited from behavioural or cognitive treatments was powerfully influenced by the extent to which the rationales of these treatments "meshed" with the pre-existing "views" of depression held by patients.

This analysis suggests that effective psychological treatments combine (1) procedures that replace patients' models of depression (and related problems) as signs of personal inadequacy about which nothing can be done (or of otherwise hopeless situations) by models that view depression as a controllable state; and (2) arrange for patients to "rehearse" the use of these new models frequently e.g. by training them in the use of compensatory skills that are related to the new models. On this view, the combination of an alternative model of depression with practice in its use in related coping responses is critical; the model without the coping responses is unlikely to be implemented or maintained; on the other hand, training in coping responses alone, without the model, is unlikely to maintain the execution of coping responses, particularly in the period after the intensive treatment phase is over.

Repeated use of more adaptive schematic models related to depression will populate the recent sections of the Implicational memory record with representations that will reduce the risk of reverting to depressive interlock. From the ICS perspective, such a store of adaptive depression-related Implicational memories is also an important aspect of the long-term, prophylactic effects of psychological treatments, which we now discuss.

Long-term Effects of Psychological Treatments for Depression

It is increasingly recognised that depression is often a relapsing and recurring condition. Consequently, the prevention of future onsets has to be a key goal for therapy. There is encouraging evidence for prophylactic effects of certain psychological treaments, especially cognitive therapy. For example, at least four studies (Simons, Murphy, Levine, & Wetzel, 1986; Blackburn, Eunson, & Bishop, 1986; Evans et al., 1992; Shea et al., 1992) provide evidence that cognitive therapy is superior to antidepressant medication in preventing relapse and recurrence of depression, or in reducing the need for further treatment after the initial treatment phase is over.

As in its analysis of vulnerability to the onset of depression (p. 219), the ICS approach identifies the tendency to establish a depressive interlock configuration in situations of mild negative affect as the crucial factor in vulnerability to relapse following treatment. On this view, prophylactic effects of psychological treatments depend on patients acquiring the capacity to respond to initial symptoms of depression by active coping responses or, at a minimum, by "distancing" from symptoms, rather than by ruminations related to hopelessness or personal inadequacy. In this way, mild depressed states that might otherwise "spiral" into more severe and prolonged conditions are "nipped in the bud" and relapse is prevented.

We can illustrate the ICS perspective on relapse prevention in depression by looking to the operation of lower-order information codes, where specific experimental evidence is available, for insights into activity at the Implicational level, where such information is not yet available.

Completion of a word fragment or stem (such as MOU_ _) can be affected powerfully by prior presentation of one possible completion (e.g. MOUND) rather than another (e.g. MOUSE). In this way, subjects' predominant tendencies to complete stems with popular endings can be counteracted so that they produce responses that are less common. This and similar effects of prior exposure to words can operate at both "automatic" and "conscious" levels. Considerable evidence (e.g. Jacoby & Kelley, 1990; Jacoby, Ste-Marie & Toth, in press) suggests that often both forms of memory process are in operation, and that "automatic" effects can occur that are independent of "conscious" effects: Subjects' performance can be affected by prior exposure to words even when they have no conscious recollection of previously seeing the word.

Jacoby and Kelley (1990) suggest that such "automatic" effects are mediated through access to episodic memory records of the earlier presentations. Presentation of the word stem or fragment acts as a cue to access episodic representations encoding prior presentation of the words.

These are then used in the current stem- or fragment-completion task. Previously presented uncommon endings can be produced, without the need for any conscious recollection of the previous presentation. It is suggested that the extent to which such effects of "automatic" memory persist or generalise will depend on the number of prior episodic encodings and the range of contexts in which they have occurred (Jacoby & Kelley, 1990).

Let us now, by extrapolation, apply these findings to understanding the persistence of the effects of synthesising alternative schematic models related to "depression about depression". We can regard the "core" Implicational pattern related to "depression" (common to a range of models concerning depression-as-a-state) as analogous to a word fragment or stem. This core pattern can be completed by the addition of further elements to create either the pattern of ["depression-about-depression"] (corresponding to completion of the word stem with a common ending) or the pattern of ["depression-as-a-normal-state-to-be-dealt-with"] (corresponding to completion of the word stem with an uncommon ending). The task of therapy is seen as providing experiences that encourage synthesis of the latter class of schematic models rather than the former (such experiences correspond to prior presentation of the word made by the uncommon ending).

The persistence of therapeutic effects, in particular the prevention of relapse in the face of mild states of depression after treatment is completed, will depend on completing the core "depression" pattern with additional patterns that yield "coping" schematic models rather than "depressogenic" schematic models. The analogy suggests that, at times of potential relapse, synthesis of "coping" models will depend on fragmentary "depression" patterns acting as cues to access episodic memory records in which this "core" pattern forms part of a total ["depression-as-a-normal-state-to-be-dealt-with"] pattern rather than part of a ["depression-about-depression"] pattern. Such access will depend on the presence, in the Implicational memory record, of many episodic representations including the former pattern, in conjunction with a wide variety of contexts. These representations, in turn, will have to have been created on many occasions, in many different contexts, if they, rather than ["depression-about-depression"] representations, are subsequently to be accessed.

The account that emerges by analogy with memory for lower-level representations has a number of attractions. First, it explains why evidence of prophylactic effects in preventing depressive relapse is currently most convincing for structured treatment approaches, such as cognitive therapy. These treatments involve repeated "homework" experiences of practising coping skills in many different contexts. More traditional "office-based" psychodynamically oriented therapies tend to have weaker long-term effects in preventing relapse or reducing further need for treatment, even when they are effective in reducing symptoms in the short term (Shea et al., 1992; Thompson & Gallagher, 1984).

From the ICS perspective, the importance of practising coping skills is not primarily to establish a "habit" or "repertoire" of skills per se. Rather, it is to acquire a stock of episodic records of "coping" Implicational patterns. Subsequently accessing these patterns in states of mild depression will prevent the "escalation" to more intense and persistent states that might otherwise occur. Accessing these memory representations may also lead to performance of coping behaviours. However, reflecting the fact that a general "coping set" has been accessed, these coping behaviours may be quite variable and flexible and need bear no close relation to the specific coping skills taught in therapy.

Finally, the analogy raises very interesting questions concerning the type of memory that may mediate the long-term effects of treatment. It may be that prophylactic effects depend on consciously "remembering" to perform the coping responses that have been learned, or the "view" of depression that has been conveyed in therapy. Alternatively, and more interestingly, it may be that prophylactic effects are mediated through "automatic" access to related Implicational memory records. In this case, a person might be aware that they are responding to an incipient depression, or problematic situation, with a "sense" or "set" of control, coping, or problem-solving, without any conscious recollection of aspects of the therapy they have received (see Brewin, 1989, for a discussion of related issues).

Synthesis of Alternative Schematic Models

ICS suggests that the task of therapy is to replace the schematic models maintaining depression with more adaptive schematic models related to the same topics. We can think of schematic models in terms of patterns of values across a number of generic variables. In changing maladaptive models into more adaptive ones we have to retain certain core elements of the original, maladaptive patterns at the same time as changing other elements to create a different total pattern. How is this to be achieved?

One possibilty is to change the values on a limited number of "critical" elements of the maladaptive pattern so that it encodes a less depressogenic higher-order meaning. For example, to a student who is depressed as the result of synthesising the ["stupid-worthless-me"] schematic model following failure on an examination, the specific information that 95% of all candidates also failed will change the value of the related Implicational element, and this may be sufficient to disrupt the wider, depression-maintaining Implicational pattern.

A second possibilty is to change coherent sub-patterns of elements, or to "nest" the maladaptive pattern within a wider "frame", to create a substantially different total pattern with a different higher-order meaning. An example of this approach is provision of a different "view", or model of depression, coupled with the enactment of active coping responses, as in our discussion of the "generic" effects of structured psychological treatments on "depression-about-depression". In Chapter 14 (p. 206) we indicated how, in principle, the negative higher-order meaning derived from an aspect of spouse behaviour could be changed by "reframing" the information related to a specific instance in a wider model in which personal happiness depended on spouse complementarity rather than spouse similarity.

A further approach derives from a basic feature of the ICS cognitive architecture. This is that the Implicational subsystem, just like all other subsystems, has a memory store specialised for recording all the information that it has ever taken as input. It follows that the ICS approach suggests that we can exploit the "stored treasures" of the Implicational memory records to modify the schematic models currently being synthesised. So, for example, one might "psych" oneself up to tackle a difficult task by accessing the "feel" of a previous experience of mastery, thereby making stored mastery-related Implicational patterns available for incorporation into the schematic models currently synthesised. Similarly, in our analysis of the long-term effects of psychological treatments, we suggested that prophylactic effects depend on accessing, at times of potential relapse, Implicational patterns encoded during previous coping experiences.

Over the course of a lifetime, Implicational patterns corresponding to an enormous range of higher-level meanings, or "modes of being", will have been stored in the Implicational memory records. The therapeutic challenge is to find ways to access adaptive patterns from this enormous potential repertoire and to use them to modify the maladaptive patterns currently being synthesised.

Implicational representations are at an implicit, generic level of representation at which it is difficult to communicate, characterise, or to identify what needs to be changed and how to change it. It is wholly understandable, then, that although (from the ICS perspective) the Implicational level is where the "action" is, psychological treatments have often focused at more specific levels of representation. Let us now focus on the most successful of these, cognitive therapy, and see how it is to be understood from the ICS perspective that we have outlined.

Cognitive Therapy for Depression

The development of cognitive therapy by Beck and his colleagues (Beck et al., 1979) is rightly regarded as one of the major advances in the history of psychological treatments. There is convincing evidence that, on average, this treatment approach is as effective as antidepressant medication in the treatment of out-patients with major depression (Hollon et al., 1991; Williams, 1992). As we noted earlier (p. 231), there is also encouraging evidence for prophylactic effects of cognitive therapy.

Cognitive therapy (Beck et al., 1979, p. 3) is "an active, directive, time-limited, structured approach" based on the clinical cognitive model of depression that we described in Chapter 1. Consistent with Beck's theoretical stance, the aim of treatment is to modify both the negative cognitions (consciously accessible thoughts and images) that are viewed as antecedents to depression, and also the underlying dysfunctional beliefs or attitudes assumed to underlie production of negative cognition.

A detailed manual describing cognitive therapy for depression is available (Beck et al., 1979). Here we summarise the key features of this treatment approach (Beck et al., 1979, pp. 3–5). Cognitive therapy includes both cognitive and behavioural strategies.

Cognitive Techniques.   These are aimed at identifying and testing patients' specific misconceptions and maladaptive assumptions. Specific learning experiences are used to teach patients: (1) to monitor negative automatic thoughts; (2) to recognise the connections between cognitions, affect, and behaviour; (3) to examine the evidence for and against distorted automatic thoughts; (4) to substitute more reality-oriented interpretations for the biased cognitions; and (5) to learn to identify and alter the dysfunctional beliefs that are assumed to predispose patients to distort their interpretation of experience.

Treatment begins with an explanation of the rationale for cognitive therapy. Next, the patient learns to recognise, monitor, and record his or her negative thoughts on specially designed forms. Cognitions and underlying assumptions are discussed and examined for logic, validity, adaptiveness, and enhancement of positive behaviour versus maintenance of pathology. For example, a depressed student expressed her belief that she would not get into one of the colleges to which she had applied (Beck et al., 1979, p. 153). When the therapist explored the reason for this, the patient responded that her grades had not been very good. Closer probing revealed that her grades had all been As, apart from two Bs the preceding semester. When the therapist asked for the average grade necessary to enter the college of her choice, the patient revealed that a B+ average would be sufficient. She then conceded that her grades would allow her to pursue her desired course of action. The therapist's aim in such interchanges is to help the patient question the validity of the thoughts or beliefs that are assumed to be creating the depression.

As a general strategy, cognitive therapy focuses on specific "target symptoms" (for example, suicidal impulses). The cognitions supporting these symptoms are identified (for example, "My life is worthless and I can't change it") and then subjected to logical and empirical investigation (Beck et al., 1979, p. 4).

Behavioural Techniques.   These are used both to change behaviour directly and also to elicit cognitions associated with specific behaviours. For example, in Graded Task Assignments, the patient undertakes a sequence of tasks to reach a goal that he or she considers difficult or impossible. Such behavioural assignments are designed to help patients test the maladaptive cognitions and assumptions that may be blocking them from undertaking constructive action. The interlinked use of challenging maladaptive cognitions that are preventing constructive behaviour, and "behavioural experiments" that provide "evidence" to disconfirm maladaptive cognitions, appears to be one of the most powerful features of cognitive therapy.

As symptoms remit, following the use of behavioural and cognitive techniques, therapeutic efforts switch to identifying and modifying underlying dysfunctional basic assumptions and beliefs. It is assumed that these more enduring beliefs are the basis for the production of negative automatic thoughts and constitute a continuing vulnerability to depression. The validity and utility of patients' assumptions are examined using a combination of cognitive techniques and behavioural experiments, broadly similar to those used in dealing with the more consciously accessible negative thoughts.

The ICS Perspective on Cognitive Therapy

ICS and the clinical cognitive model suggest different relationships between negative automatic thoughts and depression (Fig. 12.6). The clinical cognitive model suggests that such thoughts or images (or the specific meanings that they reflect) are the immediate antecedents to depression and so should be the target of treatment. Cognitive therapy, of course, aims to do just that, with many procedures designed to invalidate, discredit, or disprove negative automatic thoughts. By contrast, ICS suggests that the immediate antecedent to depression is the processing by the Implicational subsystem of generic meanings prototypical of previous depressing situations. It follows that change at this higher level of meaning must be the central goal of therapy; the aim should be to replace patterns of Implicational code related to depressive schematic models with alternative patterns related to more adaptive higher-level meanings or schematic models.

Beck's clinical cognitive model (as described in Beck et al., 1979) and ICS differ fundamentally in their view of the central effective mechanisms of therapy. How are we to understand the effectiveness of cognitive therapy from the ICS viewpoint? Specifically, given that ICS emphasises the importance of change at the generic schematic level, how does it explain the effectiveness of a treatment targeted explicitly at the level of thoughts and specific meanings?

First, negative thoughts may be useful markers of the state of the "parent" schematic model from which they were derived, or of the total processing configuration of which they are one aspect. Consequently, by applying interventions that change these thoughts we may also change the parent schematic model and so reduce depression.

Second, although they have no direct effects on depression production, specific meanings (and related thoughts and images) may have indirect effects through their contribution, as one of a large number of elements, to the production of depression-related schematic models. It follows that techniques that change negative thoughts and specific meanings may have useful effects in reducing depression. So, as already noted, to a student who is depressed as the result of synthesising the ["stupid-worthless-me"] schematic model following failure on an examination, the specific information that 95% of all candidates also failed may be sufficient to disrupt the wider, depression-maintaining Implicational pattern.

Third, it is likely that the very action of attempting to deal with negative thoughts, in common with other active coping procedures, leads to synthesis of schematic models related to "taking control". As we indicated earlier in our discussion of "depression-about-depression", synthesis of such coping-oriented models, in place of the schematic models related to themes of helplessness and hopelessness that maintain depression, may be an important mechanism through which a range of psychological treatments have their effects. Somewhat paradoxically, it seems likely that a focus on dealing systematically with specific issues, using explicitly described and monitored procedures as in cognitive therapy, may be an essential feature of treatments if they are to facilitate synthesis of generic schematic models related to "taking control".

ICS and Difficulties for the Clinical Cognitive Model's Account of Cognitive Therapy of Depression

Cognitive therapy is undoubtedly effective. However, there have been increasing doubts that its effects can adequately be explained by the clinical cognitive model. The ICS analysis, by providing an alternative perspective on cognitive therapy, overcomes a number of these difficulties:

1. Cognitive therapy is not uniquely more effective than other forms of psychological treatment that do not explicitly target negative thinking (e.g. see review by Williams, 1992). When such treatments alleviate depression they also reduce most measures of negative thinking to an extent similar to comparably effective cognitive therapy (e.g. Rehm et al., 1987; Wilson, Goldin, & Charbonneau-Powis, 1983; but see Imber et al., 1990 for preliminary evidence suggesting that cognitive therapy may have specific effects on selected measures).

These findings suggest that cognitive therapy may achieve its effects, not by changing negative thinking, but by some other mechanism, shared with noncognitive treatments. Changes in negative thinking as a result of cognitive therapy might then be seen as a consequence of the change in depression, rather than the means of achieving that change.

Although problematic for the clinical cognitive model, the finding that "noncognitive" treatments are effective in reducing both depression and negative thinking is quite consistent with the ICS analysis that has been presented. This analysis suggests that many, superficially different, structured psychological treatments may operate by a common mechanism at the generic level, namely, disrupting "depression-about-depression". Such treatments may also disrupt depressive interlock through their effects on specific components of total processing configurations. In either case, it would be expected that a range of treatments, when they are effective in reducing depression, would also reduce negative thinking.

2. It is a common clinical observation that patients in therapy often experience emotional reactions without being able to identify any related negative automatic thoughts, or any negative thoughts commensurate with the intensity of the reaction. And yet, Beck's cognitive model proposes that such thoughts or images are the immediate link in emotion production.

From the ICS perspective, such observations are not unexpected: The schematic models producing emotion may not produce "downline" related verbalised thoughts, and, even when they do, such thoughts can, at best, only partially express the content of their "parent" schematic models.

3. Within cognitive therapy, "rational" argument or "corrective" information is frequently ineffective in changing emotional response, even when the patient acknowledges "intellectually" the logical power of the evidence. This contrast between "intellectual" and "emotional" belief, or "knowing with the head" versus "knowing with the heart" poses recurring problems for clinicians. For example, depressed patients will often say "I know I'm not worthless but I don't believe it emotionally". We saw (p. 216) that the clinical cognitive model deals with this difficulty by asserting that these are merely quantitative variations of the same Propositional level of

belief or meaning. Clinical experience suggests that this is not a convincing solution to this difficulty.

As we have already noted (pp. 92, 216), the ICS analysis recognises a qualitative distinction between "intellectual" and "emotional" belief, the former corresponding to Propositional representations, the latter to affect-related Implicational representations. Within the ICS framework, only the latter are directly causally related to emotion. Consequently, dissociations between "belief" at the two levels are to be expected, and change in "intellectual" belief, unaccompanied by change in "emotional" belief, would not be expected to change emotional response.

4. There is a tendency for cognitive therapy to include in its techniques anything that "works" or "makes clinical sense", even if there is little basis for it in the explicitly stated clinical cognitive model.

This tendency is particularly evident in the use of "non-evidential" techniques that cannot be justified rationally in terms of the invalidation of the specific, distorted meanings emphasised by the clinical cognitive model. The use of such techniques is widespread in recent developments of cognitive therapy.

As cognitive therapy has been applied to more long-standing clinical problems, it has become clear that the conventional cognitive therapy for depression programme, focusing on negative automatic thoughts, is frequently ineffective. In response, treatment procedures have been imported wholesale, on an ad hoc basis, from other therapy traditions based on quite different underlying rationales, notably Gestalt therapy (Perls, 1973). Many of these procedures, although apparently clinically effective, have little to do with the acquisition of evidence in relation to the truth value of specific thoughts or meanings. For example, a popular therapeutic technique is to use guided imagery as a way of "replaying" early traumatic events so that they have a less traumatic outcome (e.g. Edwards, 1990; Young, 1990). A client might be asked, for instance, to relive in imagery a scene of childhood abuse but to introduce into the imagined scenario the elements of control and power that they now have as an adult but lacked at the time. Such an exercise, however clinically effective it may be, has no worth as evidence for refuting specific propositional meanings.

One might choose to include such procedures in a total therapy package simply on the pragmatic grounds that they "work". However, in doing so there is a danger of losing any theoretical coherence in cognitive therapy, or of creating a situation in which the implicit theories guiding clinicians practising cognitive therapy and the explicit statements of the cognitive model become discrepant. Neither outcome would seem to offer a firm foundation for the future development of cognitive therapies.

In the ICS analysis, the "action" as far as emotion production is concerned is at the generic Implicational level of representation, rather than the specific Propositional level. Implicational representations encode complex inter-relationships between patterns of elements derived from clusters of specific meanings and sensory features. It is not meaningful to think in terms of evaluating the "truth" value of such schematic representations, in the way that the validity of more specific Propositional statements can be assessed. Consequently, ICS envisages a potential role for non-evidential therapeutic procedures that are effective at creating change at the Implicational level, even when they are of no value in providing evidence to invalidate specific negative beliefs.

From the ICS perspective, it comes as no surprise that major recent importations into cognitive therapy have come from experientially oriented approaches such as Gestalt therapy. Like ICS, these approaches recognise the importance of holistic levels of representation, the role of body-state, and of the wider semantic context. ICS provides a framework within which the effectiveness of experiential therapy techniques, for which there is little justification in the clinical cognitive model, can be understood.

Gains from the ICS Perspective

The ICS analysis overcomes some of the explanatory difficulties encountered by the clinical cognitive model. ICS also provides a fruitful shift in emphasis in the way that both established and recently introduced cognitive therapy techniques are viewed and used.

A Focus on the Schematic Level

The clinical cognitive model, with its emphasis on the truth value of specific propositional statements, can lead to a strategy in which negative automatic thoughts are identified and then systematically invalidated. By contrast, ICS suggests that the task of therapy is to replace the schematic models maintaining depression with more adaptive alternative schematic models.

Changing schematic models is likely to require attending to a wider semantic context than if our aim is to invalidate specific meanings. Rather than a "search and destroy" strategy aimed at specific negative thoughts, the aim should be to create coherent, alternative, semantic "packages". It is interesting to note that the highly successful cognitive therapy for panic (Clark & Salkovskis, 1991) aims to do just this by creating whole alternative "views" or models of anxiety and panic, rather than by invalidating specific negative beliefs serially (D. M. Clark, personal communication, July 1991).

In the ICS view "enactive" procedures, such as the behavioural experiments of cognitive therapy, are important not simply because they provide "evidence" to evaluate the truth value of specific hypotheses, but because they also include a wider, coherent set of meanings incompatible with maladaptive schematic models. For example, deliberately to enter a situation and take control in order to find out what happens is rich in implicit meanings incompatible with ["helpless-hopeless"] schematic models.

Skilled and sensitive clinicians are "shaped up" by the realities of clinical experience to adopt, often implicitly, "working" theories that may not coincide exactly with explicit statements of the clinical cognitive model. The ICS analysis provides an explicit formulation of "implicit" theories that are probably shared by many experienced cognitive therapists. The advantage of an explicit articulation of underlying theoretical views is that it may decrease the variance between therapists in the way that cognitive therapy is implemented. Most importantly, it may also provide a firm foundation for further improvements in treatment. By explicitly identifying the creation and maintenance of alternative schematic models as the central therapeutic process in the psychological treatment of depression, the ICS analysis points to the need to design treatment interventions with the deliberate aim of creating such models.

For example, our earlier analysis of the effects of psychological treatments on "depression-about-depression" suggested that at least some of the effects of cognitive therapy, and of other psychological treatments for depression, were the result of changes in schematic models concerning the symptoms and effects of depression. The effectiveness of psychological treatments for depression could further be enhanced by explicitly designing treatments to change schematic models of depression, or by deliberately matching treatments carefully to pre-existing schematic models. At present, treatment effectiveness seems to depend on these effects happening "accidentally" or "implicitly". Deliberately encouraging these effects by appropriately designed procedures would be expected to yield considerable gains in effectiveness and efficiency.

A Role for Non-evidential Interventions

In contrast to Beck's cognitive model, ICS suggests a place for techniques that modify purely sensory elements. The high-order meaning I create following a failure experience may be quite different if I combine specific failure-related meanings with elements related to the sensory feedback from a smiling facial expression rather than a frown, or from high bodily arousal and an erect posture rather than from a sluggish body-state and bowed, "beaten" posture. Purely physical interventions, such as changes in facial expression (e.g. Laird et al., 1982) or physical exercise (e.g. Clark, Milberg, & Ross, 1983, discussed on p. 139, this volume) have produced mood-related biases in memory and judgement. These findings are wholly consistent with the ICS proposal that these "cognitive" effects are mediated through schematic models with important sensory components. Applied to treatment, the ICS analysis suggests a very useful place for purely physical "non-evidential" interventions, such as training in maintaining a half-smiling expression or vigorous physical exercise, in the "cognitive" therapy of depression.

Clearly, direct manipulations of bodily state, although of value in changing schematic models, will often provide little of value as evidence for evaluating the truth of specific propositions. Similarly, the synthesis of alternative schematic models can be assisted by a range of other "non-evidential" techniques, such as those recently introduced ad hoc into cognitive therapy.

For example, the use of guided imagery in child abuse, in the way that we described earlier, can be seen as potentially a very powerful way of introducing new elements into patterns of Implicational code related to helplessness, domination, betrayal, and suffering. By this means, new high-order meanings, related to mastery, control, and assertion, can be created that will allow clients to free themselves from the domination of the dysfunctional childhood schematic models.

The ICS analysis suggests that in this situation it is not the imagery, per se, that is the important factor in therapeutic change. Rather, it is only to the extent that imagery is a useful vehicle for creating change in high-order Implicational meanings that beneficial effects will arise. This explains the clinical observation that an emotional reaction to imagery of the traumatic experience in therapy is frequently a prerequisite for change. ICS suggests that this is not a result of the beneficial effects of "catharsis" or "getting in touch with one's feelings" per se. From the ICS perspective, an emotional reaction is an indication that the relevant high-level meanings have been accessed and are available for modification. Imagery that does not elicit an emotional reaction indicates that only visual-object level (OBJ) representations have been accessed. Creating changes only at the visual-object level without corresponding changes at the Implicational level would not be expected to have beneficial effects.

Summary

Cognitive therapy for depression is encouragingly effective in the treatment and prevention of unipolar neurotic depression in out-patient populations. However, the clinical cognitive model does not provide a wholly satisfactory account of cognitive therapy. ICS provides a better account. In particular, by placing emphasis on a more generic level of representation in the production and treatment of depression than the clinical cognitive model, ICS is better able to account for the effectiveness of a range of psychological treatments for depression and to provide a rational justification for the use of "non-evidential" therapy techniques, including physical approaches such as exercise.

Further improvements in psychological treatments are likely to depend on an interactive, symbiotic relationship between clinical insight and creativity, empirical evaluation of the effectiveness of treatment procedures, and explicit, research-based information-processing analyses of both the problem being treated and the psychological treatments being used. We have argued that ICS provides a useful framework within which such analyses can be formulated.

Conclusions

This book began with the description of a depressed young woman ruminating negatively as she reviewed the state of her life. At that point, we raised the following questions: (1) Does her depression make her think in this gloomy pessimistic way? (2) Does her negative thinking contribute to keeping her depressed? (3) If we were to change the way she thinks would this change the way she feels? (4) If we change the way she feels would this change the way she thinks? (5) Can we, by helping her to change the way she thinks and feels, help reduce the chances that she will continue to be depressed, both now and in the future?

The answer that we can now propose to all these questions is: "Yes, depending exactly what you mean by the terms 'depression', 'thinking', and 'feeling' ". The thrust of our argument throughout the book has been that the applied science approach provides us with a way of refining both what we might mean by each of these terms, and our understanding of how they might interact. Specifically, we have suggested that the ICS framework has the potential to operate as an heuristic "interface" between the concerns of experimentalists, and the concerns of clinicians. ICS provides a common language in which each group can express its concepts and theories in a way that is both relatively precise and accessible to members of the other group. In the concluding chapter we consider more fully wider issues related to the need for comprehensive, applicable theories in psychology.

PART VI

Afterword

CHAPTER SEVENTEEN

Applicable Theory:
A Puzzle in Three
Dimensions

In the previous chapter we reached a degree of closure on the problem that has provided our continuing point of reference throughout the book. We now consider the wider implications of the exercise in which we have been engaged.

The Value of Unified Theories

Traditionally, experimental psychology has sought to advance understanding by "breaking down" the general problem into successively smaller bits. We have psychologies of memory, human development, general learning, emotion, cognition, etc. Within cognitive psychology we have quite distinct areas such as attention, language understanding, thinking and reasoning, etc. Where a human information-processing perspective is adopted, the prevailing assumption is that we can isolate individual processes and look at their effects separately. In each area, topic, and theoretical approach, we have different languages for expressing the substance of theories. All too often, each area comes to the conclusion that the particular focus of their enquiry is related to many other issues.

Much of what we now do as a research community has been shaped by the failure of the monolithic theories of behaviourists like Hull (1952) and Skinner (1957). The cognitive revolution was accompanied by a move to more tractable theories of limited scope. In context, these moves were highly productive in advancing our understanding.

In many Western economies, success is viewed primarily in terms of short-term profit at the expense of longer-term investment for systematic growth. In an analogous way, local theories may be the best route to immediate scientific success in the understanding of particular phenomena. However, as the inter-relationships among the different facets of mental life become increasingly prominent, there is a danger that any underlying order will be obscured by a very wide differentiation of theories, models, and the languages in which that order is expressed. Contrastive tests in the context of alternative local theories may lead us only to see the properties of "local valleys" not connected within the broader topography of the full mental landscape. As a research community, we may need to invest proportionately more effort in developing unified frameworks within which the properties of the broader landscape are most likely to emerge.

As a framework, ICS is not only comprehensive in its coverage of domains of mental life; rich inter-relationships are built in from the ground up. We have argued both here and elsewhere (Barnard & Teasdale, 1991) that the operation of many individual mental resources cannot productively be studied in isolation from the wider system within which they are inter-functioning. We have also argued that knowledge-based and process-based considerations need to be dealt with concurrently (see also Barnard, 1985). Through the specific problems of cognition and emotion that we have considered here, we are seeking to support the wider movement toward "unified theories of cognition" (Newell, 1990).

There are, of course, short-term costs—both in the building and understanding of appropriate theoretical frameworks of this type. It is usually not hard to understand the communalites and points of contrast that hold over a range of local theories. It may prove quite difficult to arrive at a position where we can understand the communalities and points of contrast over a range of unified theoretical frameworks. However, even within an individual framework of this type, it should be possible to advance our understanding by specifying alternative conjectures and hypotheses and to build systematically upon the range of known empirical phenomena.

In this book, we have repeatedly pointed out that the empirical phenomena associated with cognition and affect were intricate, displayed many inter-relationships, and called for a comprehensive theoretical framework to promote an appropriate synthesis and understanding. At this point we remain convinced that the investment of effort required to develop and use such a framework offers the prospects of long-term benefit.

If we are to make the move towards unified theories of cognition, we have to address the wider questions: How can we communicate and work with candidate theories?

Theoretical Complexity in ICS

The basic constituents of the ICS framework are relatively straightforward. However, when these constituents are placed within the context of the full system there are many potential inter-relationships to consider. This is one of the major barriers to using and communicating the ICS framework. For example, a single process in ICS can do nothing by itself; the control of overt behaviour or internal mental activity arises out of a configuration in which several processes are involved. These processes may be using memory records or direct input, they may be interacting in reciprocal cycles or they may be operating in sequence. Parallel processing may be going on by different processes in the same subsystem and by-products of the interlinked processing activity may be multiply represented in the memory records of different subsystems. The forms of knowledge represented and manipulated by the different subsystems are also inter-related. The central codes are actually built out of the products of sensory-effector activity and subject to feedback influences from other central subsystems.

There are also rich inter-relationships within the short-term dynamics of system operation and in the dynamics of its long-term development and change. So, in the very short term, an individual process may be a part of one larger configuration at one moment, then be called upon by another at the next moment. At one stage of development the knowledge built into a transformation process may differ substantially from that at a later stage of development. Both the short-term dynamics of system operation and long-term dynamics of development are effectively determined by the content of representations being passed from one subsystem to another. The use of memory resources is also intimately intertwined with all aspects of process functioning and development. Copying information into memory is assumed to form the basis of our phenomenological awareness. The information stored in these records is assumed to represent the sequential interdependencies that form the feedstock of the mechanism through which the input-output relationships embodied in a particular process are acquired or proceduralised.

The theoretical complexity that we have just illustrated has profound implications for the future applicability of ICS—how is the approach to be communicated and how is it to be applied by anyone not intimately involved in its original development?

Our strategy in this book has essentially involved communication by gradual infusion. In many respects, our aim has been implicitly to communicate "schematic models for ICS, its operation, and its scientific use", by illustration and example. This, of course, is the traditional form of learning "by apprenticeship".

It may also be that, for the immediate future, using and applying ICS has to remain essentially a "craft skill". However, it is important to ensure that this does not remain the basis for applying ICS in the future. We now consider some alternative options.

How to Apply ICS in the Future

One way to get round the use of craft skill is to produce explicit running models of ICS in the form of simulations. However, even in its own terms, simulation of ICS is probably not the best route forward. Simulation is intractable because everything is related to everything else. Although we might be able to show, via simulation, that the system could behave like a human would in a given setting, this would actually miss an important theoretical point. Within ICS, processing and knowledge inter-relate across the whole mechanism. We could not expect "to carve out a little bit" and simulate it. Carving out some part would be to deny the arguments we have made earlier concerning interdependence. Trying to do the whole thing would be intractable. In this respect we believe explicit simulation techniques to be of strictly limited value for the furtherance of this sort of theoretical framework. What is at stake is the logic of the inter-functioning of the entire architecture and the relationship this logic bears both to subjective experience and to the empirically observed properties of overt behaviour. We need to look to the possibility of developing other techniques rather more appropriately tailored to reasoning about the logic of interacting processes and how to derive formal predictions from them.

In these respects we are encouraged by three developments:

1. In computer science there is now considerable emphasis on developing mathematical models that capture properties of the operation of multiprocessor architectures (e.g. CSP, Hoare, 1985). Out of these techniques is growing a whole range of agent-based languages that enable us to understand and model interactions between inter-functioning units. These formal languages offer the prospect of being able to prove that a system actually possesses the properties claimed for it.

2. In artificial intelligence, work is under way to produce formal specifications of cognitive architectures (Fox, Cooper, Farringdon, & Shallice, 1992). This work also offers the prospect of laying out, in formal terms, the fundamental theoretical claims that are embodied within a particular cognitive architecture. The formalisation provides a direct means by which simulation methods can be made more readily accessible and called upon systematically to test the fundamental theoretical claims.

These two developments suggest that our understanding of multiprocessor architectures, such as ICS, and their behaviour can be placed on a more explicit basis. We may even be able to reason formally from theoretical claim to consequence logically, rather than by simulation.

3.   One simple and practical way of representing theoretical arguments of the type advanced here is to make the rules explicit within an "expert system". Within such a system, the rules embody knowledge of the ICS architecture and the logic of its interfunctioning. The rules are used to build models that describe properties of cognitive activity and these properties are used to generate predictions about human behaviour. Versions of this particular modelling technique have so far only been developed in the specific applied context of research in human-computer interaction (Barnard, Wilson, & MacLean, 1988; Barnard, Blandford, & May, 1992). However, the same modelling approach could equally well be applied in the area of cognitive-affective interaction.

Utility and Validity

The basic ICS framework obviously cannot be tested without making additional assumptions about how the underlying architecture is actually working. Throughout this endeavour, our scientific use of ICS has been structured at three levels. At one level we have the basic ICS framework itself and its principles of operation. At the next level we have abstract conjectures about its operation, and at the third level we have specific hypotheses concerning the intricacies of the performance of individual tasks. This layered approach enables us to organise our assumptions and take a systematic view about what is being "tested".

The definition of the underlying architecture basically provides us with a systematic "language" for expressing conjectures and more detailed hypotheses. The actual models of classes of phenomena are expressed as a set of inter-related conjectures. At the end of Chapter 14, we expressed three basic conjectures that captured our overall model of cognitive-affective interaction and change. These are essentially abstract summaries of the key communalities that bind our more specific hypotheses together and link them to the broader framework. The specific hypotheses express yet more detailed assumptions that enable us to understand the phenomena we see and to generate new empirical tests of those ideas.

Within the "language" of the ICS framework, we can elaborate a number of alternative conjectures and a much larger range of hypotheses. We would expect many of the specific hypotheses to be refuted by the normal process of empirical testing. However, since they are phrased in more abstract terms, we would expect a model, as expressed by a set of inter-related conjectures, to be more robust. We would expect to change it only over a slower time cycle as the evidence for common factors or systematic differences built up concerning the causation of phenomena.

For example, the three conjectures we have advanced (p. 207) specify the level at which cognitive-affective synthesis occurs, the idea that processing priority is given to discrepancies, and the possibility of interlock within the central engine of cognition. In the verbal expression of each one we incorporated relatively little in the way of qualification or elaboration. In each case our more detailed working hypotheses are more specific. Within this layered approach we would naturally expect there to be substantial hypothesis revision. We would also expect the form and content of our more abstract conjectures to evolve.

We would expect much less change to the underlying principles that constrain the ICS architecture itself. As a language within which conjectures and hypotheses can be phrased, it is a potentially powerful tool. Rather than fall as a consequence of simple experimental test, we would expect the overall structure of conjectures to be placed under increasing strain until the wider edifice falls into disuse and collapses. The underlying architecture, like the production systems of artificial intelligence or mathematical modelling techniques, is a particular form of tool for thought. In this case, the purpose of the tool is to help us to reason about the complex inter-dependencies that might hold in the causation and modification of mental activity. The underlying framework should be evaluated, not in terms of its truth or falsity, but in terms of its utility in enabling us to synthesise what is known and to generate new research.

A Puzzle in Three Dimensions

Our objective in this book has been to develop a unified theoretical framework for understanding human affect, cognition, and change. In the first chapter, we committed ourselves to operating within an applied science paradigm. The theoretical framework we have described is intended to be of some practical and personal use outside the confines of the laboratory.

The development of a comprehensive cognitive theory that deals adequately with a broad range of phenomena would in itself be a considerable advance for psychological science. Some now believe that this kind of advance is potentially within our grasp (Newell, 1990). Its attainment would, however, be a relatively hollow victory unless we can use that theory to enhance the quality of people's lives—whether that enhancement comes through the development of therapeutic procedures to alleviate psychological suffering or, for example, to help develop new generations of more humanly useful technologies out of the present generation of computers or video-recorders.

It has long been part of the culture of the particular research unit in which we both work that an applied dimension enriches theory development (Baddeley, 1990). Amongst other things, the real world provides a very strong forcing function for theory development and an equally powerful source of validation. This can help us to avoid what have aptly been described as the "tar-pits" of experimental paradigms closely confined to the laboratory. All too often, perhaps, ideas evolve into theories about behaviour in the paradigm rather than theories of more general relevance and applicability (e.g. Norman, 1983)

In practice, movement towards these objectives is hard to achieve. The development of the ideas presented here and the writing of the book (and, presumably, the reading of it!) has been very much like trying to solve a three-dimensional puzzle such as Rubik's cube. The basic scientific problem is laid out in two of these dimensions. In our own case, one of these dimensions details the known empirical phenomena of cognition and affect. The other dimension lays out the ICS theoretical framework with its assumed mental codes, its subsystem organisation, its short-term dynamics of process operations, and its longer-term dynamics of learning and change. The third dimension of the puzzle links the laboratory to the real world. At one extreme our laboratory tasks are often rather simplified and idealised shadows of the settings in the natural world that they are designed to represent (e.g. see Barnard, 1991). At the other extreme lies the rich cognitive-affective behaviour and experience of individuals of very different characters.

In this book, we have repeatedly pointed out that the empirical phenomena associated with cognition and affect were intricate, displayed many inter-relationships, and called for a comprehensive theoretical framework to promote an appropriate synthesis and understanding. This defined the first two dimensions of our basic scientific puzzle. The area of cognition and affect thus provided a very suitable vehicle for us to pursue our broader objectives. Given the potential importance of such basic research to the clinical domain, the area of cognition and affect is also highly relevant to the third dimension of our wider puzzle, that of theoretical applications in the real world.

Non-clinical Applications

As a framework that lays claim to being both comprehensive and applicable, ICS should be of use in other settings. Indeed, our proposed conjectures concerning cognitive-affective interaction have some rather strange bedfellows within the overall ICS project. ICS was originally developed as a way to explain performance in short-term verbal memory tasks within a wider structure for language comprehension, language production, and reading (Barnard, 1985). It has subsequently been applied in the area of human-computer interaction. In this very different setting, the ideas have been developed to cover detailed aspects of the mental representation of complex tasks and their processing (Barnard, 1987); the role of wider knowledge in the procedural, declarative, or exploratory learning of technological devices (Duff, 1992); and the representation of complex visual objects, and the dynamics of their processing (May, Böcker, Barnard, & Green, 1991).

These other domains of enquiry have focused upon classically "cognitive" concerns. Nonetheless, the theoretical claims made in these domains are expressed in fundamentally the same way as they have been in this book. Not surprisingly, much of this other work shares many themes with the material discussed here—most notably at the level of the central engine of Propositional/Implicational processing, and how the products of its activity relate to the uptake of perceptual information and the control of overt action. Communalities at this level can only readily be seen because the same forms of mental code, the same processes and memory records, are assumed to mediate the performance of very different "external" tasks and domains of application.

Clinical Extensions

Accounts of other types of cognitive-affective dysfunction can be articulated within the ICS framework. We have already developed a preliminary account of post-traumatic stress disorder (Barnard, Foa, Teasdale, & Linehan, in prep.). This account, like that of depression, focuses on the inter-relationships between the central engine of cognition, the Body-state loop, and the schematic models being processed. However, reflecting the differences in the clinical conditions modelled, the account of post-traumatic stress disorder uses a different set of conjectures than the account of depression.

Through such extensions within the clinical domain, we anticipate that the wider value of a framework like ICS, and the general theoretical language it provides, will become more fully apparent. The overall language should enable us to establish relationships, and see contrasts, that would not emerge so readily if we were working on various dysfunctions from different theoretical perspectives.

Our three-dimensional puzzle has a lot of basic rules. In our overall scientific search for order in the broader mental landscape, it is clear that we will, in any event, have to start with a lot of basic bits and pieces. The rules that apply to their integration may come from many different local theories, or they may come from an initially more complex but unified framework. The great attraction of the latter strategy is that we may be able to re-use explanatory themes across a range of laboratory contexts and both clinical and nonclinical applications. We believe the initial investment of effort in developing, understanding, and communicating the rules will ultimately pay off in terms of parsimony in theoretical explanations of behaviour and in the application of theory.

Further, in the course of moving toward these objectives, we hope to make the application of theory more relevant to the understanding of ourselves.

An Applied Psychology of Personal as well as Practical Relevance?

We currently apply the products of experimental psychology in many domains. Typically, when we seek to apply the products of our laboratory psychology, we primarily think in terms of doing things with our theories and methods out there in the world. In order to effect useful and productive change, we think in terms of modifying the environment or what people do in terms of tasks.

On the other hand, when we want to talk about our own thoughts, feelings, and concerns, the language of experimental psychology is rapidly discarded. For example, if we wish to initiate personal understanding and change, these issues are more likely to be addressed in the languages of the various schools of psychotherapy, meditational traditions, or religion. More widely, personally relevant understandings are communicated indirectly through poetry and literature.

If we want a science of mental life, then it should ideally be applicable and also of personal relevance. We should be able to use the products of our theoretical enquiries, not only to help modify things out there in the world, but also to help individuals deal with the personal meaning of what is going on in themselves.

Cognitive psychology has, of course, a long tradition of concern with ecological aspects of perception (e.g. Gibson, 1979), memory (e.g. Baddeley, 1990), and wider aspects of cognition (e.g. Neisser, 1976). However, experiential issues still remain very much on the fringes of what is studied and taught.

There are two aspects of the ICS framework that we hope can function to reduce the general gap between our standard, experimentally derived theories and the more experientially oriented ones. One aspect involves the contrast between Propositional meaning and Implicational meaning. It will be remembered that Implicational meaning represents highly abstract schematic models. This level of representation takes inputs from the external world, the internal world of the body, and the mental world of propositions. Implicational coding therefore integrates over the principal aspects of the human "existential space" (Barnard & Teasdale, 1991). It is the cognitive-affective crossroads and it captures abstractions over both the "cold" cognitive dimensions of experience and the "hot" hedonic ones. In the level of Implicational representation, ICS provides the means through which, potentially, concern with more experiential, existentially important, issues can be brought within the ambit of an explicit information processing framework.

The second aspect concerns the way in which phenomenological awareness is handled within the ICS framework. On the one hand, ICS specifies direct parallels between qualitatively distinct forms of subjective experience and the particular information codes that underlie them. On the other hand, ICS also asserts that the distinction between buffered and direct processing is marked, subjectively, by the distinction between focal and diffuse awareness. In this way, ICS provides us with a rational basis on which we can use subjective experience, both our own and that reported to us by subjects and patients, to make inferences about the state of underlying processing configurations. Further, we can use changes in subjective experience as a result of specific interventions as a marker of whether those interventions have been successful in changing the underlying configurations, and in what direction change has occurred.

ICS is comprehensive in its coverage of different types of information. Consequently, we can, in principle, use subjective experience as a way to illuminate many aspects of information processing, from the perception of sensory qualities, such as sounds, through to the most subtle forms of implicit meaning that may be the focus of experientially oriented psychotherapeutic approaches.

The combination of the Implicational level of representation together with an explicit statement of the relationship between aspects of subjective experience and aspects of processing means that ICS provides the means to incorporate experiential issues into an applied science approach. The concept of Implicational representation allows us to think systematically about experiential issues. The rules relating subjective awareness to underlying processing allow us to relate this thinking to our own experience.

The development of a personally relevant applied cognitive psychology would be attractive in many ways. The possibility that ICS may provide a useful contribution to such an enterprise is a fitting point on which to bring this book to a close. In Chapter 16, we suggested that the scale of human distress and depression meant that traditional forms of psychotherapy were never likely to make a substantial impact on the problem. We argued for the development of radically different interventions. An obvious possibility is to exploit self-help and peer-help approaches. ICS has a potentially fruitful role to play in the systematic understanding, evaluation, and development of these approaches.

For example, the ICS analysis suggests that the most direct approach to changing problematic emotions and action tendencies is, first, to access or synthesise the patterns of Implicational code from which the problems arise. Next, those patterns have to be placed on the cognitive "work-bench" of the recent sections of the Implicational memory record. There, via buffered processing, they can be modified by subsequent interaction with representations derived from other sources. A definite, holistic, subjective sense of "all of the problem" would "tell" one that the essential problem-related information had been accessed, that the appropriate processing configuration was in place, and that effective psychological "work" could now begin. Establishing such an holistic "felt sense" of a problem is, in fact, the first stage of Gendlin's (1981) focusing, an experiential self-help technique, designed to embody in a procedure that takes only a few minutes the core effective ingredients identified by process research on traditional, extended, forms of psychotherapy.

By enabling such mapping of aspects of experientially oriented psychotherapeutic approaches into an explicit information-processing framework, ICS holds out the possibility of more systematic understanding of the effective mechanisms of those approaches. This, in turn, is likely to lead to further increases in their effectiveness and efficiency. A clearer understanding of the operation of experientially oriented techniques may make them both more useful to those already familiar with them and more acceptable to a wider range of people.

By providing a framework in which we can think systematically about what goes on in our minds and in our "hearts", ICS may enable us not only to help depressed individuals help themselves more effectively, but also help us to know ourselves a little better. We hope so.

References

Abramson, L.Y., Metalsky, G.I., & Alloy, L.B. (1989). Hopelessness depression: A theory-based subtype of depression. *Psychological Review, 96,* 358-372.

Abramson, L.Y., Seligman, M.E.P., & Teasdale, J.D. (1978). Learned helplessness in humans: Critique and reformulation. *Journal of Abnormal Psychology, 87,* 49–74.

Addis, M.E., Truax, P., & Jacobson, N.S. (1991). *Client understanding of the problem and response to cognitive therapy.* Paper presented at 25th Annual Convention of the Association for the Advancement of Behavior Therapy, New York City, November.

Allport, D.A. (1980). Attention and performance. In G. Claxton (Ed.), *Cognitive psychology: New directions.* London: Routledge & Kegan Paul.

Anisman, H., & Zacharko, R.M. (1982). Depression: The predisposing influence of stress. *Behavioral and Brain Sciences, 5,* 89-137.

Antrobus, J.S. (1968). Information theory and stimulus-independent thought. *British Journal of Psychology, 59,* 423-430.

Baddeley, A.D. (1986). *Working memory.* Oxford: Oxford University Press.

Baddeley, A.D. (1990). *Human memory: Theory and practice.* Hove, UK: Lawrence Erlbaum Associates Ltd.

Barnard, P. (1985). Interacting cognitive subsystems: A psycholinguistic approach to short-term memory. In A. Ellis (Ed.), *Progress in the psychology of language, Vol. 2,* (pp. 197-258). Hove, UK: Lawrence Erlbaum Associates Ltd.

Barnard, P. (1987). Cognitive resources and the learning of human-computer dialogues. In J.M. Carroll (Ed.), *Interfacing thought: Cognitive aspects of human-computer interaction* (pp. 112-158). Cambridge, Mass.: MIT Press.

Barnard, P.J. (1991). Bridging between basic theories and the artifacts of human-computer interaction. In J.M. Carroll (Ed.), *Designing interaction: Psychology at the human-computer interface* (pp.103–127). Cambridge: Cambridge University Press.

Barnard, P.J., Blandford, A., & May, J. (1992). *A demonstration of expert system capability*. Esprit Basic Research Action 3066, Deliverable D19, Brussels: Commission of the European Communities DG XIII.

Barnard, P.J., Foa, E., Teasdale, J.D., & Linehan, M. (In prep.). *Post-traumatic stress disorder: An Interactive Cognitive Subsystems (ICS) analysis.*

Barnard, P.J., & Teasdale, J.D. (1991). Interacting cognitive subsystems: A systemic approach to cognitive-affective interaction and change. *Cognition and Emotion, 5,* 1-39.

Barnard, P., Wilson, M., & Maclean, A. (1988). Approximate modelling of cognitive activity with an expert system: A theory-based strategy for developing an interactive design tool. *The Computer Journal, 31,* 445-456.

Barnett, P.A., & Gotlib, I.H. (1988). Psychosocial functioning and depression: Distinguishing among antecedents, concomitants, and consequences. *Psychological Bulletin, 104,* 97-126.

Bartlett, J.C., Burleson, G., & Santrock, J.W. (1982). Emotional mood and memory in young children. *Journal of Experimental Child Psychology, 34,* 59-76.

Bartlett, J.C., & Santrock, J.W. (1977). Affect-dependent episodic memory in young children. *Child Development, 50,* 513-518.

Beck, A.T. (1967). *Depression: Clinical, experimental and theoretical aspects.* New York: Harper & Row.

Beck, A.T. (1976). *Cognitive therapy and the emotional disorders.* New York: International Universities Press.

Beck, A.T. (1983). Cognitive therapy of depression: New perspectives. In P. J. Clayton & J.E. Barrett (Eds.), *Treatment of depression: Old controversies and new approaches* (pp. 265-284). New York: Raven Press.

Beck, A.T., Epstein, N., & Harrison, R. (1983). Cognitions, attitudes and personality dimensions in depression. *British Journal of Cognitive Psychotherapy, 1,* 1-16.

Beck, A.T., Rush, A.J., Shaw, B.F., & Emery, G. (1979). *Cognitive therapy of depression.* New York: Guilford Press.

Berkowitz, L. (1993). Towards a general theory of anger and emotional aggression: Implications of the cognitive-neoassociationistic perspective for the analysis of anger and other emotions. In R.S. Wyer & T.K. Srull (Eds.), *Advances in social cognition, Vol.6.* Hillsdale, NJ: Lawrence Erlbaum Associates Inc.

Blackburn, I.M., Eunson, K.M., & Bishop, S. (1986). A two-year naturalistic follow-up of depressed patients treated with cognitive therapy, pharmacotherapy, and a combination of both. *Journal of Affective Disorders, 10,* 67-75.

Blaney, P.H. (1986). Affect and memory: A review. *Psychological Bulletin, 99,* 229-246.

Borkovec, T.D., & Inz, J. (1990). The nature of worry in generalised anxiety disorder: A predominance of thought activity. *Behaviour Research and Therapy, 28,* 153-158.

Bower, G.H. (1981). Mood and memory. *The American Psychologist, 36,* 129-148.

Bower, G.H. (1985, September). *Review of research on mood and memory.* Presented at the Symposium on Affect and Cognition, British Psychological Society Cognitive Psychology Section, Oxford, England.

Bower, G.H., & Cohen, P.R. (1982). Emotional influences in memory and thinking: Data and theory. In M.S. Clark & S.T. Fiske (Eds.), *Affect and cognition.* Hillsdale, NJ: Lawrence Erlbaum Associates Inc.

Bower, G.H., Gilligan, S.G., & Monteiro, K.P. (1981). Selectivity of learning caused by affective states. *Journal of Experimental Psychology: General, 110,* 451-473.

Bower, G.H., & Mayer, J.D. (1989). In search of mood-dependent retrieval. In D. Kuiken (Ed.), Mood and memory: Theory, research, and applications (Special Issue). *Journal of Social Behaviour and Personality, 4,* 121-156.

Bower, G.H., Monteiro, K.P., & Gilligan, S.G. (1978). Emotional mood as a context for learning and recall. *Journal of Verbal Learning and Verbal Behavior, 17,* 573-578.

Brewin, C.R. (1989). Cognitive change processes in psychotherapy. *Psychological Review, 96,* 379-394.

Brown, G.W., Andrews, B., Harris, T.O., Adler, Z., & Bridge, L. (1986). Social support, self-esteem, and depression. *Psychological Medicine, 16,* 813-831.

Brown, G.W., Bifulco, A.T., Veiel, H., & Andrews, B. (1990). Self-esteem and depression: II. Social correlates of self-esteem. *Social Psychiatry & Psychiatric Epidemiology, 25,* 225-234.

Brown, G.W., & Harris, T. (1978). *Social origins of depression.* London: Tavistock.

Brown, J., & Taylor, S.E. (1986). Affect and the processing of personal information: Evidence for mood-activated self-schemata. *Journal of Experimental Social Psychology, 22,* 436-452.

Carney, M.W.P., Roth, M., & Garside, M. (1965). The diagnosis of depressive syndromes and the prediction of ECT response. *British Journal of Psychiatry, 139,* 181-189.

Carr, S.J. (1987). *Mood and self-related cognition.* Unpublished DPhil Thesis, University of Oxford.

Carver, C.S., & Ganellen, R.J. (1983). Depression and components of self-punitiveness: High standards, self-criticalness, and overgeneralization. *Journal of Abnormal Psychology, 92,* 330-337.

Carver, C.S., & Scheier, M.F. (1981). *Attention and self-regulation: A control theory approach to human behavior.* New York: Springer-Verlag.

Carver, C.S., & Scheier, M.F. (1990). Origins and functions of positive and negative affect: A control-process view. *Psychological Review, 97,* 19-35.

Clark, D.M. (1983a). On the induction of depressed mood in the laboratory: Evaluation and comparison of the Velten and musical procedures. *Advances in Behavior Research and Therapy, 5,* 27-49.

Clark, D.M. (1983b). *Differential effects of mood on the accessibility of positive and negative information.* Unpublished DPhil Thesis, University of Oxford.

Clark, D.M., & Martin, M. (in press). *Effects of induced mood on recall of adjectives encoded by self- or other- reference.* Submitted for publication.

Clark, D.M., & Salkovskis, P.M. (1991). *Cognitive therapy with panic and hypochondriasis.* Oxford: Pergamon Press.

Clark, D.M., & Teasdale, J.D. (1982). Diurnal variation in clinical depression and accessibility of memories of positive and negative experiences. *Journal of Abnormal Psychology, 91,* 87-95.

Clark, D.M., & Teasdale, J.D. (1985). Constraints on the effects of mood on memory. *Journal of Personality and Social Psychology, 48,* 1595-1608.

Clark, D.M., Teasdale, J.D., Broadbent, D.E., & Martin, M. (1983). Effect of mood on lexical decisions. *Bulletin of the Psychonomic Society, 21,* 175-178.

Clark, M.S., & Isen, A.M. (1982). Towards understanding the relationship between feeling states and social behavior. In A.H. Hastorf & A.M. Isen, (Eds.), *Cognitive social psychology* (pp. 72-108). NY: Elsevier North Holland.

Clark, M.S., Milberg, S., & Ross, J. (1983). Arousal cues arousal-related material in memory: Implications for understanding effects of mood on memory. *Journal of Verbal Learning and Verbal Behavior, 22,* 633-649.

Coyne, J.C., & Gotlib, I.H. (1983). The role of cognition in depression: A critical appraisal. *Psychological Bulletin, 94,* 472-505.

Dent, J., & Teasdale, J.D. (1988). Negative cognition and the persistence of depression. *Journal of Abnormal Psychology, 97,* 29-34.

Duff, S. (1992). Mental models as multi-record representations. In Y. Rogers, A. Rutherford, & P. Bibby (Eds.), *Models in the mind: Theory, perspective and application* (pp.173-186). London: Academic Press.

Dweck, C.S., & Leggett, E.L. (1988). A social-cognitive approach to motivation and personality. *Psychological Review, 95,* 256-273.

Edwards, D.J.A. (1990). Cognitive therapy and the restructuring of early memories through guided imagery. *Journal of Cognitive Psychotherapy: An International Quarterly, 4,* 33-50.

Eich, J.E. (1977). State-dependent retrieval of information in human episodic memory. In I.M. Birnbaum & E.S. Parker (Eds.), *Alcohol and human memory.* Hillsdale, NJ: Lawrence Erlbaum Associates Inc.

Ellis, E.A. (1983). *Emotional mood as a context for state-dependent retention: Some limitations of the phenomenon.* Unpublished Senior Honours Thesis, University of Toronto, Canada.

Ellis, H.C., & Ashbrook, P.W. (1988). Resource allocation model of the effects of depressed mood states on memory. In K. Fiedler & J. Forgas (Eds.), *Affect, cognition, and social behaviour.* Toronto: Hogrefe.

Evans, M.D., Hollon, S.D., De Rubeis, R.J., Piasecki, J., Grove, W.M., Garvey, M.J., & Tuason, V.B. (1992). Differential relapse following cognitive therapy and pharmacotherapy for depression. *Archives of General Psychiatry, 49,* 802-808.

Eysenck, H.J., & Eysenck, S.B.G. (1964). *The Eysenck Personality Inventory.* London: University of London Press.

Fennell, M.J.V., & Campbell, E.A. (1984). The Cognitions Questionnaire: Specific thinking errors in depression. *British Journal of Clinical Psychology, 23,* 81-92.

Fennell, M.J.V., & Teasdale, J.D. (1984). Effects of distraction on thinking and affect in depressed patients. *British Journal of Clinical Psychology, 23,* 65-66.

Fennell, M.J.V., & Teasdale, J.D. (1987). Cognitive therapy for depression: Individual differences and the process of change. *Cognitive Therapy and Research, 11,* 253-271.

Fennell, M.J.V., Teasdale, J.D., Jones, S., & Damlé, A. (1987). Distraction in neurotic and endogeneous depression: An investigation of negative thinking in major depressive disorder. *Psychological Medicine, 17,* 441-452.

Fiedler, K., Pampe, H., & Scherf, U. (1986). Mood and memory for tightly organized social information. *European Journal of Social Psychology, 16,* 149-164.

Fodor, J. (1983). *The modularity of mind. An essay on faculty psychology.* Cambridge, Mass. : MIT Press/Bradford.

Forgas, J.F. (1992). Affect in social judgement and decisions: A multi-process model. In M. Zanna (Ed.), *Advances in experimental social psychology.* New York: Academic Press.

Forgas, J.P., & Bower, G.H. (1988). Affect in social and personal judgements. In K. Fiedler & J.P. Forgas (Eds.), *Affect, cognition and social behaviour* (pp. 183-208). Toronto: Hogrefe.

Forgas, J.P., Bower, G.H., & Krantz, S. (1984). The influence of mood on perceptions of social interactions. *Journal of Experimental Social Psychology, 20,* 497-513.

Forgas, J.P., Bower, G.H., & Moylan, S. (1990). Praise or blame? Affective influences on attributions for achievement. *Journal of Personality and Social Psychology, 59,* 809-819.

Forgas, J.P., & Moylan, S.J. (1987). After the movies: The effects of transient mood states on social judgments. *Personality and Social Psychology Bulletin, 13,* 478-489.

Forrest, M.S., & Hokanson, J.E. (1975). Depression and autonomic arousal reduction accompanying self-punitive behavior. *Journal of Abnormal Psychology, 84,* 346-357.

Fox, J., Cooper, R., Farringdon, J., & Shallice, T. (1992). Building computational models of cognition. In B. Silverman (Ed.), *Proceedings of workshop on expert judgement, human error and intelligent systems.* 10th European Conference on Artificial Intelligence, Vienna, 1992.

Gallagher, D., & Clore, G.L. (1985, May). *Effects of fear and anger on judgments of risk and blame.* Paper presented at the meetings of the Midwestern Psychological Association, Chicago.

Gendlin, E. (1981). *Focusing.* New York: Bantam Books.

Gibson, J.J. (1979). *The ecological approach to visual perception.* New York: Houghton Mifflin.

Gilligan, S.G. & Bower, G.H. (1983). Reminding and mood-congruent memory. *Bulletin of the Psychonomic Society, 21,* 431–434.

Gilligan, S.G. & Bower, G.H. (1984). Cognitive consequences of emotional arousal. In C.E. Izard, J. Kagan, & R. Zajonc (Eds.), *Emotion, cognition and behavior* (pp. 547-588). New York: Cambridge University Press.

Goerss, J.C., & Miller, M.E. (1982). *Memory and mood: State-dependent retention and induced affect.* Meeting of the Midwestern Psychological Association, Chicago.

Haaga, D.A.F., Dyck, M.J., & Ernst, D. (1991). Empirical status of cognitive theory of depression. *Psychological Bulletin, 110,* 215-236.

Hamilton, E.W., & Abramson, L.Y. (1983). Cognitive patterns and major depressive disorder: A longitudinal study in a hospital setting. *Journal of Abnormal Psychology, 92,* 173-184.

Hartlage, S., Alloy, L.B., Vázquez, C., & Dykman, B. (1993). Automatic and effortful processing in depression. *Psychological Bulletin, 113,* 247–278.

Hasher, L., & Zacks, R.T. (1979). Automatic and effortful processes in memory. *Journal of Experimental Psychology: General, 108,* 356-388.

Higgins, E.T. (1987). Self-discrepancy: A theory relating self and affect. *Psychological Review, 94,* 319-340.

Higgins, E.T., Rholes, W.S., & Jones, C. (1977). Category accessibility and impression formation. *Journal of Experimental Social Psychology, 13,* 141-154.

Hoare, C.A.R. (1985). *Communicating sequential processes.* Englewood Cliffs, NJ: Prentice Hall.

Hollon, S.D., Shelton, R.C., & Loosen, P.T. (1991). Cognitive therapy and pharmacotherapy for depression. *Journal of Consulting and Clinical Psychology, 59,* 88-99.

Hull, C.L. (1952). *A behavior system.* New Haven: Yale University Press.

Imber, S.D., Pilkonis, P.A., Sotsky, S.M., Elkin.I., Watkins, J.T., Collins, J.F., Shea, T.M., Leber, W.R., & Glass, D.R. (1990). Mode-specific effects among three treatments for depression. *Journal of Consulting and Clinical Psychology, 58,* 352-359.

Ingram, R.E. (1984). Toward an information-processing analysis of depression. *Cognitive Therapy and Research, 8,* 443-478.

Isen, A.M. (1984). Towards understanding the role of affect in cognition. In R.S. Wyer & T.K. Srull (Eds.), *Handbook of social cognition, Vol.3* (pp.179-235). Hillsdale, NJ: Lawrence Erlbaum Associates Inc.

Isen, A.M., Shalker, T.E., Clark, M., & Karp, L. (1978). Affect, accessibility of material in memory, and behavior: A cognitive loop? Journal of Personality and Social Psychology, 36, 1-12.

Izard, C.E. (1990). Facial expression and the regulation of emotion. *Journal of Personality and Social Psychology, 58,* 487-498.

Jacobson, N.S., Dobson, K., Fruzzetti, A.E., Schmaling, K.B., et al. (1991). Marital therapy as a treatment for depression. *Journal of Consulting and Clinical Psychology, 59,* 547-557.

Jacoby, L.L., & Kelley, C.M. (1990). An episodic view of motivation: Unconscious influences of memory. In E.T. Higgins & R.M. Sorrentino (Eds.), *Handbook of motivation and cognition: Foundations of social behavior, 2* (pp. 451-481). New York: Guilford Press.

Jacoby, L.L., Ste-Marie, D., & Toth, J.P. (in press). Redefining automaticity: Unconscious influences, awareness and control. In A.D. Baddeley & L. Weiskrantz (Eds.), *Attention, selection, awareness and control. A tribute to Donald Broadbent.* Oxford: Oxford University Press.

James, W. (1890). *The principles of psychology.* New York: Henry Holt & Company.

Johnson, E.J., & Tversky, A. (1983). Affect, generalisation, and the perception of risk. *Journal of Personality and Social Psychology, 45,* 20-31.

Johnson-Laird, P.N. (1983). *Mental models.* Cambridge: Cambridge University Press.

Johnson-Laird, P.N. (1988). A taxonomy of thinking. In R.J. Sternberg & E.E. Smith (Eds.), *The psychology of human thought.* New York: Cambridge University Press.

Kavanagh, D.J., & Bower, G.H. (1985). Mood and self-efficacy: Impact of joy and sadness on perceived capabilities. *Cognitive Therapy and Research, 9,* 507-525.

Kihlstrom, J.F., Cantor, N., Albright, J.S., Chew, B.R., Klein, S.B., & Niedenthal, P.M. (1988). Information processing and the study of the self. In L. Berkowitz (Ed.), *Advances in experimental social psychology, Vol.21,* (pp. 145-177). New York: Academic Press.

Klein, S.B., & Loftus, J. (in press). The mental representation of trait and autobiographical knowledge about the self. In T.K. Srull & R.S. Wyer (Eds.), *Advances in social cognition, Vol.5.* Hillsdale, NJ: Lawrence Erlbaum Associates Inc.

Klein, S.B., Loftus, J., & Burton, H.A. (1989). Two self-reference effects: The importance of distinguishing between self-descriptiveness judgements and autobiographical retrieval in self-referent encoding. *Journal of Personality and Social Psychology, 56,* 853-865.

Kovacs, M., & Beck, A.T. (1978). Maladaptive cognitive structures in depression. *American Journal of Psychiatry, 135,* 525-533.

Kuhl, J. (1981). Motivational and functional helplessness: The moderating effect of state versus action orientation. *Journal of Personality and Social Psychology, 40,* 5-170.

Kuhl, J., & Helle, L. (1986). Motivational and volitional determinants of depression: The degenerated-intention hypothesis. *Journal of Abnormal Psychology, 95,* 247-251.

Kuhl, J., & Kazen-Saad, M. (1988). A motivational approach to volition: Activation and de-activation of memory representations related to uncompleted intentions. In V. Hamilton, G.H. Bower, & N.H. Frijda (Eds.), *Cognition, emotion, and affect: A cognitive science view.* Dordrecht, The Netherlands: Martinus Nijhoff.

Kuhl, J., & Weiss, M. (1985). *Performance deficits following uncontrollable failure: Impaired action control or generalised expectancy deficits?* Munich: Max Planck Institute for Psychological Research, Paper No.5/84.

Laird, J.D., Wagener, J.J., Halal, M., & Szegda, M. (1982). Remembering what you feel: The effects of emotion on memory. *Journal of Personality and Social Psychology, 42,* 646-657.

Laird, J.E., Newell, A., & Rosenbloom, P.S. (1987). SOAR: An architecture for general intelligence. *Artificial Intelligence, 33,* 1-64.

Lang, P.J. (1985). The cognitive psychophysiology of emotion: Fear and anxiety. In A.H. Tuma & J.D. Maser (Eds.), *Anxiety and the anxiety disorders* (pp.131-170). Hillsdale, NJ: Lawrence Erlbaum Associates Inc.

Lang, P.J. (1988). Fear, anxiety, and panic: Context, cognition, and visceral arousal. In S. Rachman & J.D. Maser (Eds.), *Panic: Psychological perspectives* (pp. 219-236). Hillsdale, NJ: Lawrence Erlbaum Associates Inc.

Lanzetta, J.T., Cartwright-Smith, J., & Eleck, R.E. (1976). Effects of nonverbal dissimulation on emotional experience and autonomic arousal. *Journal of Personality and Social Psychology, 33,* 354-370.

Leight, K.A., & Ellis, H.C. (1981). Emotional mood states, strategies, and state-dependency in memory. *Journal of Verbal Learning and Verbal Behavior, 20,* 251-275.

Leventhal, H. (1979). A perceptual-motor processing model of emotion. In P. Pilner, K. Blankstein & I.M. Spigel (Eds.), *Perception of emotion in self and others*, *Vol.5* (pp. 1-46). New York: Plenum.

Leventhal, H. (1984). A perceptual-motor theory of emotion. In L. Berkowitz (Ed.), *Advances in experimental social psychology, Vol.17* (pp. 117-182). New York: Academic Press.

Leventhal, H., & Scherer, K. (1987). The relationship of emotion to cognition: A functional approach to a semantic controversy. *Cognition and Emotion, 1,* 3-28.

Levey, A.B., Aldaz, J.A., Watts, F.N., & Coyle, K. (1991). Articulatory suppression and the treatment of insomnia. *Behaviour Research and Therapy, 29,* 85-89.

Lewicki, P., Czyzewska, M., & Hoffman, H. (1987). Unconscious acquisition of complex procedural knowledge. *Journal of Experimental Psychology: Learning, Memory and Cognition, 13,* 523-530.

Lewinsohn, P.M., Steinmetz, J.L., Larson, D.W., & Franklin, J. (1981). Depression-related cognitions: Antecedent or consequence? *Journal of Abnormal Psychology, 90,* 213-219.

Lloyd, G.G., & Lishman, W.A. (1975). Effect of depression on the speed of recall of pleasant and unpleasant experiences. *Psychological Medicine, 5,* 173-180.

Macht, M.L., Spear, N.E., & Levis, D.J. (1977). State-dependent retention in humans induced by alternatives in affective state. *Bulletin of the Psychonomic Society, 10,* 415-418.

MacLeod, C., Mathews, A., & Tata, P. (1986). Attentional bias in emotional disorders. *Journal of Abnormal Psychology, 95,* 15-20.

Madigan, R.J., & Bollenbach, A.K. (1982). Effects of induced mood on retrieval of personal episodic and semantic memories. *Psychological Reports, 50,* 147-157.

Martin, M. (1985). Neuroticism as cognitive predisposition toward depression: A cognitive mechanism. *Personality and Individual Differences, 6,* 353-365.

Mathews, A.M., Gelder, M.G., & Johnston, D.W. (1981). *Agoraphobia—Nature and treatment.* New York: Guilford Press.

Mathews, A., & MacLeod, C. (1985). Selective processing of threat cues in anxiety states. *Behavior Research and Therapy, 23,* 563-569.

May, J., Böcker, M., Barnard, P., & Green, A. (1991). Characterising structural and dynamic aspects of the interpretation of visual interface objects. In: *Esprit '90.* Dordrecht: Kluwer Academic Publishers, 819-834.

McKinney, W.T., & Bunney, W.E. (1969). Animal model of depression.I Review of evidence: Implications for research. *Archives of General Psychiatry, 21,* 240-248.

Mecklenbräuker, S., & Hager, W. (1984). Effects of mood on memory: Experimental tests of mood-state-dependent retrieval hypothesis and of a mood-congruity hypothesis. *Psychological Research, 46,* 355-376.

Miranda, J., & Persons, J.B. (1988). Dysfunctional attitudes are mood-state dependent. *Journal of Abnormal Psychology, 97,* 76-79.

Miranda, J., Persons, J.B., & Byers, C.N. (1990). Endorsement of dysfunctional beliefs depends on current mood state. *Journal of Abnormal Psychology, 99,* 237-241.

Mogg, K., Mathews, A., & Weinman, J. (1987). Memory bias in clinical anxiety. *Journal of Abnormal Psychology, 96,* 94-98.

Morris, W.N. (1989). *Mood. The frame of mind.* New York: Springer-Verlag.

Morrow, J., & Nolen-Hoeksema, S. (1990). Effects of responses to depression on the remediation of depressive affect. *Journal of Personality and Social Psychology, 58,* 519-527.

Morton, J., Hammersley, R.H., & Bekerian, D.A. (1985). Headed records: A model for memory and its failures. *Cognition, 20,* 1-23.

Musson, R.F., & Alloy, L.B. (1988). Depression and self-directed attention. In L.B. Alloy (Ed.), *Cognitive processes in depression.* New York: Guilford Press.

Nasby, W. (1988). *Induced moods and selective encoding of personal information about the self.* Unpublished manuscript, Boston College.

Nasby, W., & Yando, R. (1982). Selective encoding and retrieval of affectively valent information: Two cognitive consequences of children's mood states. *Journal of Personality and Social Psychology, 43,* 1244-1253.

Natale, M., & Hantas, M. (1982). Effect of temporary mood states on selective memory about the self. *Journal of Personality and Social Psychology, 42,* 927-934.

Neisser, U. (1976). *Cognition and reality.* New York: W.H.Freeman.

Newell, A. (1990). *Unified theories of cognition.* Cambridge, Mass: Harvard University Press.

Nezu, A.M. & Perri, M.G. (1989). Social problem-solving therapy for unipolar depression: An initial dismantling investigation. *Journal of Consulting and Clinical Psychology, 57,* 408-413.

Nolen-Hoeksema, S. (1987). Sex differences in unipolar depression: Evidence and theory. *Psychological Bulletin, 101,* 259-282.

Nolen-Hoeksema, S. (1991). Responses to depression and their effects on the duration of depressive episodes. *Journal of Abnormal Psychology, 100,* 569-582.

Nolen-Hoeksema, S., & Morrow, J. (submitted). *The effects of rumination and distraction on naturally occurring depressed moods.*

Nolen-Hoeksema, S., & Morrow, J. (1991). A prospective study of depression and distress following a natural disaster: The 1989 Loma Prieta earthquake. *Journal of Personality and Social Psychology, 61,* 115-121.

Nolen-Hoeksema, S., Morrow, J., & Fredrickson, B.L. (submitted). *The effects of response styles on the duration of depressed mood: A field study.*

Nolen-Hoeksema, S., Parker, L., & Larson, J. (submitted). Depression in family members of the terminally ill.

Nolen-Hoeksema, S., Wolfson, A., Mumme, D., & Guskin, K. (submitted). *Maternal influences on children's mastery-orientation and problem-solving: Comparisons of depressed and non-depressed mothers.*

Norman, D.A. (1983). Design principles for human-computer interfaces. In *Proceedings of CHI'83 Human Factors in Computing Systems* (pp. 1-10). New York: ACM.

Norman, D.A., & Bobrow, D.G. (1979). Descriptions: An intermediate stage in memory retrieval. *Cognitive Psychology, 11,* 107-123.

Oatley, K., & Johnson-Laird, P.N. (1987). Towards a cognitive theory of emotions. *Cognition and Emotion, 1,* 29-50.

Parrott, G.W., & Sabini, J. (1990). Mood and memory under natural conditions: Evidence for mood incongruent recall. *Journal of Personality and Social Psychology, 59,* 321-336.

Perls, F.S. (1973). *The Gestalt approach: An eyewitness to therapy.* Palo Alto, California: Science & Behavior Books.

Power, M.J., & Champion, L.A. (1986). Cognitive approaches to depression: A theoretical critique. *British Journal of Clinical Psychology, 25,* 201-212.

Pyszczynski, T., & Greenberg, J. (1987). Self-regulatory perseveration and the depressive self-focusing style: A self-awareness theory of reactive depression. *Psychological Bulletin, 102,* 122-138.

Pyszczynski, T., Hamilton, J., Herring, F., & Greenberg, J. (1989). Depression, self-focused attention, and the negative memory bias. *Journal of Personality and Social Psychology, 57,* 351-357.

Pyszczynski, T., Holt, K., & Greenberg, J. (1987). Depression, self-focused attention, and expectancies for future positive and negative events for self and others. *Journal of Personality and Social Psychology, 52*, 994-1001.

Rehm, L.P., Kaslow, N.J., & Rabin, A.S. (1987). Cognitive and behavioral targets in a self-control therapy program for depression. *Journal of Consulting and Clinical Psychology, 55*, 60-67.

Reps, P. (1971). *Zen flesh, zen bones*. Harmondsworth: Penguin Books.

Rinck, M., Glowalla, U., & Schneider, K. (1992). Mood-congruent and mood-incongruent learning. *Memory and Cognition, 20*, 29-39.

Riskind, J.H. (1989). The mediating mechanisms in mood and memory: A cognitive-priming formulation. In D. Kuiken (Ed.), Mood and memory: Theory, research and applications (Special Issue). *Journal of Social Behaviour and Personality, 4*, 173-184.

Riskind, J.H., Rholes, W.S., & Eggers, J. (1982). The Velten mood induction procedure: Effects on mood and memory. *Journal of Consulting and Clinical Psychology, 50*, 146-147.

Rogers, T.B. (1977). Self-reference in memory: Recognition of personality items. *Journal of Research in Personality, 11*, 295-305.

Rumelhart, D.E., & McClelland, J.L. (1986). *Parallel distributed processing: Explorations in the microstructure of cognition, Vol.1: Foundations*. Cambridge, Mass.: MIT Press.

Rumelhart, D.E., & Norman, D.A. (1983). *Representation in memory*. Centre for Human Information Processing, University of California, San Diego, CHIP 116, June.

Rumelhart, D.E., Smolensky, P., McClelland, J.L., & Hinton, G.E. (1986). Schemata and sequential thought processes in PDP models. In J.L. McClelland & D.E. Rumelhart (Eds.), *Parallel distributed processing. Explorations in the microstructure of cognition, Vol.2: Psychological and Biological Models*. Cambridge, M.A.: MIT Press.

Salovey, P., & Singer, J.A. (1989). Mood congruency effects in recall of childhood versus recent memories. In D. Kuiken (Ed.), Mood and memory: Theory, research, and application (Special Issue). *Journal of Social Behaviour and Personality, 4*, 99-120.

Schare, M.L., Lisman, S.A., & Spear, N.E. (1984). The effects of mood variation on state-dependent retention. *Cognitive Therapy and Research, 8*, 387-408.

Schwarz, N., & Clore, G.L. (1983). Mood, misattribution, and judgements of well-being: Informative and directive functions of affective states. *Journal of Personality and Social Psychology, 45*, 513-523.

Schwarz, N. & Clore, G.L. (1988). How do I feel about it? The informative function of affective states. In K. Fiedler & J.P. Forgas (Eds.), *Affect, cognition and social behaviour*. Toronto: Hogrefe.

Schwarz, N., Strack, F., Kommer, D., & Wagner, D. (1987). Soccer, rooms and the quality of your life: Mood effects on judgments of satisfaction with life in general and with specific life-domains. *European Journal of Social Psychology, 17*, 69-79.

Seligman, M.E.P. (1975). *Helplessness: On depression, development and death*. San Francisco: W.H.Freeman & Co.

Shah, I. (1974). *Thinkers of the East*. Harmondsworth: Penguin Books.

Shallice, T. (1988). *From neuropsychology to mental structure*. Cambridge: Cambridge University Press.

Shea, T.M., Elkin, I., Imber, S.D., Sotsky, S.M., Watkins, J.T., Collins, J.F., Pilkonis, P.A., Leber, W.R., Krupnick, J., Dolan, R.T., & Parloff, M.B. (1992). Course of depressive symptoms over follow-up: Findings from the National Institute of Mental Health Treatment of Depression Collaborative Research Program. *Archives of General Psychiatry, 49*, 782-787.

Shiffrin, R.M., & Schneider, W. (1977). Controlled and automatic human processing: (2) Perceptual learning, automatic attending, and a general theory. *Psychological Review, 84*, 127-90.

Simon, H.A. (1982). Comments. In M.S. Clarke & S.T. Fiske (Eds.), *Affect and Cognitio,* (p. 339). Hillsdale, NJ: Lawrence Erlbaum Associates Inc.

Simons, A.D., Garfield, S.L., & Murphy, G.E. (1984). The process of change in cognitive therapy and pharmacotherapy for depression: Changes in mood and cognition. *Archives of General Psychiatry, 41*, 45-51.

Simons, A.D., Murphy, G.E., Levine, J.L., & Wetzel, R.D. (1986). Cognitive therapy and pharmacotherapy for depression: Sustained improvement over one year. *Archives of General Psychiatry, 43*, 43-48.

Simons, A.D., et al. (1985). Exercise as a treatment for depression: An update. *Clinical Psychology Review, 5*, 553-568.

Singer, J.A., & Salovey, P. (1988). Mood and memory: Evaluating the network theory of affect. *Clinical Psychology Review, 8*, 211-251.

Singer, J.L. (1966). *Daydreaming: An introduction to the experimental study of inner experience*. New York: Random House.

Singer, J.L. (1988). Sampling on-going consciousness and emotional experiences: Implications for health. In M.J. Horowitz (Ed.), *Psychodynamics and cognition*. Chicago: The University of Chicago Press.

Skinner, B.F. (1957). Verbal behavior. New York: Appleton Century Crofts.

Snyder, M., & White, P. (1982). Moods and memories: Elation, depression, and the remembering of the event of one's life. *Journal of Personality, 50*, 142-167.

Teasdale, J.D. (1983a). Affect and accessibility. *Philosophical Transactions of the Royal Society, 302*, 403-412.

Teasdale, J.D. (1983b). Negative thinking in depression: Cause, effect or reciprocal relationship? *Advances in Behaviour Research and Therapy, 5*, 3-25.

Teasdale, J.D. (1985). Psychological treatments for depression: How do they work? *Behaviour Research and Therapy, 23*, 157-165.

Teasdale, J.D. (1988). Cognitive vulnerability to persistent depression. *Cognition and Emotion, 2*, 247-274.

Teasdale, J.D. (1989). Daydreaming, depression and distraction (abstract). *The Psychologist*, 189-190.

Teasdale, J.D. (1991). Cognitive vulnerability to persistent depression. In P. Slade (Ed.), *The psychology of depression: Current issues in research and practice*. Sheffield: Department of Psychology, Sheffield University.

Teasdale, J.D., & Dent, J. (1987). Cognitive vulnerability to depression: An investigation of two hypotheses. *British Journal of Clinical Psychology, 26*, 113-126.

Teasdale, J.D., & Dritschel, B. (submitted). *Mood congruous memory: Self-relevance is not sufficient.*

Teasdale, J.D., Dritschel, B., Taylor, M.J., Proctor, L., Lloyd, C., Nimmo-Smith, I., & Baddeley, A.D. (submitted). *Production of stimulus-independent thought depends on central executive resources.*

Teasdale, J.D., & Fogarty, S.J. (1979). Differential effects of induced mood on retrieval of pleasant and unpleasant events from episodic memory. *Journal of Abnormal Psychology, 88,* 248-257.

Teasdale, J.D., Proctor, L., & Baddeley, A.D. (submitted). *Working memory and stimulus-independent thought: The role of the phonological loop.*

Teasdale, J.D., Proctor, L., Lloyd, C.A., & Baddeley, A.D. (submitted). *Working memory and stimulus-independent thought: Effects of memory load and presentation rate.*

Teasdale, J.D., & Rezin, V. (1978). The effects of reducing frequency of negative thoughts on the mood of depressed patients—Tests of a cognitive model of depression. *British Journal of Social and Clinical Psychology, 17,* 65-74.

Teasdale, J.D., & Russell, M.L. (1983). Differential effects of induced mood on the recall of positive, negative and neutral words. *British Journal of Clinical Psychology, 22,* 163-171.

Teasdale, J.D., & Taylor, R. (1981). Induced mood and accessibility of memories: An effect of mood state or of induction procedure? *British Journal of Clinical Psychology, 20,* 39-48.

Teasdale, J.D., Taylor, M.J., Cooper, Z., Hayhurst, H., & Paykel, E. (in prep.). *Depressive thinking: Shifts in construct accessibility or in schematic mental models?*

Teasdale, J.D., Taylor, R., & Fogarty, S.J. (1980). Effects of induced elation depression on the accessibility of memories of happy and unhappy experiences. *Behavior Research and Therapy, 18,* 339-346.

Thompson, L.W., & Gallagher, D. (1984). Efficacy of psychotherapy in the treatment of late life depression. *Advances in Behaviour Research and Therapy, 6,* 127-139.

Tulving, E., & Thomson, D.M. (1973). Encoding specificity and retrieval processes in episodic memory. *Psychological Review, 80,* 352-373.

Turner, R.G. (1980). Self-consciousness and memory of trait terms. *Personality and Social Psychology Bulletin, 6,* 273-277.

Tversky, A., & Kahneman, D. (1973). Availability: A heuristic for judging frequency and probability. *Cognitive Psychology, 5,* 207-232.

Van den Bergh, O., & Eelen, P. (1984). Unconscious processing and emotions. In M.A. Reda & M.J. Mahoney (Eds.), *Cognitive psychotherapies.* Cambridge, Mass: Ballinger.

Velten, E. (1968). A laboratory task for induction of mood states. *Behavior Research and Therapy, 6,* 473-482.

Watts, F.N. (1993). Problems of memory and concentration. In C.G. Costello (Ed.), *Symptoms of depression.* New York: John Wiley.

Watts, F.N., McKenna, F.P., Sharrock, R., & Trezise, L. (1986). Colour naming of phobia-related words. *British Journal of Psychology, 77,* 97-108.

Weingartner, H., Miller, H., & Murphy, D. (1977). Mood-state-dependent retrieval of verbal associations. *Journal of Abnormal Psychology, 86,* 276-284.

Weissman, A., & Beck, A.T. (1978, November). *The Dysfunctional Attitudes Scale.* Paper presented at the annual meeting of the Association for the Advancement of Behavior Therapy, Chicago.

Wells, G.L., Hoffman, C., & Enzle, M.E. (1984). Self- versus other-referent processing at encoding and retrieval. *Personality and Social Psychology Bulletin, 10,* 574-584.

Wells, G.L., & Petty, R.E. (1980). The effects of overt head movement on persuasion: Compatibility and incompatibility of responses. *Basic and Applied Social Psychology, 1,* 219-230.

Wetzler, S. (1985). Mood-state-dependent retrieval: A failure to replicate. *Psychological Reports, 56,* 759-765.

Williams, J.M.G. (1992). *The psychological treatment of depression (2nd edition).* London: Routledge.

Williams, J.M.G., Watts, F.N., Macleod, C., & Mathews, A.M. (1988). *Cognitive psychology and emotional disorders.* Chichester: John Wiley.

Williams, R.M. (1988). *Individual differences in the effects of mood on cognition.* Unpublished DPhil Thesis, University of Oxford.

Willner, P., & Neiva, J. (1986). Brief exposure to uncontrollable but not to controllable noise biases the retrieval of information from memory. *British Journal of Clinical Psychology, 25,* 93-100.

Wilson, P.H., Goldin, J.C., & Charbonneau-Powis, M. (1983). Comparative efficacy of behavioral and cognitive treatments of depression. *Cognitive Therapy and Research, 7,* 111-124.

Wright, J., & Mischel, W. (1982). Influence of affect on cognitive social learning person variables. *Journal of Personality and Social Psychology, 43,* 901-914.

Young, J. (1990). *Cognitive therapy for personality disorder.* Sarasota, Florida: Professional Resource Exchange, Inc.

Zeiss, A.M., Lewinsohn, P.M., & Munoz, R.F. (1979). Nonspecific improvement effects in depression using interpersonal skills training, pleasant activity schedules, or cognitive training. *Journal of Consulting and Clinical Psychology, 47,* 427-439.

Author Index

Subject Index

ANXIETY

The Cognitive Perspective

MICHAEL W. EYSENCK
(Royal Holloway University of London)

Theorists are increasingly arguing that it is fruitful to approach anxiety from the cognitive perspective, and the empirical evidence supports that contention. The cognitive perspective is also adopted in this book, but the approach represents a development and extension of earlier ones. For example, most previous theories and research have been based on anxiety either in clinical or in normal groups. In contrast, one of the central themes of this book is that there are great advantages to be gained from a joint consideration of clinical and normal anxiety.

Another theme of this book is that it is of major importance to establish whether or not there is a cognitive vulnerability factor which is associated with at least some forms of clinical anxiety. It is argued (with supporting evidence) that there is a latent cognitive vulnerability factor for generalized anxiety disorder which manifests itself under stressful conditions. This vulnerability factor is characterized by hypervigilance, and is found predominantly in normals high in the personality dimension of trait anxiety.

The scope of the book extends to the effects of anxiety on performance and to the phenomenon of worry, which is regarded as the cognitive component of anxiety. In both cases, a new theoretical framework is presented.

Contents: Introduction. Theories of Anxiety and Cognition. Theoretical Framework. Attentional Processes. Comprehension and Memory. Worry. General Processing. Summary.

ISBN 0-86377-071-1 1992 198pp. $26.95 £14.95 hbk

For UK/Europe, please send orders to: *Lawrence Erlbaum Associates Ltd., Mail Order Department, 27 Church Road, Hove, East Sussex, BN3 2FA, England. Note, prices shown here are correct at time of going to press, but may change. Prices outside Europe may differ from those shown.* **Please send USA & Canadian orders to:** *Lawrence Erlbaum Associates Inc., 365 Broadway, Hillsdale, New Jersey, NJ07642, USA.*

Titles in the Series
Essays in Cognitive Psychology
Series Editors: Alan Baddeley, Max Coltheart, Leslie Henderson
& Phil Johnson-Laird

WORKING MEMORY AND LANGUAGE

SUSAN E. GATHERCOLE (Lancaster University) and ALAN D. BADDELEY (Director, MRC Applied Psychology Unit, Cambridge)

This book evaluates the involvement of working memory in five central aspects of language processing: vocabulary acquisition, speech production, reading development, skilled reading, and comprehension. The authors draw upon experimental, neuro- psychological and developmental evidence in a wide-ranging evaluation of the contribution of two components of working memory to each aspect of language. The two components are the phonological loop, which is specialised for the processing and maintenance of verbal material, and the general-purpose processing system of the central executive.

A full introduction to the application of the working memory model to normal adults, neuropsychological patients and children is provided in the two opening chapters. Non-experts within this area will find these chapters particularly useful in providing a clear statement of the current theoretical and empirical status of the working memory model. Each of the following chapters examines the involvement of working memory in one specialised aspect of language processing, in each case integrating the available experimental, neuropsychological and developmental evidence. The book will therefore be of direct relevance to researchers interested in both language processing and memory.

Working Memory and Language is unique in that it draws together findings from normal adults, brain-damaged patients, and children. For each of these populations, working memory involvement in language processing ranging from the speech production to comprehension are evaluated. *Working Memory and Language* provides a comprehensive analysis of just what roles working memory does play in the processing of language.

Contents: Introduction to Working Memory. The Development of Working Memory. Vocabulary Acquisition. Speech Production. Introduction to Reading Development. Phonological Processing and Reading Development. Visual Word Recognition. Language Comprehension. Theoretical and Practical Issues.

ISBN 0-86377-265-X 1993 288pp. $46.95 £24.95 hbk

For UK/Europe, please send orders to: Lawrence Erlbaum Associates Ltd., Mail Order Department, 27 Church Road, Hove, East Sussex, BN3 2FA, England. Note, prices shown here are correct at time of going to press, but may change. Prices outside Europe may differ from those shown. Please send USA & Canadian orders to: Lawrence Erlbaum Associates Inc., 365 Broadway, Hillsdale, New Jersey, NJ07642, USA.

---

*For UK/Europe, please send orders to: Lawrence Erlbaum Associates Ltd., Mail Order
Department, 27 Church Road, Hove, East Sussex, BN3 2FA, England. Note, prices shown
here are correct at time of going to press, but may change. Prices outside Europe may
differ from those shown. Please send USA & Canadian orders to: Lawrence Erlbaum
Associates Inc., 365 Broadway, Hillsdale, New Jersey, NJ07642, USA.*